Praise for *Shepherding Women in Pain*

Shepherding Women in Pain fills a real void in the Christian Pastoral and Counseling library. Dr. Hislop helps caregivers to see more clearly the unique ways in which women have been sinned against and the wounds they carry. Additionally, she provides us with helpful information and strategies to bring healing and wholeness in the lives of women. I highly recommend this book.

—RONALD E. HAWKINS, EdD, DMin, licensed professional counselor; served on the Executive Board for American Association of Christian Counselors; pastor, speaker, and Provost and Chief Academic Officer at Liberty University; author of *Strengthening Marital Intimacy* and *The Quick Reference Guide to Biblical Counseling* with Dr. Tim Clinton

Shepherding Women in Pain is a book every Christian leader needs! Dr. Bev Hislop has thoroughly addressed all of the major issues we encounter in the process of providing ministry to women. With true stories, outstanding input from professionals, unprecedented how-tos and practical suggestions, this book will help you to confidently identify tough issues and provide grace, resources, personal involvement, and action steps that are needed. This is the most thorough, up-to-date ministry tool I've read in years.

—CAROL KENT, founder and director of Speak Up; cofounder with her husband, Gene, of Speak Up for Hope; author of over 20 books, including *When I Lay My Isaac Down*, *A New Kind of Normal*, and *He Holds My Hand*

Bev Hislop has written a wonderfully practical go-to book tha within an arm's reach of everyone who cares about women.

—KAY WARREN, international speaker and author of several b(including *Choose Joy*, *Say Yes to God*, and *Sacred Privilege*; b member of the National Action Alliance for Suicide Preventi founder of the HIV/AIDS Initiative; cofounder of Saddleback with her husband, Rick

Shepherding Women in Pain is long overdue. For years I have needed such an insightful resource—addressing biblically and sensitively a broad scope of gender-specific issues of half our world's population. Bev Hislop is certainly correct: men and women do process pain differently. This book explains how they differ, and it will help to maximize the ministry of anyone with a heart for helping people.

—WILLIAM J. MCRAE, President Emeritus, Tyndale University College and Seminary, Toronto; author of *Preparing for Your Marriage, The Dynamics of Spiritual Gifts*, and *A Book to Die For*

The information this wonderful book contains is invaluable. Bev Hislop has gathered together experts on a wide variety of issues who give needed information and insights into both effective and ineffective ways to respond to and care for hurting women. It is a book to better equip caregivers to offer God's love and hope to women in pain.

—JOYE BAKER, DMin, Women's Adviser and Adjunct Professor in Educational Ministries and Leadership, Doctor of Ministry Studies at Dallas Theological Seminary; Chair of the Board of the AWMP

Finally . . . a book to help those of us in the trenches of ministering to hurting women! I am grateful to the Lord that He has used Dr. Hislop to bring a critical understanding of how to shepherd the millions of women who are dealing with life's most terrible circumstances. This will become the how-to for ministry leaders for decades to come!

—JENNIFER KEITT, founder and radio host of the nationally syndicated *Today's Black Woman Radio Show* and the *Jennifer Keitt Show* podcast; cofounder along with her daughter, Morgan, of The Keitt Institute

This is an amazing resource, not just for professional shepherds but for ordinary women who are committed to living out Christ's call to walk alongside those who are hurting. It gives her the tools needed to be a conduit of God's hope and love.

—ROSEMARY FLAATEN, MA in Counseling, Speaker and author of *A Woman and Her Relationships*

shepherding
women in pain

REAL WOMEN, REAL ISSUES, AND
WHAT YOU NEED TO KNOW
TO TRULY HELP

BEV HISLOP

GENERAL EDITOR

MOODY PUBLISHERS
CHICAGO

All Scripture quotations, unless otherwise indicated, are taken from the Holy Bible, New International Version®, NIV®, Copyright ©1973, 1978, 1984, 2011 by Biblica, Inc.™ Used by permission of Zondervan. All rights reserved worldwide. www.zondervan.com The "NIV" and "New International Version" are trademarks registered in the United States Patent and Trademark Office by Biblica, Inc.™

Scripture quotations marked NASB are taken from the *New American Standard Bible*®, Copyright © 1960, 1962, 1963, 1968, 1971, 1972, 1973, 1975, 1977, 1995 by The Lockman Foundation. Used by permission. www.Lockman.org

Scripture quotations marked NLT are taken from the Holy Bible, New Living Translation, copyright ©1996, 2004, 2015 by Tyndale House Foundation. Used by permission of Tyndale House Publishers, Inc., Carol Stream, Illinois 60188. All rights reserved.

Scripture quotations marked ESV are taken from *The Holy Bible, English Standard Version*. Copyright © 2000, 2001 by Crossway Bibles, a division of Good News Publishers. Used by permission. All rights reserved.

Scripture marked KJV is taken from the King James Version of the Bible.

Scripture quotations marked NKJV are taken from the *New King James Version*. Copyright © 1982 by Thomas Nelson, Inc. Used by permission. All rights reserved.

Scripture quotations marked *The Message* are taken from *THE MESSAGE*, copyright © 1993, 2002, 2018 by Eugene H. Peterson. Used by permission of NavPress. All rights reserved. Represented by Tyndale House Publishers, Inc.

All websites and phone numbers listed herein are accurate at the time of first publication but may change in the future or cease to exist. The listing of website references and resources does not imply publisher endorsement of the site's entire contents. Groups and organizations are listed for informational purposes, and listing does not imply publisher endorsement of their activities.

Names and details in some stories have been changed to protect the privacy of individuals.

Edited by Pam Pugh
Interior Design: Ragont Design
Cover Design: Erik M. Peterson

Library of Congress Cataloging-in-publication Data

Shepherding women in pain : real women, real issues, and what you need to know to truly help / [compiled by] Bev Hislop.
p. cm.
Includes bibliographical references.
ISBN 978-0-8024-7705-7
1. Church work with women. 2. Christian women—pastoral counseling of. 3. suffering—Religious aspects—Christianity. i. Hislop, Beverly White
Bv4445.s54 2010
259.082--dc22

2009051292

ISBN: 978-0-8024-1996-5

Originally delivered by fleets of horse-drawn wagons, the affordable paperbacks from D. L. Moody's publishing house resourced the church and served everyday people. Now, after more than 125 years of publishing and ministry, Moody Publishers' mission remains the same—even if our delivery systems have changed a bit.

Moody Publishers
820 N. LaSalle Boulevard
Chicago, IL 60610

1 3 5 7 9 10 8 6 4 2

Printed in the United States of America

*This book is dedicated
to the women who have honored me
by sharing their emotionally painful experiences,
allowing me into that sacred place of vulnerability and pain.
Thank you for trusting me enough to risk.
Thank you for allowing me to walk with you
to the foot of the cross and together experience
the power of the grace of the Lord Jesus Christ in our lives.*

Contents

Section 3: Healing Women in Pain
What the Healing Community Needs to Know

Foreword

*P*ain has few boundaries—it barges in uninvited at every age and stage of life—both inside and outside our faith communities. Jesus-followers often come through the more visible and common forms of suffering with the much-valued support of Scripture, the Holy Spirit, and caring people.

But sadly, deeper emotional and relational scars are often hidden from the eyes of even family and friends. They can be chronic, isolating, shame-based, and hope-depleting. Regrettably, many pastoral teams are not equipped to shepherd people through these kinds of pain very effectively. They pray and give their best—but often are tapped out by the sheer variety, complexity, and volume of pain.

Bev Hislop has given us a pastoral care gift that has the potential to change that paradigm. I really could have used this resource when I began my "trial and error" counseling/care approach. But it is never too late to learn—even for a pastoral veteran. I witnessed the formation of this equipping model, and in the first six months saw my pastoral care load decrease.

Bev's shepherding model has been gestating much of her adult life. She has listened, learned, and ministered to untold numbers of women in pain—as a pastor's wife, as a pastor to women, and as a seminary professor. She has also selected some seasoned experts to address significant subjects. Their experience and expertise, as devoted Jesus-followers and caregivers, will inform, sober, counsel, and inspire you.

If you need additional reasons for reading this book, consider these:

- Most male pastors are not equipped to be the primary processors of emotional pain for women.
- The gap between what pastors and professional caregivers can provide often leaves people in limbo. Neither one has the time to track them once they leave our offices.
- Pain that is not processed well builds up scar tissue and usually surfaces in unexpected ways. Have you ever wondered why some mature believers behave the way they do? Sometimes the cause may be more related to suffering than to sin.
- Being more informed about pain can produce greater compassion for people as well as heightened authenticity and relevance in public ministries.

Pastors and leaders, please *become familiar with this resource.* The potential payoff in terms of emotional and spiritual health is immeasurable. Refer to it for invaluable insights. And if you want to extend God's grace more effectively, prayerfully place this book in the hands of a few women who, along with you, can become a catalyst for creating a new culture and a safe place for people to heal, as they follow Jesus.

DENNIS FRIESEN, DMin
Pastor Emeritus at
Grace Community Church, Gresham, Oregon

Introduction

*A*my and Ryan were so excited! After three miscarriages the hope of another pregnancy was finally realized—the pregnancy test was positive! Immediately Amy called the doctor's office and set up an appointment. Amy had an early ultrasound that revealed she was six weeks and two days along and the baby had a strong heartbeat. They stopped on the way home from the hospital to celebrate with ice cream while revising the nursery plan. There was much to do before the due date. The evening was spent calling family and friends to share in the joy of this fabulous news.

Several weeks later, a second ultrasound initially verified the good news of the first. Amy and Ryan had already chosen a name—Elijah Daniel if the baby was a boy—after two of their most admired biblical men. Friday was spent making a second round of phone calls, followed by friends coming by to congratulate the happy parents.

Later that evening, the doctor's call came through. He had received the initial report and suggested they look at the ultrasound together on Monday. The sound of his voice was unsettling. It was Good Friday. Amy and Ryan went to church services acknowledging that the God of the resurrection who "knit us together in our mothers' wombs" had the ability to form a healthy baby. Amy prayed the Lord would heal any problem with their baby. But if God chose not to heal, then God would not put her and her husband in the place of having to decide if the baby should live or die.

On Monday more ultrasounds were taken and read by the specialists in perinatology. A second ultrasound, which confirmed that the baby was a boy, seemed to show that his heart was on the wrong side and there appeared to be a cyst in the chest.

Further investigation showed three major defects. The baby had a chromosomal defect, a congenital diaphragmatic hernia (CDH), and a hypoplastic left heart. The perinatologist gave a grim outcome. He actually said that he expected the baby to die anytime in utero because he said a CDH found this early was extremely severe. Amy and Ryan made it clear they would not terminate the pregnancy. They felt God had made this baby for this family and God had a plan for him. This was an answer to their prayers, but it was not the answer for which they had hoped. The incredible joy celebrated with family and friends so quickly turned to sorrow as they began to face the tough reality.

At times Amy was overwhelmed with confusion, doubt, and questions. Feelings of fear and love simultaneously swirled within her, each competing for control. Love for her baby drove her to cry out to God demanding He confound the medical professionals and heal their baby. She wanted more than anything to carry this baby to full term, to hold him and caress him, and celebrate his life. Amy's own feelings and thoughts seemed unmanageable. The equilibrium of life suddenly was out of kilter. She wondered if she would make it through the next hour.

What hope and comfort could a shepherd possibly bring to these young parents? Unlike many parents in pain, Amy and Ryan were fortunate to have trustworthy friends and spiritual advisors who offered to pray for them. Caregivers were invited to bring biblical perspective and encouragement. Amy and Ryan did a lot of talking and praying with valued friends. Admittedly, caregivers often felt impotent and incompetent amidst such a traumatic life event. Yet, shepherds who understood the trauma of fetal loss were the most consoling and accepting. They understood that typically men and women process emotional pain differently. They communicated a message of "these feelings are normal" given the present circumstance. They were present, extended love, and spoke appropriate words of compassion and support to Amy and Ryan.

Elijah Daniel was delivered full term at eight pounds and eleven ounces. Amy's prayer was answered in being able to hold, caress, and love little Elijah, if only for fifty-four hours. Amy would remember the final moments with these words:

He passed away very quickly. We all started crying hard at that moment. Even though we knew he was dying, that was the final moment he was with us, and it hit us all pretty hard. I just held my baby boy. I remember saying, "Oh my sweet boy!" My heart wanted him back so badly. . . . Many of our friends were in the hall and were able to see him. I was given hugs and felt so loved. There were so many tears in the hallway that day—tears that said how much our baby boy was loved!

Pictures with family and friends, a birth certificate with precious tiny footprints, poems, and the pathology report were gathered and treasured. Although the report confirmed the outcome of the three major defects, Amy and Ryan today rest in the assurance that the resurrected body of their precious Elijah Daniel is whole.

As feelings of anger, sadness, and even denial emerged, Amy felt the freedom to express her grief, to process her pain in the safe company of understanding friends. In the midst of her own emotionally painful weakness, Amy would later realize the strength she drew from her caring friends. Certainly no caregiver would assume to have all the answers, nor should she. The "why" will likely not be known in this life. Typically answers are not the greatest contribution to be made by a caregiver in the fog of an emotionally painful life event. Appropriate cognitive processing is important; caregivers who are able to integrate an understanding of a given emotionally painful issue with a loving presence will maximize their shepherding effectiveness.

Crises are a part of the landscape of life. No one gets through life without them. Some storms of life are more devastating than others. Some are more disruptive, some more life-threatening than others. A crisis is often a point where people determine whether they will turn to God or walk away from Him. Women in crisis may be eternally influenced at this critical life juncture by a well-prepared shepherd.

A few years ago my husband and I built a home in a south Florida location that required over twenty-five truckloads of dirt to be brought in to raise the ground level before the foundation of the house could be built. This requirement was both unexpected and costly and it remained in question until the "hundred-year flood" came in 1995. Torrents of rain pounded at the rate of twenty-two inches every twenty-four hours. Neighbors were Jet Skiing and even boating in what were normally the roadways in our development. Homes that were built before the new building codes were flooded. Ours remained high and dry. We understood in a new way the value of a solid foundation. The cost of building that foundation when the weather was dry and seemingly indifferent to the possibility of floodwaters proved to be well worth the investment.

Jesus tells us:

"Therefore everyone who hears these words of mine and puts them into practice is like a wise man who built his house on the rock. The rain came down, the streams rose, and the winds blew and beat against that house; yet it did not fall, because it had its foundation on the rock." (Matthew 7:24–25)

In a similar way, an investment in our relationship with Jesus Christ *daily* will lay a strong foundation of hope and truth that will remain solid amidst the storms of life. If we as caregivers continue to grow in our relationship with the Good Shepherd and expand our understanding of what is needed to bring health to women who are in pain, we will be better prepared to shepherd those in the storms of life.

Fortunately, Amy and Ryan had a strong foundation of faith built in good times that would remain solid in the hard times. They certainly experienced painful emotions and asked hard questions, but their faith in God kept them afloat. Their informed support system contributed greatly to their ability to process the painful reality of their experience, to make tough decisions, and to celebrate the short life of Elijah Daniel.

Caregivers may encounter other challenging life events such as those listed below and wonder how to give comfort and encouragement.

- Sheryl, in the face of infertility, experiences the repeated agony of grieving the loss of a child *every* month and seeks to isolate herself, suffering silently.
- Beth is worn down emotionally by the silent, relentless "impacted grief" of a past abortion, yet has no understanding of her own seemingly irrational behaviors indicative of post-abortion stress.
- Cassie anxiously hurries out the church door the minute an event is over, fearing her husband will inflict further emotional or physical abuse on her or the children if she is even one minute late coming home.
- Monique's disproportionate focus on dieting, exercising, and body image has drawn her into unhealthy obsessions.
- Feelings of betrayal from her recent divorce are sabotaging Shannon's ability to generate healthy friendships.

What will an understanding pastor, leader, or friend say or do to bring comfort, hope, and healing to women struggling with issues such as these? Caregivers can provide help that is truly encouraging and beneficial, but this requires an understanding of the many issues that cause emotional pain. Women in pain desperately need effective shepherding! This book is written for that purpose.

My previous book, *Shepherding a Woman's Heart*, gave an overview of the key elements of shepherding women. This book goes further. *Shepherding Women in Pain* addresses specific issues that will be encountered as leaders shepherd women like Monique and Amy in their churches and communities. The three sections of this book address these aspects of shepherding: what the woman in pain wants to know, what the shepherd needs to know, and what the healing community needs to know.

Amy and Ryan realize how unusually blessed they were to have spiritual encouragers who had adequately prepared themselves to shepherd others through these kinds of life storms. The need for this kind of well-prepared shepherd is enormous. *Shepherding Women in Pain* is written with the hope of providing easily accessible understanding to those who care about the emotional health of women of all ages. The church, as a reflection of Jesus Christ, is beginning to more fully express the grace-filled acceptance and unconditional love of our Savior. May this book advance that purpose.

Understanding Women in Pain

What the Woman in Pain Wants to Know

Chapter 1

How Can I Stop the Pain?

*L*indsey married her high school sweetheart, Brandon. A few months after their honeymoon, Brandon was accepted into the navy and eventually was assigned to submarine duty. He served six months out at sea and six months in port. The first six months of separation were very difficult, but both survived and felt their relationship was stronger than before the separation. Two years later, Brandon returned home and announced to Lindsey that he needed a little space in their relationship to determine whether he had "it" with other women. Brandon said they had married young, so he had not dated much prior to their marriage. Now Brandon wanted to stay married while dating other women.

Lindsey was devastated. Brandon had promised fidelity on their wedding day. Lindsey's love for Brandon had only grown deeper over the three years of their marriage. And now this? Lindsey was devastated to think she was not enough for Brandon. What had she neglected? In what way should she have given him more? She began to blame herself. The thought of other women in his life was more than she could bear. The pain became so intense. At times she did not think she could draw her next breath.

Lindsey's words awkwardly tumbled out intermittently between heavy sobs and a flood of tears as she worked to tell me her story. As each sentence seemed to intensify her feelings of emotional pain, she came to the conclusion that somehow she had to find a way to stop the pain. She hurt so much! What could she do to stop the pain? Direct questions exposed thoughts of suicide and even murder. Lindsey did not remember ever feeling this much emotional pain in her life. She quickly remembered her grandfather's suicide as a means of ending his pain when his wife left him.

Lindsey clearly felt out of control. Although thoughts of committing suicide might bring a feeling of control in the immediate, the intensely negative outcome needed to be brought into perspective. Reframing her current situation with expressions of hope would prove to be life-giving. Involving family and close friends was an appropriate next step.

The immediate responses to Lindsey's outbursts included determining whether immediate intervention was needed. Contact information for local crisis intervention resources was close at hand. Listening well—without judgmental responses—was critical. Maintaining a calm demeanor without minimizing Lindsey's emotional pain allowed her to freely express what she was really feeling. Communication with Lindsey needed to be simple and directive. It was helpful to remember that Lindsey's ability to think and plan was likely to be inhibited in the immediate crisis.

Lindsey needed the ongoing support and understanding of those who would provide the safe environment in which she could be honest about her feelings. This in turn would likely enable her to begin the journey of facing the pain in a way that would enhance her ability to understand her own responses and realize this present distress was not endless.

Several issues interplayed with Lindsey's ability to process the emotional pain and eventually move into a place of healing. The essential human need to be loved and accepted had been violated. The level of pain was particularly deep because that violation occurred by someone who not only promised to be loyal, but who expressed love and understanding to her on a very intimate level. It was the first time in her adult life that she had received such understanding and expression of love.

Secondly, the number of losses Lindsey would experience was great. Not only would she lose the love of her husband and identity as a wife, but her future life as a mother and grandmother as well. The death of a marriage and the sting of divorce were deeply felt by Lindsey. The loss of a home, a house, vacations, anniversary celebrations, family life—her entire future seemed in peril. Asking Lindsey to list her losses was the beginning of a process of grief and recovery.

Grief is the normal reaction to loss of any kind. The feelings associated with the loss are also normal. The tension lies in the fact that we have been socialized to believe these feelings are abnormal. The feelings associated with loss are some of the most neglected and misunderstood emotions.[1] All relationships are unique. No one can assume they know how another feels, even if they have experienced some aspect of a similar grief.

Yet, can pain be accurately measured or compared? Many would think the grief of losing a mother, wife, and daughter to death in one vehicle accident would be the "worst." Although that horrific experience was Jerry Sittser's, he writes that the grief an individual bears is the "worst" to her or him.[2] Pain, agony, and anguish are defined by the one experiencing the loss. How can one say because you lost only one loved one to death, your pain is less than the pain of one who lost three? Sittser would conclude experiences of severe loss cannot be quantified or compared.

> Loss is loss, whatever the circumstances. All losses are bad, only bad in different ways. No two losses are ever the same. Each loss stands on its own and inflicts a unique kind of pain. What makes each loss so catastrophic is its devastating, cumulative, and irreversible nature.[3]

Losses—such as moving, starting school, graduation, health changes, financial changes, or empty nest—may result in emotional pain. Grief is the conflicting feelings caused by the end of or change in a familiar pattern of behavior.[4] Some losses, like graduation, may bring a positive feeling. At the same time, the graduate may realize she will no longer share experiences with classmates and friends at the school from which she is graduating. The uncertainty of her next step in life might add further anxiety and intensify the emotional feelings surrounding graduation. These are conflicted feelings, feeling both positive and negative feelings simultaneously.

A woman who has been physically abused by her father may have feelings of relief at his death. These positive feelings may generate feelings of guilt because she is feeling positive at a time when others are mourning a loss. Often the negative feelings overtake the positive feelings and the pressing question becomes, "How can I stop the pain?"

Typically the intensely painful feelings override clear thinking in the immediate. Too often a woman in pain may focus on immediate relief of her emotional pain instead of short- and long-term processing that leads to healing. Addictive behaviors may be a default response. Quick and seemingly easy relief is sought. Numbness and altered thinking may skew her reality. It is clear that her *perception* of her reality will be what triggers her emotional response. Her perception is her reality.

A caregiver can begin to enter her perceived reality by encouraging the woman to talk about the situation, about her thoughts and feelings. The memory will linger, but the painful impact may eventually lessen by knowing someone is traveling alongside the woman in pain and is willing to listen to her expressions of excruciating confusion and emotional agony. A caregiver who will be directive when intervention is needed, empathetic when listening is required, and understanding in the journey toward recovery will bring hope in the midst of pain. The care receiver may begin to see that this level of pain is not endless and that she is not powerless in her circumstances. She does have choices and recovery will begin with a series of very small but critical decisions.

Some people tend to avoid the reality of the problem and thus hope to avoid pain. Part of our task is to help them face the pain, but this must be done gradually so they are not overwhelmed. We can create an environment in which they feel safe and comfortable enough to face their situation fully.[5]

Too often well-meaning people or ill-prepared shepherds may hinder this process by giving a woman in pain comments that may be intellectually accurate but do not bring healing to a broken heart. For example, a woman, who after miscarrying a much-wanted baby may be physically able to get pregnant again, is not comforted by the words, "Don't feel bad, you're young. You can have another child." Neither is a woman whose husband has just walked out on her comforted by hearing, "Don't worry, you'll find a better man next time." Shepherds who realize "Grief is about a broken heart, not a broken brain"[6] will more likely respond with words that bring healing to a broken heart.

The caregiver who understands that God's purpose may unfold in the midst of painful situations will be challenged to communicate this truth appropriately. Although the woman may ask, "How can I stop the pain?" this may not be the most pressing issue. An effective shepherd will have looked deeper into the purpose of pain.

Gabby was born with a rare disorder. She has no ability to feel physical pain. On the surface we may all wish for this. However, the reality is that this inability to experience pain is incredibly destructive to one who feels no consequences of harm done to her body. Young Gabby would bite her tongue and fingers until they bled and "looked like hamburger." She unknowingly tried to destroy her own eyes before the intervention of doctors to sew her eyelids shut and later her parents insisting she wear eye goggles. Her mother had to check her feet several times a day to see if thorns, glass, or stones may have imbedded themselves and infection might have set in. Gabby could not tell from "feeling pain" whether she had injured her body. So even though her parents tried to watch her every move, little Gabby was literally demolishing her own body.[7]

The result of not feeling physical pain can be self-destruction. Pain is really a gift that no one wants, but none of us can do without. The ability to feel physical pain actually is a God-given means of preserving life.

> Because we were created in the image of God we are pro-life—
> meaning pro my life. When we sense a threat to our existence and
> well-being, we spontaneously act to protect and preserve our lives . . .
> we normally adopt defensive, self-protective thinking and behavior
> patterns when we feel emotionally or relationally threatened and
> wounded. Emotional pain, like physical pain, draws attention to the
> fact that something needs to change.[8]

Touching a hot stove sends the message to the brain that says, "Stop!
Remove finger from stove immediately." In a similar way, emotional pain
alerts a woman to the fact that alerts a woman to the fact that she should
seek relief. Relief is seldom as simple or easy as removing one's finger
from a stove top. A woman in emotional pain is alerted to finding the
source of the pain and, like cutting an onion, peeling away the layers of
thinking and behavior patterns she has acquired through her lifetime that
intensify the painful responses to her immediate circumstances.

Perhaps the caregiver's job is to help women understand the message
or purpose of pain. Too often the shepherd herself feels a discomfort with
the pain of another and instinctively joins the help-seeker in finding ways
to cover up the sensation. This is more likely to occur if the shepherd's
pattern of dealing with her own pain is to simply find quick relief.

Pain may send a message that life, as it is, is not working. The status
quo has become painful enough to reconsider. It is the continual uninterrupted pain that comes as a consequence of an alcoholic's decision to
medicate his pain through drinking that breaks through his *modus operandi*. Family and friends clearly communicate the pain they have experienced as a consequence of his decision to drink. If the alcoholic hears
their pain and the pain he feels as a result is *greater* than the pain that
precipitates his *modus operandi*, then he is likely to stop and reconsider
his choices. This opens the door to make life work better.

Pain also tells a woman that she is not as much in control as she had

thought. Pain that is not easily dismissed or relieved sends a ⟍
that it is bigger than the person bearing the pain. Once she sees ⟍ ... ⟍er
attempts to relieve the pain are futile, she may be tempted to think less of
herself or even shame herself. The next step of asking someone to help is
prefaced by her own admission that *she needs help* and is inadequate in
her independence. Some stay stuck in this stage until the pain becomes so
intolerable that they are finally willing to give up their fierce self-sufficiency
for the sake of relief.

Pain takes on a lot of faces. Antonyms for *pain*[9] are joy and delight.[10]
This is quite telling. Often when loved family members or friends experience emotional pain, those observing spontaneously attempt to change
their emotional suffering to joy or delight. Additional efforts may include
changing the subject, telling a joke, or suggesting a trip to the mall.
Our human instincts—unless trained otherwise—tend to trigger such
responses.

Life is filled with pain. In the midst of pain is it possible to feel joy or
delight? True joy and delight are found in the hope we have in the presence of Jesus—now and in eternity. Jesus endured the cross "for the joy
set before him" (Hebrews 12:2). We have that same hope.

The understanding of a "present" shepherd is often what a woman
in pain really needs. Pain is a part of life. For the believer in Christ the
understanding that human suffering brings opportunity to become more
like Christ provides a foundational strength. For the unbeliever the pain
of life may be a catalyst to begin seeking God. Compassion, support, and
understanding from another are among the greatest gifts a shepherd can
provide. A woman in pain needs someone to walk alongside her in the
pain, someone who will bring the hope of Jesus Christ.

In this chapter's opening story, Brandon's decision ultimately proved
to be one that dissolved their marriage. Lindsey would discover that
although the immediate circumstance of Brandon's unfaithfulness was
reason enough to experience myriad painful emotions, Lindsey also
would uncover several other major losses in her life that had not been fully
grieved. In fact, even the death of her grandfather was hushed and not

discussed in her family. The messages she received from her family were
(1) Don't feel bad, (2) Don't talk about it, (3) Pretend it didn't happen,
and (4) Be happy for others. As Lindsey looked back on the losses in her
life, she realized this is how she approached each of them. However, no
matter how hard she tried, she was not able to keep the unspoken family
rules in her most recent loss. She felt horrible and could not pretend this
was not happening any more than she could act happy. At times she was
afraid she would never quit crying.

What Lindsey did not realize was the way in which we grieve our first
loss, unless we have had intervention, will be the way we experience each
subsequent loss.[11] The emotions Lindsey allowed herself to express were
in essence a collection of feelings that she had stored away from previous
losses in life. It was time to begin peeling back the layers and revisit that
first experience of grief. A helpful process for Lindsey was to ask in each
loss she had listed, What do I wish had been different, more, or better?[12]
enabling Lindsey to communicate messages that brought completion to
each loss. Lindsey came to realize that she could not change the actions
of others, but she could take responsibility for her current reaction to
what happened in the past. This realization opened the door for Lindsey
to identify her choices and respond by making small but important decisions that eventually led her to a place of resolve and wholeness.

Lindsey would acknowledge the value of a shepherd expressing
hope, especially when Lindsey saw none. Extreme and long-term pain
can result in a feeling of despair. This may lead to an absence of hope.
No matter the extent of the pain, hope is a key ingredient that is needed.
When pain is extensive, the clear meaning can diminish or seem obscure.
The purpose may be lost in the dailyness of simply trying to cope. Henri
Nouwen affirms that the hope we as "wounded healers" bring is the truth
that the wound "which causes us to suffer now, will be revealed to us later
as the place where God intimated his new creation."[13]

Often women on painful journeys similar to Lindsey's ask, "When
will life be normal again?" The next chapter will take us further in exploring this aspect of understanding a woman in pain.

Chapter 2

When Will Life Be Normal Again?

*A*fter a long day in the office, Jackie walked slowly to her car in the parking lot. Before she knew what happened, she was assaulted and robbed. Fortunately a coworker appeared and was able to get her home. How does Jackie process this heinous injustice? Although she healed physically in a few weeks, the feelings of violation, immobilization, fear, and anger began to haunt her. Conversations revealed her strong feelings of resistance. "Why should I forgive him after what he did to me? All he deserves is punishment and I hope he gets the full extent of the law and more." Jackie could not imagine giving him compassion or forgiveness. Others in her family felt she was fully justified in her bitterness toward him.

This reaction is certainly normal and expected immediately after such a crime. Yet, when more of the story was divulged, it became clear that Jackie was not in a good place. The attack occurred over *four years* prior to this conversation. She still thinks about him every day, and relives the humiliation she felt that night. Every time she goes out to her car—day or night—she is nervous, sometimes panic-stricken when she sees someone else in the vicinity. She relives the attack in her thoughts by day and her dreams by night. She quit the job she loved out of fear. Now she rarely goes outside, even in the daytime. The few times she allows herself to be with a man, she fears he might attack her and is unable to build a relationship of trust with him.

Clearly this attack has affected every aspect of Jackie's life. It is obvious she is a victim and wrong was committed against her; she is justified in feeling angry about the injustice. But is she justified in her fears, anxieties, and inability to trust anyone? Would life ever be normal again? She allowed the original attack to dominate her whole existence, to define her existence. The attack had nearly destroyed her life. The effects thrive in part because Jackie had not forgiven the man who attacked her.

Jackie is a person with intrinsic value, created in the image of God. God has a purpose for her life. She is a visual example of the truth of John 10:10, "The thief comes only to steal and kill and destroy; I came that they may have life, and have it abundantly."[1]

Through forgiveness the pain caused by the original wrong can be released. The victim in essence is saying the wrong caused me pain but I will not allow it to hurt me anymore. I am putting the injustice in its proper place, as one thing that happened in my past, which I have dealt with, for which I forgive you, something that is only one small part of my whole life story. If I can forgive him, then I will not be totally destroyed by his actions. I am someone over and above the harm that he has done to me. Otherwise I could not be offering him forgiveness here and now.[2]

Forgiveness is not as simplistic as this might imply. It is a process. Too often women assume it is a matter of just saying, "I forgive Steve," and that is all there is to it. Then she wonders why the pain never subsides, and why it actually increases each time she sees Steve. "When you can't let go of the pain, when the act of betrayal or brutality still burns in your memory, there is some unfinished business. That business is typically guilt or resentment. They are opposite sides of the same coin. When you feel guilty, you feel you owe somebody something. When you feel resentful, you feel that somebody owes you something."[3] Both require further processing.

There are several aspects to forgiveness that will prove helpful in shepherding women in pain. Three important ones are understanding what forgiveness is *not* saying, the levels of forgiveness, and the forgiveness process.

Forgiveness Is Not

It is helpful in shepherding a woman in pain to underscore what forgiveness is *not* saying. Forgiveness is not saying:[4]

1. *It is no big deal.* It *is* a big deal. An offense, a sin, has been committed and needs to be addressed. Forgiveness is saying it is big enough to require a process to move forward.
2. *Now everything will be as it was before.* Just the opposite is true. The victim, the abused, the one treated unjustly will never be the same. So "everything" will never be as it was before the offense.
3. *I will never have to think about this again.* Forgiveness is not the same as forgetting or hoping I can forget the offense. Forgiving is releasing the debt.
4. *Welcome back into every area of my life.* Forgiveness should not be confused with reconciliation. Reconciliation is about a restored relationship. Forgiveness focuses on the debt, not the debtor. The integrity and sincerity of the debtor is not critical for true forgiveness to be given. Forgiveness may have no impact on the one whose debt is cleared. He may not even be aware of the forgiveness. If we look to the offender for healing, restitution, or compensation, we will continue in our bondage. The one who has caused the pain does not have the means to repay the debt or remove the pain from

us. If we look to the perpetrator to fill the void, we will always be disappointed.[5]

The forgiving victim will need to make good decisions regarding future contact with the perpetrator. Even if it is a family member and family events seem to demand attendance, the woman who has gone through the forgiveness process will set wise boundaries. She will not intentionally leave the door open for future offenses.

5. *Well, that takes care of that.* The impact—both negative and positive—will linger on. Likely shrapnel will surface at various points throughout life. Typically this may indicate yet another corner of pain, anger, or fear that needs to be brought out into the open and processed.

6. *I can do it by myself.* This is a huge misconception for a woman in pain. Although a woman familiar with the Bible may know well the biblical texts about forgiveness, the process needs to include another person. Most offenses were committed in relationship, and it is in relationship that most healing occurs—in many cases not with the same person who committed the assault but certainly with an understanding shepherd.

Three Levels of Forgiveness[6]

Jackie finally made a decision to forgive her perpetrator. She realized the potential value forgiveness might bring to her life. She was ready to make a change. She did not emotionally feel like forgiving; she felt no compassion toward her offender. She simply made a cognitive choice to forgive. She said the words to a shepherd and she said the words to God in prayer. She wrote them down as if she were saying them to the perpetrator. This was most challenging. Jackie made the decision on the cognitive level and she restated words of forgiveness as she worked through the forgiveness process.

This first level took some time to process. After significant time in this level, the forgiver will slowly begin to understand several things.

- Harm comes to everyone.
- Moral contracts cannot prevent injury.
- No one is immune from it.
- Test of character is how well one functions even when one does not understand God's plan.
- God can redeem our injuries and use them for good.[7]

Level two is emotional forgiveness. This is the level in which the victim comes to understand the above truths about life. Growth in understanding the weaknesses and life struggles of the offender is the major path that leads to emotional forgiveness. Jackie slowly began to see the man who assaulted her as Jesus Christ would see him: a person with great spiritual and personal need. This was preceded by her entry into the third level of forgiveness, the spiritual. The spiritual level is one that says, "Lord, please help me to forgive him. I want to forgive him. You have forgiven me. Please enable me to forgive him. He needs to know Your forgiveness in his own life."

Scripture clearly mandates forgiveness. Jesus told Peter to forgive seventy times seven, which essentially meant no limit should be set on how many times we need to forgive. Peter thought he was being generous suggesting seven times, for the traditional rabbinic teaching was that an offended person needed to forgive a brother only three times.[8] Jesus tells a parable to illustrate the point that to the extent we have been forgiven, we should forgive. Unlike the first servant who was forgiven all his debt (likely several million dollars), he was not willing to forgive another servant who only owed a laborer's one day's wages—a much, much smaller amount. A follower of Jesus has been forgiven all her sins by accepting Jesus' payment for her sins. Therefore, she should be willing to forgive others (Matthew 18:21–35).

Ephesians 4:31–32 clearly says, "Get rid of all bitterness, rage and anger, brawling and slander, along with every form of malice. Be kind and compassionate to one another, *forgiving each other, just as in Christ God forgave you*" (emphasis added). Jesus tells us in the model prayer of Matthew 6:9–13, "Forgive us our debts, as we also have forgiven our debtors." There is a relationship between the two.

The beautiful story in Luke 7 is worth taking the time to ponder further. The religious leaders are appalled that Jesus would allow "a woman in that town who lived a sinful life" to enter the same room with them. They assumed Jesus did not know who she was. Jesus responded by giving a parable that illustrated the one who is forgiven much, loves much. Jesus reiterated this point referring to the woman as one who was forgiven much and so loved much. Her actions were an expression of her love for Jesus, the one who had forgiven her. In case the listeners missed it, Jesus also said, "But whoever has been forgiven little loves little."[9]

Jesus Himself was able to extend forgiveness for those who abused Him when going to the cross.[10] Jesus extends the limitless offer of forgiveness to us, "If we confess our sins, he is faithful and just and will forgive us our sins and purify us from all unrighteousness" (1 John 1:9). Forgiveness is a priceless gift we receive and we give. Scripture clearly mandates it. Often the process is assumed to be simply saying three words, "I forgive you" and it is all over. Yet we wonder why the bitterness and anger linger, along with the emotional pain.

Forgiveness does not always resolve all the emotional pain resulting from traumatic life events. However, it does bring the victim to a place of newfound freedom from being held in bondage to the victimization and the ability to move forward in life.

All hurt comes from loss, whether it is real or imagined loss: past, present, or anticipated loss. There is the loss of love or lovability when a loved one dies or a relationship ends. Betrayal or infidelity of a spouse may shatter a person's self-esteem. One may lose control of her life or be forced to do something against her will. Perhaps the beliefs you always held dear are lost or no longer have meaning.

Perhaps it would be helpful to ask the injured person, "What loss have you incurred?" This informs the wounded of the area needing healing. When people experience a deep loss, they are forever changed. Even if they forgive, even if they rebuild the basic assumptions about life, love, and relationships that were shattered as a result of the injury, they are different.[11] They must be in order to have successfully integrated what has happened to them into their lives.

Certain offenses seem more difficult to forgive because they assault people's fundamental beliefs. Three basic assumptions in life are: the world is meaningful and well, people are generally benevolent, and the self is worthy.[12] When people experience traumas, their assumptions about themselves and their world are shattered. The more damage done to a person's assumptions, the more difficult it can be to forgive.

Jackie was forced to accept that her core beliefs failed and had to begin rebuilding them. She assumed because she was a good employee and did a very conscientious job, she would be safe walking to and from her car each day. She believed people were generally good and that she was worth being treated kindly. She also thought because she was a Christian, God would protect her from things like assaults. All of these assumptions had to be reconfigured. Careful study of Scripture with a shepherd helped her in this process. She began to change her perception, behavior, values, and expectations. She realized she could be wounded again, but with the strength of this process behind her, she now knows that through God's empowering Spirit, she will not only be able to survive the woundedness but see God redeem it.

The Process of Forgiveness[13]

Forgiveness is best understood as a process, a process that takes time. The first step in the forgiveness process is to clearly identify the hurt done to you. Lily's father was abusive to all three of her siblings. Yet, Lily needed to identify the painful abuse she experienced, apart from that of her siblings, to begin her forgiveness process. She needed to admit the harm done to her, the dimensions of the injury in terms of its duration, controllability, consequence, and perhaps its cause. Lily made a list of very specific wounds inflicted by her father. She stopped trying to pretend nothing happened. She began to take ownership of the injuries and stopped defending herself against them. She stopped rationalizing the behaviors of the offender or giving justifications for his abuse. She had to own the wounds in order to fully forgive the one who wounded.

Blaming the injurer was hard for Lily. She felt that was not a Christian thing to do. Yet, until she was able to put blame where it belonged, she could not fully forgive. The American myth of no-fault injuries does not apply in the forgiveness process. To blame the injurer is to hold them morally accountable for causing an event to happen. Blaming separates the victim from the offender, clarifying the two roles. This is the place where the victim begins to regain some ability to make choices that she felt she lost in the offense. Lily named each offense, named the injurer, and made the choice to forgive each one.

Forgiving comes from a position of strength, not weakness. It changes people from objects of other people's choices to people who create their own choices. This is a major step in the process of healing. A crime, abuse, or injustice robs the victim of choice. It disrupts the balance of personal choice. Forgiveness restores choice.

Forgiveness means you no longer expect that person who injured you to owe you anything. You forgive the debt of the offender. This includes giving up the option of blaming the injurer for personal pain or attitudes. These personal attitudes once again become the sole property of the wounded, who alone has the choice of what to do with them. Forgiveness cuts the bond that held her to the offender and chooses to look ahead, not back.

This process leads to the emergence of a new perspective. Lily became a different person through the process of forgiving her father. Granted, it took time. A shepherd assisted her in studying the Scripture to learn that unlike her earthly father, her heavenly Father valued her and would redeem her painful experiences. Jesus Christ died, was buried, and rose from the dead for the purpose of providing forgiveness, righteousness, and eternal life for Lily. Lily had not only the hope of heaven when she died, but the power of the Holy Spirit in her life while on this earth. She embraced God's love but it took her a long time for her default

perspective of God to be gracious and compassionate rather than puni-
tive. Eventually, she began to see ways she could encourage other young
women who had experienced abusive pasts. She was effective because in
part she understood their pain and the healing process. As a follower of
Jesus Christ, Lily experienced redemption.

Neither Jackie nor Lily would ever again see what *was* their normal.
Rather, both women would construct a new normal for their lives.
The pain of injury and process of recovery forge new life patterns and
insights. Greater understandings of the world, of faith, and of God are
likely to generate a different chapter in the story of the life of a woman
who experiences emotional pain. This is a gift.

"This gift of meaning is not a piece of artwork that you contemplate
and enjoy. Instead, it is a gift of lumber, hammer and nails, and a saw. You
must build something. Making meaning out of what happened to you is
seeing the possibilities that are now open to you as a direct result of your
suffering."[14]

Chapter 3

What Does Healing Look Like?

August 24, 1992 is a day many south Floridians will always remember. Hurricane Andrew was the second most powerful and the last of three Category 5 hurricanes (top gusts reached 175 mph) that made US landfall during the twentieth century.[1] In August of 1992, my husband and I were living within a few miles of the incalculable devastation in south Florida where most of the damage occurred.[2] Hours before Hurricane Andrew hit land, we filled our bathtub and boarded up windows. If the circumference of Hurricane Andrew had been typical, our home would have been in its path. After the storm moved out into the Gulf and on to Louisiana, we took supplies to a sister church in the distressed area for distribution to hurricane victims.

The church was sweltering hot in the Florida heat. There was no electricity or running water within miles of the church. To our astonishment, Lynn welcomed us with a warm smile and offered us a cup of water. The source of that one cup of water was the only plastic jug of water on the premises, with no promise of additional water arriving soon. Jesus' words, "And if you give even a cup of cold water to one of the least of my followers, you will surely be rewarded,"[3] suddenly had new meaning. Lynn, a woman who'd lost so much, offered us a cup of water! She ministered to us in a way words could never describe. I felt the presence of Jesus in her act of kindness.

This scene is one I replay often as a caregiver. Sometimes when I feel this is the last cup of water I have to give today, yet it is still to be given, with the hope that Jesus will multiply its effect. Too often we underestimate the value of seemingly small kindnesses, of giving what we have for the benefit of others. As caregivers, we may be surprised how those we assume need *our* help actually minister to us.

I recall conversations with women like Lynn who could not even get to their houses, who had no idea if anything was left standing, but who were grateful to be alive. There were no moorings, no land markings, such as traffic lights, street signs, trees, or buildings, to identify where a particular house used to stand. *Nothing* was left standing. "Normal" as Lynn knew it was gone. Her church, which thankfully was still standing, offered shelter and supplies as people brought them in from surrounding areas.

Lynn eventually found her property. Rebuilding seemed impossible and initially undesirable. How could she set herself up for the possibility of another hurricane by living in this hurricane-prone area? That assessment would require more than her immediate ability to make a logical decision. Lynn was a woman in pain. The recurring dreams of a violent storm, losing everything, and standing alone on her street corner plagued her for many months. As the reality of her situation settled in, Lynn entered into a deep depression.

What would healing look like for Lynn? Would she ever recover from this "natural disaster"? How does a woman find a new "normal" after such an unwarranted, unjustifiable, or inexplicable life event? What can a shepherd bring to help Lynn in this journey?

> Crisis intervention is giving emotional first aid. . . . In its simplest form, the goal of crisis intervention is to stop the psychological deterioration, stabilize the person's thinking and emotional processes, manage stress symptoms, and either restore him or her to a functional level or find the necessary help for continuing acute care. . . . This is *not* therapy. It is intervention and support.[4]

Initial efforts of support are for the purpose of restoring equilibrium. People cannot tolerate the stress of a crisis for long. Efforts to find quick relief will not be well thought out and could be counterproductive, worsening the problem or crisis. Find out what happened and let the woman describe it from her perspective. A shepherd may need to prompt her: "And then what occurred?" "What thoughts went through your mind initially?" "What was your reaction to this?" Normalize her feelings and reactions. Help her understand the crisis. Determine what you can do to bring a greater sense of order to her environment. She may feel her world is falling apart and everything is spinning out of control. Listening and encouraging are your primary tools. Eventually you and the woman in pain will focus on setting goals and walking through them step-by-step.[5]

The first step for Lynn is to fully acknowledge her new reality. Denial is a mechanism that serves a purpose temporarily. It gives the person time to integrate the new reality into existing ones. Lynn's willingness to receive needed items delivered to her church was one way she was able to slowly receive messages of the disaster she would later fully embrace. Her ability to welcome warmly and express kindness was clearly at the heart of who Lynn is as a follower of Jesus. Similarly she would emerge from this disaster a woman of warmth and kindness, but with an intensified, life-altering passion to serve others. Granted, Lynn would never be the same neighbor, family member, coworker, or follower of Jesus as she was before Hurricane Andrew. But she would weave through the passageways in the circle of loss endless times before emerging the woman she is today.

The process of acknowledging loss followed by needful grieving has been given a variety of configurations. Certainly there is agreement that no matter how this process is described, it is not predictable. That is, not every person going through emotional pain will walk an identical path. It is not a linear experience. The value of knowing the elements of the journey is in assuring women in pain that it is "normal" to feel the feelings they experience, given the trauma they have endured. It also provides a direction in which shepherds can encourage women to walk. Hope comes in seeing what is possible for a woman who may be experiencing the harshest of emotions as she fully embraces the reality of her painful situation.

Typically the first stage is protest. She will be disoriented, nonfunctioning, and have a sense of numbness. The woman in pain may be using words such as, "Nothing is wrong. I'm fine." She needs a shepherd primarily to be present. The shepherd may be able to assess the situation and gently draw her into acknowledging the reality. The woman in pain needs to discover the normalcy of her responses. Lynn's first step was to accept the reality of the losses of her home and life as she knew it.

The second stage is despair. She may feel confusion, anger, rage, fear, sadness—the gamut of emotions. Her thinking and ability to problem-solve will be severely limited. The woman in pain will likely express, "I know I can't make it. I am sure I will not survive." She longs to recover what was lost and may dream of her "before" life. She may have repeated dreams of her first discovery of the loss. The griever's main task in this stage is to fully experience the pain of grief. The shepherd should focus on (1) listening and being and (2) gently giving small task-oriented guidance so when the shepherd leaves, the woman in pain realizes she *can* do something. That task may be as simple as finding clothes to wear for the next day, or putting a load of clothes in the washer, or identifying what she will eat for breakfast.

Typically this phase will take longer than stage one. The caregiver should look for ways this stage may be short-circuited by (1) denying pain or (2) entering into a period of exaggerated grief and refusing to take care of minimal self-care. Either of these may reveal one or more losses in the past that were not fully grieved or processed. Lynn's depth of grief revealed previous life losses that surfaced and increased her level of pain. Lynn had assumed a "buck up and move on" mentality reflecting her family's response to life's losses. She agreed to see a professional counselor who specialized in the kind of trauma she had experienced. Lynn did the hard work of grieving multiple losses, with the consistent help of a shepherd and a small group in her church.

The third stage is detachment. The woman in pain will feel many of the same feelings as stage two, but will begin to realize she must adjust to an environment in which the loss exists. She will continue to feel an emptiness, deadness, and numbness. She will have a strong desire to withdraw, a loss of interest in normal activities, and a desire to give up. Again, the shepherd's tasks are similar to stage two: listen and increase the griever's sense of being able to accomplish simple daily tasks. Lynn's church small group members made contact with her regularly during these months. They invited Lynn to join them in a light task, an errand, or a fun activity. This provided opportunity for Lynn to stay engaged with people rather than isolate. Granted, there were days when Lynn chose not to go. But those became fewer each month. This regular engagement with members of her small group also motivated her to accomplish tasks or errands of her own, and the occasional fun lightened the constant heaviness of her reality. Being with people she trusted and knew cared about her also provided opportunity for Lynn to express her feelings and thoughts as she slowly began to acknowledge the fact that she would never be able to return to the familiarity of her home or neighborhood.

The fourth stage is recovery. She will begin to have positive thoughts. She will be able to do minimal problem solving. She will begin looking for something new in which to invest. Her main task is to invest energy into the new: new relationships, new job, new home, or new endeavors. Celebrate with her new feelings. Build new memories together. Typically this stage takes longer than the others.

This is the stage in which gentle conversation about God may surface. She may be ready to engage in conversation about who God *really* is and how He could let this happen to her if He really is a loving God. The need to forgive (herself or others) may also surface. As Lynn's friends encouraged Lynn to dream about a new community and a new job, deeper conversation emerged. The relationships established in Lynn's small group provided a safe environment for her to question where God was in this tragedy. Why did He not protect her house and neighborhood? Her previous understanding of who God is was not proving to be valid in this crisis. It felt disorienting to her. The hard work of reconstructing a more biblical perspective of God began.

Stage five is restoration. In this stage, hope returns and reconstruction increases self-confidence. Thinking is clearer. Conversation will enable her to normalize her experience. She may be ready to begin verbalizing what she is learning from this journey of loss and grief. She may soon be ready to come alongside others who are experiencing a similar loss. She will take initiative for progress and reattachments are occurring. Lynn's relationship with God clearly deepened, along with her appreciation of the fragility of life. Lynn began praying and searching for ways to minister to others in crisis situations. She felt her life mission was only beginning.

How long does it take to complete this cycle? As long as it takes. Not everyone grieves in the same way. The context of the loss and individuality of the griever impacts the process.[6]

In 1999 Carol and Gene Kent watched their "normal" lives take a horrible detour when their beloved only son was arrested and eventually sentenced to life in prison without the possibility of parole. Carol's book *A New Kind of Normal* attests to the fact that when faced with this kind of emotional pain, one faces a choice.

> Living in a new kind of normal has taught me that pain is pain is pain is pain. . . . Embracing your new kind of normal is the most empowering choice you will ever make. It transcends common

sense. It is resistant to old patterns. It is sticky, uncomfortable, agitating, and difficult. But it is liberating and life giving and spirit enriching. It changes your life and the lives of everyone who joins you on your journey. And then, quite unexpectedly, you realize you are splashing hope into the lives of others because you have an intimate love relationship with the Source of hope.[7]

People in pain have the power of choice. Shepherds have the opportunity to gently encourage that power of choice to be exercised. As women in pain choose to walk through the pain, the hope of healing can be a strong motivator. But what does that healing look like? Will it be obvious to all that this woman has completed all five stages of grief? Will the shepherd or the one in pain recognize healing when it emerges?

The task of quantifying healing can be challenging.

A plumb line is preset before one begins to paste wallpaper so the outcome will be uniform and "straight." In the same way, we can set a plumb line of what a healthy follower of Jesus Christ looks like from reading the Scriptures. While general principles for following Christ are clearly laid out, the specifics are influenced by culture, history, and gender. Jesus did not present the gospel to any two people in quite the same way. He challenged people at their point of need.

A woman in pain may remember with fondness the person she was before the crisis. She may see this as her plumb line. On the other hand, a woman in pain may have a strong desire to grow in maturity through this pain and desire a greater sense of intimacy with God and character development in her own life as outcomes of the crisis.

Remember, biblically the picture of health is not one of perfection but rather one of completeness or wholeness. It is one in which both soul and spirit are giving and receiving essential components of wholeness or health. James tells us that the purpose of trials (pain, crises, etc.) is the testing of our faith, which develops perseverance. "Let perseverance finish its work so that you may be mature and *complete*, not lacking anything" (James 1:2–4, emphasis added). *Complete* is "complete in all its parts, in no part lacking or unsound . . . whole."[8] Biblical health is wholeness.

How can healing be measured? Often this is difficult to assess in the midst of the crisis. After time has passed, growth may be more evident, measured against a woman's pre-crisis status. If a woman *wants* to mature and admittedly is taking steps forward in the healing process, she is likely to experience growth. Perhaps the woman herself and those closest to her are best able to measure that growth because they will have something (her pre-crisis state) with which to compare her behavior and attitude.

For example, a woman who post-crisis has a greater sense of the fragility of life may see that change reflected in expressing greater patience toward elderly people, to whom pre-crisis she expressed great impatience. This change may be measured in terms of her change in attitude, which is reflected in her change in behavior. The ability to measure this change would be dependent on the plumb line of her pre-crisis behaviors and attitudes.

The human change process takes time. Children generally do not make changes in their behavior the first time their attention is drawn to the misbehavior. It takes motivation, and that motivation is directly affected by consistent reminders and rewards. The motivation should move from extrinsic to intrinsic as the child becomes self-motivated to change.

An adult may be intrinsically motivated but will need consistent reminders in order to change established behavior patterns. The length of time the current behavior has been in place will directly impact the time line of the adult's ability to make a change. Much of adult behavior may be habitual. Breaking a habitual pattern takes time and motivation. Once an adult sees progress, that may be motivation enough to continue pressing on. There are multilevel processes through which we experience change. The end goal is not simply the elimination of pain. Change in human responses, growth as a disciple of Jesus, and maturity of perspective are some of the outcomes we are looking for. Eliminating pain is only secondary.

Walter Brueggemann provides a paradigm from the Psalms[9] for human change. He identifies three points:

1. *Orientation*—I know the questions and the answers. God is doing a good job of being God.
2. *Disorientation*—I no longer know the questions or the answers. We can't even find God and we think His way of running the world has much to be desired.
3. *Reorientation*—Now I see. I was asking the wrong question and now I see. This is a place of reshaping, of restructuring. The presence of the Holy Spirit in the person's life may be the key to the openness of process and change.

Soon Reorientation once again becomes Orientation. And we start around the cycle again. Orientation—I know the answers before the question is asked. And then the Holy Spirit nudges us and we find ourselves again at the Reorientation.

When people come for help, they are most likely to be in Disorientation. Human change comes through progress through this cycle. Brueggemann suggests we sing the Psalms in each of these phases. Healing takes place in a world in which His kingdom is here, but His redemption is not yet complete. The human change process takes place in the context of a relationship with Jesus Christ and caring people.

One of the ways a shepherd can initiate progress in the midst of Disorientation is to initiate a working alliance[10] with the woman in pain. Together you agree on the specifics of what the woman in pain will be working on with you. This may include working through the loss and grief process described above. Perhaps an initial agreement will be to identify one step and walk through it together. Perhaps the working alliance would be working with a woman recently widowed to reestablish mealtime as a meaningful time with friends and family, rather than a time of mourning for what it used to be. A working alliance may include agreeing on how a verbally abused woman will respond to her abuser the next time he speaks hurtful or demeaning words to her. A newly divorced woman may need to be held accountable for her own self-care on a given day(s).

Sometimes the woman in pain simply wants the caregiver to tell her it is okay to do something she has already decided to do, something that does not appear to be helpful or healthy. A working alliance is about talking through a plan that you both are willing to support. "I will help you with those feelings you have inside. Would you like to change those? Yes . . . well, we can have an agreement about that." Find common ground on which you can fully agree on a decision. Manipulating a wounded woman to believe what you want her to believe will backfire every time. You have to work with where the woman in pain is, not where you think she should be.

A working alliance may have more than one task, or may identify a new task after completing a previously named task. The task may be literally "how to do" something better, or it may be a better way of responding emotionally, internally or externally. It may be to increase understanding that will eventually lead to a different response. What may appear to the caregiver to be diminutive agreements and diminutive advances may in actuality be mammoth for the woman in pain. At appropriate junctures, both the woman in pain and the shepherd will identify what the working alliance agreed to do and then ask, "Did we do what we set out to do? Did we do only a part of it? What is left to do?" Celebrating what has been accomplished can be a potent reason to continue.

Jerry Sittser, after receiving news that his wife, baby daughter, and mother were killed in a car crash by a drunk driver, soon realized

> My own catastrophic loss thus taught me the incredible power
> of choice—to enter the darkness and to feel sorrow, as I did after
> the accident, even as I continued to work and to care for people,
> especially my children. . . . I wanted to integrate my pain into my life
> in order to ease some of its sting. I wanted to learn wisdom and to
> grow in character. . . . I knew that running from the darkness would

only lead to greater darkness later on. I also knew that my soul had the capacity to grow—to absorb evil and good, to die and live again, to suffer abandonment and find God. In choosing to face the night, I took my first steps toward the sunrise.[11]

Sittser realized he had no power to control the circumstances that altered the course of his life, but soon discovered he had the power to determine the course his life would take from that point forward, however limited it seemed at the time. He had the power to choose how he would respond and whether or not he would trust in God. *People in pain have the power of choice*, and shepherds have the opportunity to gently encourage that power of choice to be exercised.

One of the most helpful guidelines for use in helping women recognize progress in their healing is the following checklist taken from Marion Duckworth's book *Healing for the Empty Heart*.[12] When a woman has made progress in any *one* of these areas, the shepherd should celebrate this step of progress with her. This is a great motivator for the woman in pain to continue on in her journey toward wholeness!

Evidence of Progress in My Personal Growth

1. Once I didn't know or wouldn't admit that "something's wrong with me"
   NOW I HAVE FACED THAT FACT

2. Once I thought that I'd just have to fumble along this way
   NOW I HAVE TOLD SOMEONE

3. Once I thought it was up to me to fix myself
   NOW I KNOW THAT MY HELP COMES FROM GOD

4. Once I depended on coping mechanisms to survive
   NOW I AM SEEING THESE PRACTICES AS SELF-DEFEATING

5. Once I couldn't trust God

   NOW I'M IN THE PROCESS OF CHANGING MY PERSPECTIVE—*GOD IS NOT LIKE THE FATHER WHO ABANDONED, NEGLECTED, OR ABUSED ME. HE IS JUST AND LOVING.*

6. Once I repressed my feelings or was overwhelmed and controlled by them

   NOW I AM LEARNING TO NAME AND CONTROL MY FEELINGS AND NOT ALLOW THEM TO CONTROL MY LIFE

7. Once I didn't know how to speak appropriately about the experiences that damaged me

   NOW I AM LEARNING BOUNDARIES

8. Once I saw myself as a failure

   NOW I'M LEARNING TO PLACE BLAME WHERE IT BELONGS

9. Once I saw myself only as a victim—used and abused—

   NOW I'M LEARNING THAT, ALTHOUGH I WAS A VICTIM, CHRIST CAN PROVIDE THE GRACE AND POWER TO MAKE MY PAINFUL PAST THE FOUNDATION FOR A CONSTRUCTIVE FUTURE

10. Once I saw myself as inferior

    NOW I AM COMING TO SEE MYSELF AS A PERSON OF WORTH WHO IS HIGHLY PRIZED BY GOD

11. Once I pretended to be someone I was not

    NOW I'M LEARNING TO BE AN INTEGRATED PERSON

12. Once I ran from intimacy with God

    NOW I AM OPENING UP TO GOD

The self-portrait inside my head is subtly changing from failure, victim and reject to winner, survivor-thriver, and accepted one. I know God's arms are open, His love extended. I know I am making progress![13]

What a great declaration for a woman in pain! What a joy to witness Lynn's own journey from the unspeakable pain of losing all her earthly possessions to a place of fresh hope and renewed courage, willfully choosing to go deeper in her relationship with Jesus Christ and give others hope in the midst of their losses.

Chapter 4

Where Is God in the Pain?

Joni dove into shallow water and broke her neck. At only seventeen years old, her body was permanently disabled, and she was a quadriplegic. During the extensive months of recovery, Joni continually asked, "Oh, God, what have You done to me? How can you do this to me? How much more can I take? I'm at the end of my rope. Why, God, why? Where are You, God?"[1]

Joni had plenty of Bible verses to look at, but in the midst of such a life-altering tragedy, Bible verses would sting like salt poured on a wound. Severe chronic depression, fear, horror, shock, grief, remorse, and anger culminated in thoughts of suicide. Joni was not physically able to slit her own wrists, so demanded her friend Jackie do it for her.

One night during a desperate prayer, Joni realized she had two choices as she prayed: "God, either you exist or you don't. If you don't exist, then there is no logical reason for living. If people who believe in you are only going through the motions, I want to know. Why should we go on fooling ourselves? Life is absurd most of the time. And it seems man's only end is despair. What can I do, Lord? I want to believe, but I have nothing to hang on to. God, you've got to prove your existence to me!"[2]

As Joni closed her eyes, she began to feel a surprising calmness come over her. A still, small voice whispered, "Thou wilt keep him in perfect peace, whose mind is stayed on thee."[3] She sensed God's presence and felt Him reaching out to her in a life-changing way. Additional Bible verses—which previously were irritatingly out of touch with reality—began to flood her mind with peace and clarity. Joni Eareckson Tada's change in attitude and perspective began while in the hospital after nearly two long years of wrestling with God. One particularly meaningful moment was when she sensed God saying, "Joni, if I loved you enough to die for you, then can't you trust me with the answers?"[4]

Joni's questions are those uttered often in the midst or aftermath of tragic and unexplainable circumstances. Dealing with emotional pain presents a twofold dilemma. Something emotionally satisfying needs to be said to help bear the pain. Something acceptable to the intellect needs to be said to help understand the reason for the pain. Both are challenging.[5] While some trauma victims may not be ready to process pain's purpose until the pain has subsided, others are able to endure incredible suffering given an understanding of God's purpose in their suffering.

Unlike the pain that animals experience, humans inevitably want to know the *why* of suffering.[6]

The problem is not that suffering and pain exist in the world and that one feels them. The real problem is that suffering, like Joni's, seems random and meaningless, crushing people as often as it ennobles them. The atheist, polytheist, the dualist, the naturalist, the fatalist, the materialist, and the agnostic[7] may see accidents caused by the forces of nature or human wickedness as an annoyance, a tragedy, but not a problem.[8] Only the believer in one Creator who is both good and almighty must come to terms with the problem of suffering. The tension that exists for Christians is in trying to reconcile the truths that if God is good and has total power, why does suffering exist? Does God cause suffering? Is He able to stop it? Is He moved by it?

God's Response to Suffering

Job's experience seems to indicate that in the long-term God is both good and sovereign. But in the short-term Job's pain raises the question of the coexistence of both the goodness and ultimate power of God.

God draws Satan's attention to the fact that Job is an exemplary human. This endorsement engenders God's challenge to Satan that suffering will not change Job's reverence for God.[9] Satan is up for the challenge but God determines the extent of Satan's devastating work in Job's life. Satan's attacks are propagated in succession: possessions, family, health, and relationships.[10] But God draws a boundary of preserving Job's life and does not allow Satan to cross that line.[11] Is God moved by Job's suffering? God chose to respond to Job's insistent request for an audience with God[12] by speaking directly to Job. God could have remained silent indefinitely. Rather, God enlarges Job's understanding of God's sovereign power by giving Job a review of God's creative work.

God takes Job on an incredible verbal tour of His creation (Job 38–41) from which two penetrating questions emerge. First, who would challenge or find fault with a God who has abilities and understanding clearly displayed in His created universe, with which humans cannot begin to compete or compare? This is a God who gives and blesses His creatures even when no one sees, a God who is intuitionally good, irrationally loving, and gives for no apparent reason at all.[13] There is great disparity in the finite finding fault with the infinite Almighty Creator who has limitless understanding and ability.

The second question strikes at the heart of theodicy.[14] God asks if Job in wanting to justify himself would condemn God.[15] In the cul de sac of confusion and disorientation, one is often led to validate one's own choices while condemning God's. This is often the default defense in the midst of pain.

God does not give Job a clear explanation for his suffering.[16] Instead, He asks Job seventy questions, none of which Job could answer. Job failed the test and realized his own understanding was finite, but he met God in the process.[17]

Job repented of his previous assumptions about God and admitted his own lack of understanding, that mankind never has all the facts as God does.[18] Job acknowledged that God's plan could not be thwarted; that God is much bigger than any human.[19] Job was affirmed in the way he represented God to his friends.[20] Job's misguided friends angered God because of their erroneous perspective. Despite His anger, God made a way for their redemption.[21] God extended grace to Job and his friends. God's goodness is seen in blessing "the latter part of Job's life more than the former part."[22] Job, because he received God's grace, was able to give it—to his three friends, plus family members who virtually disowned him during his illness. Job broke culturally acceptable mores to give his daughters[23] an inheritance along with their brothers (42:15). Job is reflecting God's irrational love and goodness in this act.

The final debate is over whether the foundation of God's kingdom is built on genuine love or power. Satan has power but no love. God *is* love and God *is* power. Satan is powerless to compete when people choose to follow God because of love. Satan is out to use his power to win people's allegiance. God makes clear through Job that it is Job's love for God that underlies Job's allegiance to God. C. S. Lewis observes,

> To love at all is to be vulnerable. Love anything, and your heart will certainly be wrung and possibly be broken. If you want to make sure of keeping it intact, you must give your heart to no one, not even to an animal. Wrap it carefully round with hobbies and little luxuries; avoid all entanglements; lock it up safe in the casket or coffin of your selfishness. But in that casket—safe, dark, motionless, airless—it will change. It will not be broken; it will become unbreakable,

impenetrable, irredeemable. . . . The only place outside Heaven where you can be perfectly safe from all dangers . . . of love is Hell.[24]

"God is love. Whoever lives in love lives in God, and God in them" (1 John 4:16b).

God seems more interested in securing our love, establishing our faith, and nurturing a desire for holiness than in answering all our questions.[25] Job exemplifies this as does Naomi,[26] the female version of "Job-like suffering."[27] God gives neither clear understanding for the "why" of their pain. Yet each learns more about God in their painful journey.

The collapse of Naomi's world was spread over years of heartache and tragedy. Too quickly we read over the tragic events that precede the majority of the text in the book of Ruth. Naomi endured famine, moved to a foreign country, and raised sons as immigrants in that country. The death of Naomi's husband left her widowed in a culture that required male provision. Sons provided the only hope for a widow; two sons doubled her chances for survival. Yet in addition to the drawbacks of their immigrant status and the absence of a father, Naomi and her sons were without land, wealth, or other assets that might attract a Moabite family's interest in providing wives. Orpah and Ruth probably were not seen as cream of the crop among marriageable Moabite women and eventually had that perspective reinforced when a decade passed without children.

Then the unthinkable happened: *both* of Naomi's sons die. One could argue that at this juncture Naomi was even worse off than Job. Both lost family and the life they worked to build. But Job still had his wife and community. Job was not an immigrant and he was not a woman—both nearly impossible barriers to survival in Naomi's world.[28] Naomi's theodicy is clearly repeated to both her daughters-in-law: "It is more bitter for me than for you, because the LORD's hand has turned against me!" and to the Bethlehem women, "Call me Mara [bitter], because the Almighty has made my life very bitter. I went away full, but the LORD has brought me back empty. Why call me Naomi [pleasant]? The LORD has afflicted me; the Almighty has brought misfortune upon me."[29]

Clearly Naomi bore the devastating consequences of the decision she and Elimelech made to leave Bethlehem with their two sons and live in Moab. The death of Naomi's husband and sons led her to the decision to return to Bethlehem. Naomi could not have known that, although she was feeling empty and bitter when she chose to return to Bethlehem, God would redeem her losses and her daughter-in-law would one day be an ancestor of Jesus the Messiah.[30]

God extends His love even when humanity's choices result in hurtful consequences. The Old Testament prophets depict the metaphor of a groom (God) wooing an adulterous bride (Israel) back to Himself.[31] In the New Testament the compassionate longings of God for a restorative relationship with His erring child are seen in the parable of the father of the prodigal son.[32]

God's sovereign timetable in which He works out His purposes is far more extensive than humankind's incessant focus on the present. God's ultimate time line for the Christian leads to eternity in heaven. Shepherds have the opportunity to bring this powerful message to wounded women.

The Bible does not indicate that categorically a woman in pain is suffering because of sin she committed. The biblical text does indicate painful consequences to sin in a fallen world, effects of other people's sin on innocent victims, and personal sin.[33] The erroneous assumption of sin in the life of a wounded woman adds additional grief to the heaviness a woman in crisis is already experiencing.

Jesus dismissed any conjecture that those on whom the tower in Siloam fell were guiltier than any others living in the area.[34] Even Galileans who suffered horribly at the hand of Pilate were not "worse sinners" than other Galileans who did not suffer in this way.[35] The man born blind is not personally faulted for his biological condition.[36] Suffering, particularly victims of accidents, nature, or even human cruelty, does not identify those who are guilty of sin or evil according to Jesus.

Jesus does use the opportunity to point out to His hearers that they need to repent because everyone will eventually die. Jesus uses disaster as a megaphone to call attention to guilt and destination, to the imminence of His righteous judgment if there is no repentance. Disaster is a call to repentance.[37] Jesus uses the incidents recorded in Luke 13 as opportunities to bring the message of life.

God Suffers

God is not the unmoved observer of pain. God too feels pain.

The Hebrew word translated *pain* was first used by God in the Bible subsequent to Adam and Eve taking the forbidden fruit. After cursing the serpent, God says to the woman in Genesis 3:16a, "I will greatly multiply your sorrow and your conception; *in pain* you shall bring forth children" (NKJV, emphasis added).[38] In the next verse God says to the man, "Cursed is the ground because of you; through *painful toil* you will eat food from it all the days of your life" (emphasis added).[39]

Pain in this context is a consequence of sin, experienced by the first man and woman on Earth after the fall. Men would now suffer in the struggle to provide the necessities of life. Women would feel the impact of painful toil in conceiving and birthing children. The relationships between men and women would be marred by sin. Pain would be an inherent element of living in a fallen and broken world.

God in His mercy provided garments and clothed the naked man and woman. God also banished them from the garden of Eden so they would not eat of the Tree of Life and live forever in a sinful state. Within the first three chapters of the Bible, God is seen as a caregiver to suffering humanity.

It was in Noah's lifetime that the Creator of the world experienced pain: "The LORD regretted that he had made human beings on the earth, and his heart was deeply troubled."[40] This Scripture gives insight into a God who felt the pain of mankind's choices: "The LORD saw how great the wickedness of the human race had become on the earth" and grieved.[41] This incident of pain felt by almighty God is a precursor of the pain He would yet feel in the death of His Son Jesus.

Throughout the Old Testament there were many people who were

treated cruelly and unjustly. Women experienced the emotionally pain-
ful issues identified in this book. Reproductive issues were of particular
concern to Sarah, Hagar, Rachel, Hannah, Tamar, and Bathsheba. Hagar,
Dinah, and Abigail experienced emotional, physical, or sexual abuse.
God listened to the cry of infertile women and often provided children.
The pain of rape and abuse negatively affected families and communities.
Such atrocities were intended to be prevented by the law given to Moses.

The Old Testament highlights a God who is compassionate and cares
for His creatures, particularly those who are suffering, oppressed, and
poor. God longs for even those who have turned away from His love to
return and receive His forgiveness and favor. The law and the prophets
call God's people to care for others, the widows, poor, and young. Micah's
clear injunction to act justly and to love mercy leaves no room for followers of Christ to ignore those in pain.

Pain was an integral part of the life of Jesus Christ; He came to earth for
the ultimate purpose of suffering. God is with humans in their suffering—
the cross is the sign of what God does with suffering. Christ asked three
times to be delivered from suffering if it was the Father's will.[42] Yet, Jesus
chose the Father's will, which led to the pain of crucifixion. In the midst of
His pain on the cross, Jesus asked a question similar to the one Joni asked:
"My God, My God, why have you forsaken me?"[43] God answers the problem of human pain by identification and participation.[44]

It clearly follows that a God who suffered for His creatures would
not deal with them in a way that is meaningless. God does not perpetrate
suffering to facilitate His purpose in the lives of His creatures.[45] Yet there
is biblical support for the idea that God uses pain for the sufferer's benefit
and to bring glory to God.[46]

The apostle Paul, who experienced myriad painful experiences,
enjoins the Roman Christians to be glad in the midst of suffering because
of its purpose. "Suffering produces perseverance; perseverance, character; and character, hope."[47] That hope is a current reality of the love of
God through the Holy Spirit in Christ's followers. The future hope will

be realized in the new heaven and new earth where there will be no more tears, pain, mourning, or death.[48]

We in the Western world assume that suffering is something to avoid or to fix: illness simply requires proper medical attention; the effects of natural disasters can be restored through government funding or insurance benefits; losses are compensated for by the legal system. A comfortable life is not only our expected status quo, but an indication of God's blessing. It is difficult for those with this mind-set to embrace pain. The community of faith must challenge the mind-set of those suffering in Western cultures.

Pain and suffering make one vulnerable, and the Western Christian works hard to protect against pain by attempting to be "self-sufficient."[49] Pain is not easily accepted or embraced, and leaves one feeling helpless and out of control. We assume that one who is in control of life would find a way to eliminate the pain.[50] But this assumption lacks biblical support.

Paul focuses on suffering as if it were something those following Jesus should expect; it is the result of living a faithful life.[51] David expressed both pain and joy in songs to the Lord.[52] Many of these Psalms could serve our churches well as liturgies needed in times of suffering and mourning.

The Bible is filled with people who also wondered *where is God in the pain.* Job in his pain was insistent on knowing where God was. Naomi accepted the fact that God was present in her pain. Both Naomi and Job, in trying to make sense of their stories, eventually realized God is intentional in using suffering for His purposes. Similarly a woman in pain is likely to focus on her story in trying to understand her hurtful situation. She assumes it is her story that gives life meaning—but her story taken alone makes no sense at all.

God Has a Story Too

It is God's story that gives our story meaning. God cares passionately about it. When we become willing to incorporate our story into His story,

He enters ours in a way that empowers us to transcend our painful world. Only one of the thieves on the cross asked to be in Jesus' story: "Jesus, remember me when you come into your kingdom," and Jesus responded, "Truly I tell you, today you will be with me in paradise."[53]

Women in pain also have the opportunity to contextualize their own story by entering God's story. Initiating this process may be one of the most important aspects of a shepherd's role, bringing life-altering meaning and hope into a woman's emotionally painful story.

Section 2

Shepherding Women in Pain

*What the Shepherd
Needs to Know*

Chapter 5

Shepherding Insights

One hour after Jane[1] received the devastating news, she packed her car and began driving the nine hundred miles to be at her mom's bedside. Jane's mom had an aggressive cancer. Nothing more medically could be done, and it was likely her mother, whom Jane loved, would die within days. How could this be happening? She declared that once she arrived she would never leave her mother's bedside until the end.

After seven nights of remaining in her mother's room throughout the night, Jane was exhausted. Her sister-in-law insisted that she leave the hospital just to get at least one good night's sleep at their house, and Jane was tired enough to agree. But to her horror, the next morning she learned that her mother had died in the middle of the night. Jane was devastated at not having been with her mother at the end. The guilt and remorse engulfed her. She began to imagine all sorts of thoughts her mother must have had when she sensed her daughter's absence. Perhaps that is why she died, Jane told herself.

As she freely talked about her remorse to those around her, it was several months later that she had opportunity to talk with a woman who chose to really listen while walking alongside Jane in her pain. In addition to the agony of her mother's death, Jane began to talk about her brother working hard to cut Jane out of her mother's will. A year before her mother's death, Jane had experienced three deaths in her family of origin—people she loved and relied on. Now there was no one. On top of these losses, Jane was laid off just weeks after she returned home from her mother's memorial service. It soon became clear that Jane had experienced multiple losses in a very short period of time. The family members with whom she could confide, her closest support system, were no longer living. She felt she had been hit with a bulldozer and just could not get up. Jane admittedly did not *want* to get up. She felt alone and beaten down. She was done with life.

How would you shepherd Jane? Would you encourage her to read her Bible more and pray? Jane would tell you she wished she could read her Bible and pray. But the pain is so intense that all she could concentrate enough to do is cry out, "Help me, Jesus!" (This, by the way, is a wonderful prayer.) Although reading and praying are certainly valuable and needful suggestions, when a woman in pain feels so beat down she does not want to get up, she also needs a referral. She may need *immediate* intervention, such as calling 911 or providing transportation to a hospital, especially if she has suicidal ideation. When deep depression is present, contact with her primary care physician is essential. Physiologically based conditions, such as continual headaches, dizziness, fainting spells, loss of appetite, sudden weight changes, may be due to toxins in the body, chemical imbalances, or a number of other physical causes. Medical intervention may save her life in the short-term. But long-term she may need the services of a psychiatrist or psychologist. Professional therapy revealed additional losses in Jane's life that she had not processed. Recent family deaths triggered previous victimizations and losses. Medication stabilized her emotional health, which then allowed her to begin the hard work of processing her losses.

Did Jane need a shepherd during this time? Absolutely! She needed professional help *and* a shepherd. *Both* are needed for women in this kind of pain. The consistency of a shepherd's presence is vital. Typically a woman in pain will see a therapist once a week for one hour. She may have a thirty-minute appointment with medical personnel and a similar time line at a social service office. Although extended stays in hospitals provide more time away from home, the actual contact time with medical personnel is limited. There are many hours in a week that a woman in pain would be unattended. In Jane's case, there was no family to support her. She certainly needed people who expressed care appropriately to consistently come alongside her. A team of people provided daily contact, a safe environment to process her feelings and thoughts, plus practical help.

The process of referral begins when, after consideration of all the aspects of the woman's problem, the shepherd realizes the problem is beyond her ability to help. It is critical for the shepherd to be familiar with behavioral, emotional, and physical indicators that suggest a referral is needed. Women in pain will benefit from three levels of intervention.

1. Professional help when needed
2. Shepherding/pastoral care
3. Group and/or community care

Indications Professional Help Is Needed

Behavioral Signs[2]
- Sudden *changes* in social behavior, such as becoming unusually outgoing or withdrawn. A major change in friendship groups. Persistent lying, stealing, or other antisocial behavior.
- Inability to concentrate or formulate sentences that convey clear meaning. Inability to make decisions. Confusion about career goals.
- Lethargy or listlessness; loss of interest in favorite activities.
- Hyperactivity or nervousness. Power struggles with authority.
- Erratic behavior or behavior that is dangerous to herself or others.

Emotional Signs

- Open talk about intense family problems. Marital distress resulting in emotional or physical trauma.
- Overwhelming sadness following the death or serious illness of a family member or friend.
- Feeling sad or down in the dumps. Mood swings. Pessimism, hopelessness, or helplessness about the future; scary thoughts.
- Talks to herself and hears voices.
- Preoccupation with physical or sexual issues.
- Extreme suspiciousness or irrational feelings of persecution. Nonsensical conversation, indications of being markedly out of touch with reality.
- Recurring thoughts of suicide or death.
- Unwarranted sense of tremendous guilt. Feelings of inadequacy or failure.

Physical Signs

- A marked change in weight or appearance. Excessive eating. Extreme loss of appetite or preoccupation with weight issues. Poor hygiene.
- Marked change in sleeping habits. Consistently fatigued.
- Use of alcohol or drugs to cope with life's traumas.
- Outbursts of anger. Accident-prone.

In a milder form, these experiences come to all normal people. However, when they are exaggerated, they are serious. Often there is a cluster of these symptoms and they need to be taken seriously. Assure the woman in pain that you will continue to walk alongside her and participate in helping her make good choices for professional help. Present a realistic picture of professional help. Continually assure her of your desire to see her get the best care possible, because "she is worth it."

Shepherding/Pastoral Care

Many of the issues causing emotional pain in women's lives result in shame, rejection, fear, and feelings of abandonment, worthlessness, and guilt. An understanding of God's love, communicated through the life and death of Jesus Christ and empowered by the Holy Spirit, has the power to bring life change in these painful areas. Faith in Jesus Christ also provides a context in which to examine the purpose of pain; Christ's love gives meaning to life and pain. A woman gains strength when others in the church offer a listening ear, practical support, and spiritual tools to assist in times of crises. This is most effective when the caregiver enters the woman's painful experience with an understanding of the context of her pain. Shepherds and pastoral caregivers are strategically prepared to offer such care and insights.

Often *pastoral care* is understood to be given by people who are part of a full-time staff in a church. This erroneous assumption has often led people to assume that only the "professionals" can give effective pastoral care to women in pain. The biblical injunction is that every believer is a caregiver.[3]

Pastoral care is the ministry of soul care, which encompasses helping acts done by Christians directed toward the healing, sustaining, guiding, and reconciling of troubled persons.[4]

The meaning of the word *pastor* is *shepherd*.[5] Pastor is one of several spiritual gifts given to the church for the purpose of preparing God's "people for works of service, so that the body of Christ may be built up . . . mature . . ."[6] Because spiritual gifts are not gender specific,[7] this allows all believers with this spiritual gift to shepherd in the appropriate contexts.

The terms *shepherding* and *pastoral care* may be used interchangeably.[8] The term *shepherding* draws one to imitate the model of Jesus Christ in caring for others. *Shepherd* is used repeatedly in both the Old Testament and the New Testament as a metaphor for one who gives care as a shepherd does for the sheep. The term suggests endearment, life-giving care, and nurture.

Philip Keller's experience as a shepherd illustrates many of the characteristics of biblical pastoral care. Whenever the shepherd came to the fold, it was for the benefit of the sheep.[9] The shepherd's voice conveyed a positive assurance that he cared for the sheep and that he was acting in their best interests.[10] There was a special relationship between the shepherd and each of his sheep.[11] This endearing image is one that portrays the Christian's heavenly Father and is to be reflected by His followers.

Shepherding when used as a metaphor for caregiving may encompass elements of helping, spiritual direction, mentoring, discipleship, and/or pastoral counseling. The shepherd may be called on to facilitate, coach, listen, pray, or transmit information.[12] "The greatest distinction of a shepherd is that she is a woman who intentionally provides the comfort and understanding that fosters healing and growth."[13]

Relationship, which is important to women, is at the core of the shepherding concept. Shepherding will ultimately involve figuratively putting the wounded woman's hand into the hand of the Good Shepherd. A shepherd may invite others to assist her in the care, but her desire is to do what she can to ensure that the sheep "have life, and have it to the full."[14]

Jesus, using the metaphor of the good shepherd, describes His relationship with His sheep in John 10.

> "The sheep listen to his voice. He calls his own sheep by name and leads them out. When he has brought out all his own, he goes on ahead of them, and his sheep follow him because they know his voice. . . .
>
> ". . . The thief comes only to steal and kill and destroy; I have come that they may have life, and have it to the full.
>
> "I am the good shepherd. The good shepherd lays down his life for the sheep. The hired hand is not the shepherd and does not own the sheep. So when he sees the wolf coming, he abandons the sheep and runs away. . . .
>
> "I am the good shepherd; I know my sheep and my sheep know me— just as the Father knows me and I know the Father—and I lay down my life for the sheep."[15]

The ultimate desire is to see women fully embrace the purpose the Good Shepherd has for them in this life by becoming reproducing disciples of Jesus Christ.

Shepherding is grounded on the centrality of healing relationships with both *vertical* and *horizontal* dimensions. Drs. Tim Clinton and George Ohlschlager of the American Association of Christian Counselors admit, "We would . . . assert that counseling, by itself, is not enough. . . . We have all encountered persons who, after years of work, are still stuck, still oppressed. . . . We assert true freedom only comes through faith in Christ."[16]

The vertical dimension cannot be excluded. It is life-giving. Caregiving that is centered in Christ delivers a message of significance and purpose for all who embrace the gospel of Jesus Christ.[17] Followers of Jesus accept the authority of Scripture and recognize the uniqueness of human creatures made in the image of God. They recognize the effects of sin and acknowledge the redemptive initiative of God. They have accepted the forgiveness Christ's death on the cross and resurrection made possible. Christ-followers have a perspective that enables them to help people find and follow a godly plan for healing, for life. Shepherds who effectively model this in their own lives are better able to follow Christ's example of ministering with wisdom, understanding, and the empowerment of the Holy Spirit.[18]

On the horizontal level, effectively shepherding women in pain must include active listening skills and understanding of the issues causing emotional pain. This will include *attending*, undivided attention exhibited by an open posture, eye contact, forward leaning, and courteous gestures that communicate the shepherd is fully present. An *empathic response* is one from which the woman in pain feels heard, understood, and free to tell her story. Asking appropriate questions is critical for the purpose of prompting the woman to further understand and explore her pain, then develop a course of action. (For more specific instruction in acquiring these skills, please see *Shepherding a Woman's Heart*.)

The need to *belong* is at the heart of the human struggle. The community of believers gathered as the church is an ideal organism to embrace others who share the human struggle. When people see Christ in our caring, they are more open to our proclamation of the words of the gospel.

Shepherding involves caring for, binding wounds, and protecting the sheep. "When churches lean toward systems rather than shepherding, they have . . . traded the vocation of hand-crafting saints for the business of mass-producing sheep."[19] Leaders in the church would do well to prioritize shepherding on church agendas.

Leaders are to guide followers in fulfilling the biblical mandate to minister to the weak and suffering. But leaders will not be able to guide others in effectively caring for women in pain if they do not have the urgently needed awareness or skills to assist wounded women. Dr. Siang-Yang Tan, who is both a pastor and a professor of psychology, concludes, "Most of the results obtained in the secular research literature have indicated that lay helpers are generally as effective as professional therapists for most common problems."[20]

Group and/or Community Care

Since most emotionally painful experiences happen in relationship, most are healed in relationship. The value of a community of people who provide care cannot be overstated. Psychologist Larry Crabb observes, "Beneath what our culture calls psychological disorder is a soul crying out for what only community can provide."[21] Crabb further asserts we need to go further with instruction in biblical principles and live them out in community. "The greatest need in modern civilization is the development of communities—true communities where the heart of God is home, where the humble and wise learn to shepherd those on the path behind them, where trusting strugglers lock arms with others as together they journey on."[22]

A community of people provides a diversity of gifting, schedules, resources, and multiplied encouragements. Deep wounds require long-term healing and extensive investments of time and resources. The value of a single message repeatedly given in a variety of venues increases the probability of it being incorporated and acted upon by a woman who desires healing. As in the parable of the good Samaritan, the care given to the poor traveler by the staff of the inn, a community of people increases the likelihood for healing.

Chapter 6

Depression

Chantelle K. Dockter, MA, LPC
Associate Counselor of Christian Counseling Centers
of Oregon and Washington

ife had not turned out as she had anticipated. At forty-nine, Susan was disenchanted, angry, and hopeless. The sadness and hurt were clearly evident in her eyes. She stated that she did not believe counseling would work and was not sure why she had even made the appointment. One by one she listed all the situations, relationships, and events that had disappointed her. The wall she had built brick by brick around herself for protection was nearly visible. Susan reported that she was exhausted and did not believe that God had her best interests in mind. She folded her arms across her chest, sat back, and gave me a look that said, *I dare you to help me.* I was praying unceasingly that God would give me the words to help this woman and that she would have ears to hear whatever He gave me for her.

Much to my surprise, Susan kept her next appointment, and continued to come to counseling each week. After the first few visits, she stopped saying her usual mantra of "You can't help me, nobody can, not even God. Nobody cares and I am worth nothing to anyone." As Susan's story unfolded, I began to understand why she was so protective and defensive.

Susan came from an emotionally and physically abusive family. As a teen she thought she found the perfect guy, who promptly left her when she became pregnant. With virtually no support system, Susan vowed to raise her son on her own and do the very best job she could. She worked hard. Nothing seemed to come easy for them. Life was about survival, and not much more. Finally her son got married and was on his own. Susan had made a few good friends by this time and let her guard down just enough to fall in love with a man she thought God Himself had sent to her door. Tears spilled down Susan's face as she described how difficult it had been to let down her guard with this man and risk vulnerability. She prayed all along that God would make it clear if it was not meant to be. Because no doors closed, she continued to open herself up and ventured to dream of a future with this man, a future she had previously denied herself. A year before Susan met me, the relationship ended. The man Susan had finally let herself love declared he was gay and ended the relationship.

This was the final straw for Susan. She closed herself off from everyone and her anger quickly turned to bitterness. She was irritable, sad, and isolated. She presented a rough and abrasive exterior, to the point that no one wanted to get close and see what was really going on below the surface. Susan clearly was depressed. By her own admission Susan "ate" her feelings, which resulted in her being significantly overweight, which did not help her already low feelings of self-worth.

Susan slowly began to trust and open up. Tears were shed, exchanges were intense, and her resistance level was high. Susan became a hard-working client, and as we worked on the core issues, her "real" personality came through. She was witty, possessed a kind heart, and was a fighter for what was right.

After six months of weekly therapy, Susan was walking to the door at the end of that day's session. She turned to me and said, "You know, my birthday is next week and I am going to be fifty. I have had a long-time plan of how to celebrate this birthday that I have never told anyone." Thinking we were just making small talk, I asked what she had planned. She responded, "I have had the plan of killing myself on my fiftieth birthday." I stopped and looked at her, trying not to let my alarm show. I said, "And now?" Susan broke into a big grin and responded, "Plans have changed. I want to celebrate what is good about my life with my friends and family. Suicide is no longer on the table." Susan had decided to fight the grave pull of depression rather than give in to it. She was clearly winning the fight.

Understand the Issue

Depression is defined as,

> An illness that involves the body, mood, and thoughts and that affects the way a person eats, sleeps, feels about himself or herself, and thinks about things. Depression is not the same as a passing blue mood. It is not a sign of personal weakness or a condition that can be wished away. People with depression cannot merely "pull themselves together" and get better. Without treatment, symptoms can last for weeks, months, or years. Appropriate treatment, however, can help most people with depression.[1]

Common symptoms of depression include: irritability, tearfulness, loss/increase in appetite, diminished interest in or enjoyment of activities, psychomotor agitation or retardation, sleeplessness or sleeping too much, somatic complaints, lack of energy, poor concentration, difficulty making decisions, social withdrawal/isolation, suicidal thoughts or plan, feelings of hopelessness, worthlessness, or inappropriate guilt, low self-esteem, mood-related hallucinations or delusions, and thinking errors.[2]

The following statistics on depression in women come from the National Institutes of Mental Health (NIMH).

- One in four women will experience severe depression at some point in life.
- Depression affects twice as many women as men, regardless of racial and ethnic background or income.
- Depression is the number one cause of disability in women.[3]

It is important to understand that depression is an illness. It is not a sin. It is not an illusion, and it is not "all in your head." Illnesses such as depression are harder to medically define and the diagnosis is not as concrete as that of a physical illness, and much of the diagnosis is based on self-report and observation. But simply because it is more ambiguous does not mean it is any less real an illness that needs treatment and attention like any other medical diagnosis.

Medical conditions such as thyroid activity can look like depression. Many types of depression are related to a medication or a physical condition that can be treated. It is important to encourage someone who may be depressed to contact her primary care physician (PCP) and make an appointment for a complete physical, to rule out any physical causes. The person should be sure to let her PCP know if she is taking any medications, whether pharmaceutical or natural. It is also important to know if there is a family history of depression as there can be a genetic component. Depression can have a biochemical root. The more one understands how chemicals and hormones work in the body, the better prepared she can be to have a plan of attack to fight depression.

In the case of handling depression, knowledge is power. The more the depressed woman[4] and her caregiver know, the less fear they will feel. Knowing the symptoms of depression will enable a woman to more clearly discern if she meets the criteria for depression. First, rule out physical causes. Secondly, know referrals and resources. Guide women to get the help they will need. This may include a pastor, professional therapist, and/or psychiatrist. "That which we cannot see and do not understand holds the power to terrorize us." Knowing the symptoms and understanding them takes away the mystery and terror of depression.[5]

Depressed women feel tired and hopeless, and tend to give up easily. They let the disease dictate how they respond emotionally. That is why perseverance is one of the strongest weapons to fight depression.[6] Those who are depressed need to face their fear of depression and know that it can be fought and won. Every step taken toward defeating depression leads to an increase in confidence. Helpers can give the message that they will not give up on the woman who is depressed and are present to aid in the fight.

There is more to life than survival. There is something deep within each person that longs to thrive. As important as it is to understand a woman's mind and body, the spiritual component must not be forgotten. Meditation on Scripture and prayer can give a woman a more objective view of reality, rather than being stuck solely in her own emotions. When depressed, it is common for her to only see the negative aspects of her circumstances, relationships, and self. She often feels God is far away, and her depressed mind tells her that no one really cares for her, not even Him.

By meditating on the truths and promises of the Bible, she begins concentrating on the world outside her depression. As with anything else, reading the Bible and prayer probably will feel like an overwhelming task for a woman who is depressed. She can start by setting a realistic goal of reading a chapter a day, whether the desire is there or not. Encourage her to look in the concordance of a Bible and choose a subject, such as "hope" or "anxiousness," and look up the verses offered. Suggest she pick one verse that says something positive to her. Have her read it out loud, write it down, carry it with her, and ponder it when needed. Communicating needs and feelings to God in prayer can be helpful. Encourage her to simply cry out to God, especially when words seem inadequate to articulate the pain.

Communication with people in general is difficult for those who are depressed. Depression makes women want to be isolated, staying home and maybe ignoring phone calls. They may even retreat from family members within the home, preferring to spend much of their time alone. As difficult as communication is when depressed, it should still be encouraged. As a woman shares her thoughts, feelings, and anxieties with others, it can lessen the hold of depression, making it easier to manage. Many depressed clients have expressed the dread they feel anticipating attendance at any type of social event, no matter how big or small. However, after attending, they express feeling a bit more recharged and hopeful.

The depressed mind does not work the same way as the healthy mind. An important difference is that the depressed mind easily believes lies, especially about self-worth and worth to others. Thinking errors run rampant in a depressed woman's way of thinking. A woman who is depressed will generally perceive an event or situation very differently than she will when she's healthy because she views through a depressed lens, which is foggy and unclear. Most of us are able to talk a situation through in our heads and toss out the faulty thinking. For a depressed person this is much more difficult and sometimes even seems impossible.

Here are some examples of thinking errors.

- Personalization—taking everything said or done as a personal attack
- Catastrophizing—making something much bigger and worse than it actually is
- Assuming/mind reading—attributing meaning to someone else's actions or words without actually seeking clarification, and generalizing. For example, if one person is upset with me, then *everyone* must be upset with me.

Therefore, it is vital that a depressed woman learns how to effectively challenge negative and faulty thinking. Cognitive Behavioral Therapy (CBT) can be very effective in teaching how to restructure thought patterns. Most therapists are familiar with CBT and many utilize the concepts and tools in their work with clients, especially with those who are depressed. When finding a counselor to work with, the woman can ask if that particular therapist operates from a CBT framework, and request it be incorporated into their work together.

Although people tend to think of depression as a mental, emotional, or spiritual issue, it is also a physical issue. It may not have a physical cause, but it does affect the body. Many people who are depressed report physical symptoms such as headaches, stomachaches, and bowel irritations. The body also typically feels sluggish, lethargic, and achy. An effective tool to help the body as well as provide mental and emotional recharge is physical exercise. Clearly physical workouts affect us emotionally. God designed us as whole beings. "At the University of California at Berkeley, School of Public Health, an ongoing survey clearly showed a strong association between a sedentary lifestyle and depression."[7] A variety of studies have shown that exercise is necessary, almost mandatory, in the battle to defeat depression. Exercise releases endorphins, the "feel-good" hormones, as well as provides an outlet for stress.

It is common for a depressed individual to feel an abundance of guilt and/or shame. Guilt can be a helpful alarm system that signals when we have sinned against God or others. However, if the guilt is true and appropriate, then it can be dealt with in a healthy way by confession and repentance, and then moving on. Depressed individuals tend to hang on to guilt and more often than not will make it about themselves rather than their behavior, resulting in shame. If the guilt is false guilt, as is often the case in depression, or if shame exists, then the woman needs to understand the grace and mercy of God.[8]

Depression triggers are different for everyone. It is important to assist those who are depressed in identifying their particular triggers. Some of these include: work stress, burnout, family/relational conflict, poor eating/sleeping habits, alcohol/drug use, chronic medical conditions, postpartum, feeling overwhelmed, and unresolved grief. Those who are depressed become overwhelmed easily and may need assistance with setting reasonable and realistic goals. Identifying time wasters and making lists to prioritize tasks can greatly assist in small yet forward-moving steps.

It is important for the depressed woman to look at how to meet others' needs. In doing so she can meet her own needs. If she puts effort into looking for people to help or minister to around her, she will not be so focused on her own problems. This is important for the depressed person, who becomes internally focused. Investing time and energy reaching out to assist and help others gently pushes that internal focus to the external.

Shepherding Insights

It certainly helps to have an understanding of what depression is and a picture of what the depressed woman faces daily. Shepherds can have a great impact on those who are in the pain of depression. To enhance the positive impact, take note of the following list of helpful insights.

HELPFUL THINGS TO SAY AND DO

1. **DO** acknowledge that the depression exists. Caregivers, family, and friends may want to ignore what they are not comfortable dealing with and this can lead to feelings of shame and isolation for the depressed individual.

2. **DO** validate feelings. Although the depressed individual may not see her world or circumstances clearly, her feelings of pain are real and should be validated.

3. **DO** pray for and with the depressed individual. Prayer not only is a call to involve Jesus Christ but is also therapeutic and calming in the process. I have never had a client who has declined prayer when offered in session, whether she is a believer or not.

4. **DO** assist the woman in seeing that she may be depressed but that the depression itself does not define her. She is not the disease, rather she has the disease and is in the process of fighting it.

5. **DO** stay positive, hopeful, and encouraging. A shepherd can be

the surrogate for hope until the person gets there herself. Be a gentle, broken record when it comes to repeating positive and encouraging messages.

6. **DO** encourage self-care. Self-care can include eating well, sleeping enough, exercising consistently, getting fresh air/ sunlight, and investing time in hobbies.

7. **DO** encourage a depressed individual to look into volunteering her time doing something for her community or for those less fortunate. This should be something that is not too demanding or taxing, so it does not further overwhelm her. It is important because helping others can stretch the depressed woman to step out of herself and concentrate less on her own hurts and pain, even for a short period of time. This can have positive effects that last long after the actual volunteering.

8. **DO** share your own depression story if you have one. She'll see that depression is not something to be ashamed of and helps "normalize" depression; there are many others who also experience it. This is important because when in the midst of depression, a woman can feel she is the only one afflicted.

9. **DO** check in with the individual consistently. This assures her that you care. However, this comes with a caveat: caregivers need to make sure they have appropriate boundaries, particularly on the limits of assistance given as a helper. As professional helpers have a limit to their availability and know that they cannot own the problems of their clients, those participating in her support system should do the same. Be clear about these boundaries from the beginning, so both parties are on the same page. This models healthy boundary keeping and is needed for both the helper and the one being helped.

10. **DO** ask if the person is suicidal. Some shepherds worry that by asking they will plant the idea that was not present previously in a depressed person's mind. This simply is not true. If the woman

was thinking about it, then asking the question can open the doorway of communication and the appropriate intervention can be accessed.

11. **DO** reach out and touch the hurting individual . . . literally. Physical touch can provide powerful healing to those who are hurting. Do not be surprised if the depressed person shrinks from touch, or seems stiff and unresponsive. Depression can cause women not to want to physically connect with others in any way. However, as with other aspects of depression, it is important to do the opposite and to attempt to embrace those who are fighting depression.

      Jesus used touch often in the Bible. He touched those who were blind, deaf, ill, and even those who were considered repulsive to society. Jesus touched the man "covered with leprosy"[9] and he was healed. Jesus did not have to touch him. Jesus could have merely spoken the words and he would have been healed. Yet Jesus touched a man no one else in that culture would have touched.[10] What do you think that touch did to the soul and spirit of that hurting man? He probably felt deep compassion and acceptance, where he had once felt rejection and isolation. There is something strong and powerful that comes with touch.

12. **DO** refer the individual for professional help as discussed on page 70. If appropriate, suggest she meet with a pastor. The recommendation to involve professional helpers is vital so the depressed individual does not burn out her natural support system (family and friends) and end up feeling even more alone in the end. No matter what professional resources are accessed, the depressed woman will benefit from a shepherd/caregiver as a major player in her support team. "Plans fail for lack of counsel, but with many advisers they succeed."[11]

Just as important as looking at what we should say and do, we also need to know what is not helpful and what is important to try and avoid.

HURTFUL THINGS TO AVOID

1. **DON'T** preach to the depressed person. Comments such as "if you were closer to God, you wouldn't be depressed," or "your depression signifies a sin in your life that isn't being attended to," not only aren't helpful responses, they are not necessarily true. Although it may be true that a woman experiences depression when avoiding something God is trying to show her, or if she continues to engage in sin, this is not true for the majority of cases of depression. If it is apparent that sin is a major factor, then the caregiver should speak the truth in love and bring that sin to light by discussing it openly and honestly with the individual. If comfortable with the idea, the caregiver can offer to be an accountability partner for that person if they are willing to address the hold that a particular sin has on them. Sometimes it is helpful for the helper to offer to go with the woman to talk with a pastor or Christian mentor for additional accountability and spiritual guidance.

   Often I find that clients who are reaching out for help in the church tend to feel judged and given "pat answers" more than clients who are not in the church. Shepherds are more effective in caregiving when they respond as Jesus did to the pain of the individual. Jesus never negated the truth but spoke truth in an appropriate manner and in the context of love.[12] Effective shepherds recognize that there are many factors and causes to depression and will not oversimplify or overspiritualize it.

2. **DON'T** give up inviting the depressed individual to gatherings or events. Chances are she may say no as she tends to isolate. However if the invitations stop, it will only worsen her already fragile sense of self. Do not take refusals personally but keep inviting. This will send the message that you care and will not give up on her.

3. **DON'T** guilt the person into getting involved. This is true for

those who are depressed as well as those who are not. Guilt and shame are damaging and should not be used. Depressed individuals are easily overwhelmed and may have a tough time tackling even routine tasks.

4. **DON'T** treat the person as a label. Again, the depressed woman is tackling depression. She is not depression. Just like someone fighting cancer, she herself is not cancer.

5. **DON'T** treat depression as a weakness. Those who have never been depressed and do not fully understand depression sometimes do this. It is damaging and makes the woman feel like she is less than or that she herself is weak. Caregivers want to give hope and send the message to the depressed woman that she is strong and *can* tackle depression.

6. **DON'T** discount the option of medication. Depending on the person, the situation, and the severity of the depression, psychotropic medication may be recommended or may even be necessary for the woman's safety and well-being. Leave that decision to the health care professional and the individual. Although medication should not be the first or only line of defense, it has its place in treatment and should not be looked down upon. Sometimes temporary medication enables the depressed woman to better process life issues that have engendered the depression. Once she has completed the hard work of processing core issues, the level of medication may be greatly adjusted, occasionally ended.

7. **DON'T** think that you can "fix" the depressed person. It is important to understand that as much as you want to help and try to be there for her, it is still her battle to fight. Shepherds, caregivers, friends, and family can come alongside as compassionate and encouraging supports; however, they cannot own the outcome or be responsible for how much or how little the individual puts into the fight.

8. **DON'T** discount the importance of your own encouragement and prayer to the woman experiencing depression. A shepherd/caregiver extending consistent prayer, love, and care is a powerful gift to the depressed. The best care is given by multiple contributors who take initiative in surrounding her with needed resources and referrals.

Resources

Websites

http://www.christiancounselingcenters.org: Christian Counseling Centers is a nondenominational, nonprofit community mental health agency. Our mission is to provide comprehensive and effective services integrated with Christian beliefs and values.

https://www.depression.org/about-us: Depression.org – Raising awareness to overcome depression

https://www.aplaceofhopechristiancounseling.com: The Center—A Place of Hope. Whole person care addresses the entire you—your mind, body, and spirit. Christian counseling is a core element of whole person care at A Place of Hope.

Books

Backus, William, and Marie Chapian. *Telling Yourself the Truth*. Rev. ed. Minneapolis: Bethany House, 2014.

Burns, David D. *Feeling Good: The New Mood Therapy*. New York: Signet, 1999.

Cook, Muriel L., and Shelly Cook Volkhardt. *Kitchen Table Counseling*. Colorado Springs: NavPress, 2006.

Day, Larry. *Self-Esteem: By God's Design*. Portland, OR: Mt. Tabor Press, 1992, 1994, 2004.

Minirth, Frank, and Paul Meier. *Happiness Is a Choice*. Rev. and exp. ed. Grand Rapids: Baker Books, 2013.

Omartian, Stormie. *Lord, I Want to Be Whole*. Nashville: Thomas Nelson, 2000.

Quinn, Brian P. *The Depression Sourcebook*, 2nd ed.: New York: McGraw-Hill, 2000.

Stoop, David. *Self-Talk: Key to Personal Growth*, 2nd ed.: Old Tappan, NJ: Revell, 1996.

Sutton, Mark A., and Bruce Hennigan. *Conquering Depression*. Nashville: Broadman & Holman, 2001.

Thompson, Curt MD. *The Soul of Shame: Retelling the Stories We Believe About Ourselves*. Downers Grove, IL: InterVarsity Press, 2015.

Thurman, Chris. *The Lies We Tell Ourselves*. Nashville: Thomas Nelson, 1999.

VanVonderen, Jeff. *Tired of Trying to Measure Up*. Minneapolis: Bethany House, reprint, 2008.

Related Scriptures

1 Chronicles 28:9

Psalm 139:1–3, 23

Proverbs 13:12

Jeremiah 29:11

Romans 5:3; 8:24–25

1 Corinthians 2:11; 13:7

2 Corinthians 10:5

Ephesians 6:13

Hebrews 11:1; 12:1

AUTHOR BIO

CHANTELLE DOCKTER graduated from George Fox University with her master's in counseling and bachelor's in psychology. She is a licensed professional counselor and specializes in women's issues, adolescent female issues, anxiety, depression, marital and/or relational conflict, ADHD, ODD, PTSD, bipolar, physical and sexual abuse, and self-harm behaviors with couples, families, and individuals of all ages. Chantelle enjoys writing a monthly article for an online magazine for women and enjoys speaking at different seminars and events. Chantelle is married and has two young daughters. She enjoys family time, traveling, and is an avid runner.

Chapter 7

Infertility

Susan L. Suomi, MA in Counseling

The X-ray table feels hard and cold against her back as Kari lies in the sterile examination room. All alone, she shivers, not sure if it is really cold in the room, or is it that she is so anxious that she's just all shivery inside. She chokes back the tears that threaten to spill as she waits for the technician to come back and inject the dye and take the X-ray images that might give the answer to what's wrong with her. How is she flawed so that what should be the most normal thing for a woman to do is impossible for her?

Kari and her husband have been trying for four long years to conceive a child; the beautiful spontaneity of their love is becoming a clinical task: taking temperatures, counting days, running tests and more tests. Month after month there is a new disappointment with no baby to look forward to. Theirs is a deep, personal, and private pain. Not many people are aware how hurtful their innocent question "So, isn't it time you start a family?" really is. Very few people know about the tears Kari sheds when she is alone. The longing to hold a child of her own causes her arms to ache and her heart to break. Only God hears the *Why?* of her questioning heart.

Understand the Issue

What is infertility? The dictionary definition is "Incapable of produc-
ing offspring, used especially of females."[1] Infertility is recognized as a
disease or condition of the reproductive system often diagnosed after
a couple has had one year of unprotected, well-timed intercourse, or if
the woman has suffered from multiple miscarriages. According to the
Centers for Disease Control and Prevention, more than 7.3 million
Americans or one in eight couples of childbearing age are infertile.[2] The
statistics and brief description can seem meaningless because they do
not begin to touch the impact infertility has on the lives of those who
suffer this pain.

There are different conditions of infertility. *Primary infertility* is the
initial inability to conceive and bear a child. Medically, one is identified
as dealing with infertility issues after a year of trying to get pregnant
without success.

Secondary infertility is the inability to conceive or bear children after
having successfully had a child. For example, Kari eventually was blessed
with a little boy. However once again, she and her husband are dealing
with the trials of infertility due to her medical condition. Again the same
emotions and hurts are there, because each conception and each child is
a separate and individual experience. Others will experience secondary
infertility due to various medical conditions, a hysterectomy, or having
miscarried or borne stillborn children.

Impact on husbands and marriage. Although infertility is often seen
as the woman's problem, some studies indicate that when a couple deals
with infertility, about 40 percent of the time it is caused by a medical
concern of the wife, 40 percent a medical concern of the husband, and
20 percent of the time from unknown causes.[3] It is important for husbands and wives to remember that, though they may respond differently,
they are in this together. Conceiving a child is only one part of their love
for each other, and their desire to marry and be one was based on many
other areas that continue to need to be cared for and nurtured. A husband

is often caught between dealing with his own sorrow and caring for his wife. Men often see their role is to be strong and supportive. Just as a wife needs reassurance that she has not failed her husband, she also needs to know that he hurts too. For a male the hurt is often at a different level than that of his wife. He often sees it from a level of lineage and fathering his genetic child, while a female's loss is more closely tied to her self-identity and personhood.

The way each will want to deal with his/her hurt will differ. Often men want to shut down, not talk about it, and possibly do something active (i.e., sports activity, hobby, work), while women want to have someone safe with whom they can share their emotions and talk through the hurt. The book *Tear Soup* gives grieving people permission to deal with things in their own way.[4]

When a couple begins to confront the reality of infertility, they may start by seeing medical specialists to rule out or diagnose a medical cause. The decision for treatment from that point is determined by the underlying cause of their inability to conceive. The emotional impact of this process is extremely trying for the couple. Each month is spent in counting days, timing procedures, building hope, while wondering if they dare hope. Time after time those hopes are dashed when another month goes by without conception. Usually this entire process is private. Innocent comments by family and friends can feel hurtful. The couple may find it increasingly difficult to share in the joy of others who are having babies.

Some couples choose to accept not having children without knowing the cause. Depending on each person's personality and the dynamics of the couple's relationship, they may choose to accept childlessness as God's will in their lives, using their love of children to serve the Lord in other ways within His kingdom. Sometimes this might include adoption. It is important to recognize, however, that although adopting children might be the way a couple is able to fulfill their dream of having a family and parenting children, it is not a "cure" for infertility.

There are multiple medical treatments and procedures that are used to treat infertility, depending on the underlying condition. However, if you are ministering to someone dealing with these procedures, try to become somewhat educated about them in order to be able to empathize with her.

Shepherding Insights

The emotional pain of infertility often is not understood because it is such a private and personal condition. Women find it difficult to share their condition with others. So much of being able to bear a child goes to the core identity of a woman's being. There is often a sense of being flawed or "not womanly" if she cannot bear a child. To share this requires extreme emotional vulnerability. Unfortunately, the comments and attitudes of people are not always conducive to women feeling safe to open up. It can be difficult to know who is safe.

Infertility can be a major life crisis. It is important for a woman dealing with infertility to grieve the loss of her dream to have a child. The infertility experience involves many hidden losses for individuals, their loved ones, and society as a whole, including:

- Loss of the pregnancy and birth experience
- Loss of a genetic legacy and loss for future contributing citizens of the next generation
- Loss of the parenting experience
- Loss of a grandparenting relationship
- Loss of feelings of self-worth
- Loss of stability in family and personal relationships
- Loss of work productivity
- Loss of a sense of spirituality and sense of hope for the future[5]

Elisabeth Kubler-Ross describes the grief stages in her book *On Death and Dying*.[6] Each stage of loss is experienced to a greater or lesser degree, and one can go back and forth between stages before coming to acceptance. All of the grief stages apply to grieving in infertility. Examples of how to identify with each are given below.

Denial: It is often difficult for a woman who is having trouble conceiving to even use the word "infertile" because it has such a sound of finality, an end to her dream of having a child. However, denial also prevents her from being able to seek help, to look into options of testing to see if there are specific medical reasons for her inability to conceive, and to consider whether she and her husband want to consider medical treatment for infertility. Shepherds who understand this difficulty may gently coach women by asking if they have looked into other options, naming possible medical treatments. Offering a question, such as, "Have you been given any new information or diagnosis?" may be just the prompt she needs to address her reality. Even if a woman is not ready to go that next step, she will note the shepherd is a helpful resource when she and her husband are ready to discuss other options.

Anger: It is often extremely difficult for a woman to admit her anger because it can affect her at so many levels. Some women feel angry with their own bodies for "betraying" them or at their spouse if the infertility is medically attributed to the husband. She might feel anger toward other women who are able to conceive children easily and she perceives that they take it for granted that anyone can have children. She may be angry with God for not answering prayers, for not hearing, or not caring. A woman who is angry may feel guilty about her emotions and try to deny having such feelings. A shepherd may provide the safe place a woman needs to talk about the hurt, frustration, and fears that are behind her feelings of anger. She will be encouraged to express her feelings and thoughts behind the anger. She will also be encouraged to tell God directly how she is feeling about Him, and she will be assured God is big enough to handle her pain. A caregiver who listens well and prompts this woman in pain to talk will be a needed catalyst for the healing processes.

Bargaining: This seems to be a common theme in the prayers of infertile women; the promise to God that if He will answer their prayer for a child, they will use their experience to minister to others to His glory. It is sort of a "if you give me this, I'll give You that" concept. The best place for a woman struggling with infertility to grow toward is a place of being able to accept God's plan for her life, a process that takes time. A shepherd may assist by gently prompting a woman's relationship with God to move to a place of being able to answer affirmatively the question "Will you still love Me even if I do not give you what you are asking?"

Depression: When childlessness becomes the overwhelming focus of her life, a woman can become depressed past the point of experiencing sadness to not being able to find any joy in life. At this point her marriage and other relationships with friends and family are affected. Some sadness is normal but if it begins to spill into all areas of her life for an extended period of time, she should be referred to professional help. A caregiver or friend may offer lighthearted or encouraging words or experiences, but if they are met repeatedly with sadness or lack of response, further action is needful. In addition to medical and possibly psychological assistance, consistent support from those who understand and care will contribute much to a woman experiencing the emotional pain of childlessness.

Acceptance: Coming to a place of acceptance opens the opportunity to make other choices, seek medical treatment, and/or to have God use her and her husband in other ways. In accepting infertility, she can separate the fact that pregnancy and parenting are two different experiences. With acceptance comes freedom from anger and guilt. Those who care will continue to provide support and encouragement as the woman takes the next step in her journey.

There are ways to come alongside those who are suffering the pain of infertility and be an encouragement and "safe place" for them to share their hurt. First, consider how to help a woman on an individual basis, and secondly, how a church community can contribute positively to a woman grappling with infertility.

Infertility is a deep and painful wound for women because being able to have a child is often essential to a woman's identity. When a woman hears about others having babies, she can feel as though she's been stabbed in the heart. Be sensitive about sharing news, perhaps telling news about an upcoming birth in private, giving her time to deal with it in her own way before dealing with it in a group setting. Try to be available if a friend or family member wants to talk about her/his infertility problem, although it is important to let him/her guide the conversation toward or away from the topic. Often just having a caring person with a listening ear is the most important thing; it isn't necessary to offer advice. Especially be cautious of offering pat advice or answers; often these are myths that surround the problem of infertility.

Men and women have emotional differences regarding infertility, so caregivers need to be in tune where each partner is in the healing process. When questioned about the impact infertility had on their lives, 57 percent of women and 12 percent of men identified it as the most difficult challenge they have faced.[7] Be understanding if couples need to withdraw from events or gatherings that have a strong focus on children, such as baby showers, holidays, and Mother's Day. Don't force them to participate in uncomfortable situations.

There are many women in the Bible who suffered from infertility and are often referred to in ministering to women suffering with infertility. Elizabeth Price in *Stepping Stones* stated she was often given as examples, "The Infertility Hall of Fame: Sarah, Rebekah, Rachel, Hannah, and Elizabeth." Yet these women failed to encourage her because although they walked down a similar path of barrenness, their path led to giving birth to a child. Unlike these matriarchs of the faith, Elizabeth found she needed a message from God when the answer to her prayer was no. God gave her Paul's story of wanting the thorn in his flesh removed (2 Corinthians 12:7–9). Infertility also is a thorn in the flesh, a physical condition that pricks the heart of every woman (and couple) who struggles with it. God's answer to Paul became her comfort: "My grace is sufficient for you, for my power is made perfect in weakness." Elizabeth tells how she began to follow Paul's example of appreciating the work God could do in her life *because* of the weakness of infertility, not just in spite of it.[8]

Unfortunately, many women have stated that the church has not been a "safe" place for them. Often their faith is challenged by having prayers unanswered, and songs of praise are hard to sing when their hearts are hurting. It is hard to grieve publicly when the source of the sorrow is so private. Some ways those in church leadership can be more sensitive to infertile couples is to consider how to include them, particularly at times like Mother's Day. It is important that women who would want to be mothers be included in the prayers for moms.

Although some churches have support groups for those dealing with infertility, many women have not found this type of resource available. Starting a group for people to share their hurts and hopes with others who have the same concerns and emotions would be a wonderful resource. One woman stated she had attended a secular support group but did not feel like she could connect or identify with the women there because the comfort and healing of the heavenly Comforter was not a part of the process. A magazine like *Stepping Stones* (see Resources) is a wonderful comfort to many, and as one woman said, "It was my support group even if I wasn't at a meeting."

Most importantly, be a prayer supporter. Pray for the childless in your church. "Carry each other's burdens, and in this way you will fulfill the law of Christ" (Galatians 6:2).

HELPFUL THINGS TO SAY AND DO[9]

1. **DO** listen, empathize, and encourage her to talk. A woman experiencing infertility often feels out of control. Let her know you are willing to listen and let her choose whether and when to talk about it.

2. **DO** ask questions that express an appropriate level of interest in her journey such as, "Have you been given any new information or diagnosis?" Listen well and respond with care and gracious support.

3. **DO** offer words of encouragement such as, "I care about you. I want you to know I hurt with you."

4. **DO** let her know if and when she has any interest in making contact with another woman who is willing to talk about experience with infertility (or adoption), you could give her the

contact information. This of course would be offered when she may be willing to talk about her journey.

5. **DO** tell her "I am praying for you." Then pray! Occasionally send a card or email to her to let her know you have not forgotten and you are still praying for her. Offer prayers of comfort and strength.

6. **DO** ask permission *before* sharing her needs or situation with anyone else. Do proceed with caution! Prayer requests are best given *with* permission from the one who generates the request. If she is willing to have her needs given to others for prayer, you may want to ask her to put in writing how she would like those expressed. Infertility is private, personal, and needs to be handled with the greatest of discernment and care.

7. **DO** express care by expressing kindness and charity, such as offering to "be there" on the day of her monthly cycle when her hopes will be again heightened and possibly dashed. Be sensitive to the days in her cycle when she may experience "the death of a child" once again. The loss and the dashed hope will threaten to devastate and possibly immobilize her. Offer to bring her favorite latte or lunch to her. Do express words of comfort as is appropriate, but your silent presence can sometimes bring the greatest comfort.

8. **DO** realize men and women typically express emotions differently, particularly grief. Women are more likely to talk through their sorrow, to express their emotions, and to share their feelings. Men are more likely to keep it inside, to isolate themselves, and move on to another activity. Men like to find solutions and feeling unable to solve this can be very painful. Both genders *feel* sadness with varying levels of intensity; they will simply express them differently. Do help a woman to understand that this difference does not indicate her husband has a lack of support or engagement in their painful experience; rather, his response reflects their differences. Do offer words of understanding and encouragement.

HURTFUL THINGS TO AVOID

1. **DON'T** make such thoughtless comments to anyone such as, "You've been married so long and no kids. Don't you want children?" or "Why don't you have children?" or "If you had children, you would understand." This can be the most hurtful comment of all.

2. **DON'T** say things such as, "If you have faith, I know God will give you children." "God will send you kids; just be patient." *Don't place a spiritual guilt on the infertile couple.* You have no way of knowing what will happen.

3. **DON'T** say, "I know exactly how you feel." Even if you have had a similar experience, you will never know *exactly* how another person feels. Resist saying so!

4. **DON'T** give solutions or fertility treatments you've just heard about. Don't give false hope. If she is open to discuss medical options, offer a resource as something she may want to explore further. Don't present your latest discovery as "the answer."

5. **DON'T** assume it is okay for you to talk about the woman's situation to others, even other family members, or her husband. You must first ask her permission to talk with *anyone* about her situation. A woman struggling with infertility will likely feel fully exposed if she knows others are discussing her most private concern.

6. **DON'T** assume that the varying expressions of sadness or grief, or seeming lack of expression, indicate a husband or family member's lack of interest or support. Men and women often express grief differently and it is helpful to have this understanding as you come alongside a woman and her family who may be also grappling with the pain of infertility.

Resources

Websites

https://resolve.org/: Resolve Organization

https://bethany.org/: Bethany Christian Services

Books

Dobson, James R. *When God Doesn't Make Sense.* 1993. Reprint, Carol Stream, IL: Tyndale Momentum, 2012.

Flowers, Lois. *Infertility: Finding God's Peace in the Journey.* Eugene, OR: Harvest House, 2003.

Gibbs, Donna, Becky Garrett, and Phyllis Rabon. *Water from the Rock, Finding God's Comfort in the Midst of Infertility.* Chicago: Moody, 2002.

Kubler-Ross, Elisabeth. *On Death and Dying: What the Dying Have to Tell Doctors, Nurses, Clergy and Their Own Families.* 1969. Reprint, New York: Scribner, 2014.

Schalesky, Mario, *Empty Womb, Aching Heart: Hope and Help for Those Struggling with Infertility.* Bloomington, MN: Bethany House Publishers, 2001.

Schwiebert, Pat, and Chuck DeKlyen. *Tear Soup: A Recipe for Healing after Loss.* 5th ed. Portland, OR: Grief Watch, 2005.

Vredevelt, Pam. *Empty Arms: Emotional Support for Those Who Have Suffered a Miscarriage, Stillbirth, or Tubal Pregnancy.* Sisters, OR: Multnomah, 2001.

Related Scriptures

Psalm 69:1–3, 16–20; 94:22

Isaiah 26:3; 40:29; 55:8

Habakkuk 3:17–19

2 Corinthians 4:6; 12:9

Hebrews 13:5

AUTHOR BIO

SUSAN L. SUOMI received a master of arts in counseling from Western Seminary in Portland, Oregon, and a BA in psychology from Northland College, Ashland, Wisconsin. She has worked as a licensed mental health counselor at Charis Counseling Center, Vancouver, Washington, and as a counselor at North Greenville University, Tigerville, South Carolina, and the Vine Community Church in Taylors, South Carolina. Sue has counseled both clients and family members who have experienced infertility.

Chapter 8

Terminal Illness

Kay Kirkbride, BSN
Hospice and Palliative Care in Washington County, Oregon

Mom had severe heart disease the last twenty years of her life. Near the latter part, she came to live in our tri-level home as she was less able to care for herself. The most minor tasks, such as getting dressed or brushing her hair, taxed her limited energy. Rest was necessary after eating, walking a short distance, or climbing a short flight of stairs. As time progressed, her heart disease and the roller-coaster ride sped up. It started slowly, then gathered speed with each subsequent turn and scary twist of life. There were lots of highs and lows, ups and downs as her weakened body deteriorated and her heart strained to oxygenate her vital organs. The anxious rides to the hospital became more frequent while her heart struggled, racing rapidly out of control. "Will I make it to the hospital in time?" she questioned in fearful silence. "Is this it? Will the doctors be able to help me again? I am so tired. My heart is bouncing in my chest and I can hardly breathe. I feel so dizzy. I don't know if I can pull through this time . . ."

The painful thoughts were pushed aside as help rushed to her aid.

The gurney received Mom's frail body and shot through the emergency room doors with no time to waste. As doctors and nurses came running, orders were given and they efficiently went to work. Out came the needles, medications, and sometimes electric shock to treat her runaway heart. After tense, hushed seconds went by, a hesitant heartbeat began anew as her body lay wilted upon the cart. After several days of careful observation and rest, with deep gratitude, we returned home with Mom. How many more trips lay ahead? Will the next episode be the last?

We cherished our extended time with Mom as the peaceful days went by. One quiet day, Mom strolled down a short flight of stairs where my husband and I were in the kitchen preparing for the day and listening to soft background music. After a short conversation, Mom ascended to her room. After only a few moments, I turned the radio down when I thought I heard our Siamese cat beckoning. Listening closely, what I heard sounded more like singing. Intrigued, I went upstairs and knocked gently on Mom's door, which was uncharacteristically ajar and beckoned me in. And just that quickly she was gone, no longer alive. With the sweetness of angelic singing, she slipped away to be with her Lord.

Understand the Issue

Terminal illness is a term used when medical science feels there is nothing more they can do; it is when there is no known cure—barring divine intervention.[1] In effect, terminal illness is a medical or physiological condition that is *incurable and fatal.* Often, an additional parameter especially used by hospice includes that the patient has six months or less to live, although that is not always easy to assess or predict accurately. Depending on the diagnosis, patients go through similar but different types of experiences, often with unique and special needs.

Process of Dying

1. A few months before death, the terminally ill person feels a separation from the world and others. No one knows what she[2] is going

through. She begins to process her life, regrets and losses, relationships, fears of the afterlife, and so on. She may exhibit little interest in anything and begin sleeping much more. This may be an important and significant time of "grief work" as she deals with her approaching death.

Physiologically the body is slowing down and changing, not requiring the fuel and energy it once needed. The appetite diminishes and often the taste of food changes as the disease progresses. There may be little or no desire to eat. Activity is waning and her deteriorating body no longer needs the fuel as it conserves energy. This is the body's natural response in the dying process as it transitions from life to death. It can be very hard on the family who typically wants her to eat to keep up her strength. Realizing it is normal for her not to eat or drink may help the family accept this change in their loved one's behavior. After all, it is the illness that is ending her life, not the lack of water or nutrition.

2. A few weeks before death, the physical and sometimes mental deterioration continues. She may experience incontinence, irregular heartbeat, weakness, changes in body temperature, difficulty swallowing, and respiratory irregularities. Chemical changes and diminished oxygen to the brain can cause confusion. Restlessness, agitation, and reduced recognition may be present. It is helpful for family and caregivers to identify themselves as they enter the room, giving the time of day in a calm and soothing manner.

3. Days or hours before death, symptoms will be more pronounced as the body declines and the organs shut down. She may be less responsive, sleep with her eyes and mouth open, and develop noisy breathing as fluids collect in the trachea or lungs. The breathing may be irregular with long pauses in between. She may become restless or pick at the bedcovers or the air. Her state of consciousness may fluctuate. Sometimes a patient may have hallucinations and/or delusions, "seeing" people who are not there. She may talk incoherently (or so it seems to us) or perhaps may be having visions from the Lord.

Body circulation concentrates on fueling the organs, causing the skin and extremities to become cool and mottled. Having a loved one present at this stage may be a powerful support. Just the sound of your voice or touch may be very comforting. Holding her hand, reading a book, playing her favorite music, or singing may all express love and comfort as she nears the threshold of death.

Some patients become unresponsive and slip into a coma. This is common in the final minutes, hours, and sometimes even days. Even though she does not respond, family and caregivers must watch what they say in her presence and speak as if she were listening to every word. Many patients are conscious and can hear right up to the very end. Sometimes a patient will dismiss her family who may be hovering at the bedside. Not wanting her family to see her die, she might suggest, "Why don't you go get a cup of coffee?" And while the family is gone, she draws her last breath.

4. Impending death is foreshadowed by the kidneys shutting down, resulting in a decreased amount of urine, which is dark and concentrated. Her temperature will often spike high and then begin to fall. Her pulse and blood pressure also decrease. The patient may become incontinent of both stool and urine in the final hours or days as death becomes imminent.

5. Minutes before death the patient's breathing deteriorates further. Her color changes to pale or waxy yellow. The skin is cold, clammy, and mottled. The finger- and toenail beds turn blue. The patient appears to lose all contact with her environment. The heart and breathing cease as she silently slips away.

The natural processes of dying have many similarities, though they are not exactly the same for everyone. The general signs and symptoms experienced by most people are listed in the chart below. Just as each person's life is unique, so is each death. Every person may experience some or all of the signs on the next page but perhaps in a different time frame than shown.

UNDERSTANDING THE PROCESS OF DYING [3]

Months	Weeks	Days/Hours	Minutes
Decreased activity	Decreased blood	Intensification of	Decreased pulse,
Increased sleep	pressure	previous signs	blood pressure,
Lack of appetite	Increased or	Decrease in blood	and circulation
Decreased food &	decreased pulse	pressure	Breathing becomes
water intake	Respiration	Pulse weak and	weak, shallow,
Less communication	irregularities	hard to find	and erratic
Withdrawal from the	Congestion	Purplish & blotchy	Temperature can
world and others	Increased	knees, feet, and	spike high then
Introspective	perspiration	hands	drop low
	Body temperature	Irregular breathing	Cannot be
	hot or cold	(lengthy stops	awakened
	Color changes:	between breaths)	
	pale or bluish	Decreased urine	
	Decreased urine	output	
	output	Urine dark,	
	Incontinent	concentrated	
	Body feels tired	Incontinence	
	and heavy	Eyes glassy, dry/	
	Sleeping but	tearing, half open	
	responding to	Restlessness or	
	stimulation	no activity	
	Agitation	Possible surge	
	Confusion/	of energy	
	disorientation	State of	
	Talking with the	consciousness	
	unseen	fluctuates	
	Not eating, taking	Less responsive	
	little or no fluids	or coma	
		Hallucinations/	
		delusions	
		Picking at clothes	
		or the air	

**Signs of
DEATH**

Breathing has ceased. *Chest and abdomen no longer rise and fall. Airflow cannot be felt with hand in front of the patient's nose or mouth. Pulse is absent when checked at the wrist and neck.*
Patient is motionless, without speech or response.
All muscles relax:
The jaw is relaxed and the mouth slightly open.
The eyelids are slightly open.
Possible bowel or bladder incontinence

Many people associate pain with dying but that is not always the case. Some conditions may involve no pain while others may involve varying levels from little to extreme, intermittent to constant. Today, we have many excellent ways to help manage pain, leaving little reason for a lot of suffering due to out-of-control pain.

Common myths about pain:[4]

- Myth: *Dying is always painful.*
- Myth: *There are some kinds of pain that can't be relieved.*
- Myth: *Pain medications always cause heavy sedation.*
- Myth: *It is best to save the stronger pain relievers until the very end.*
- Myth: *To get good pain relief, you have to take injections and be in a hospital.*
- Myth: *Once you start taking morphine, the end is always near.*

Shepherding Insights

Death is an uncomfortable, often frightening subject for most people. Death forces us to face our own fears, frailties, and mortality. It is an unwelcome guest. Many of us have felt the gut-wrenching shock following the news of a beloved friend or family member who has been diagnosed with a terminal illness—much more so if it is a child or younger person who is robbed of life. Shepherding will not only include the patient but often the family. Each person and family navigates these disturbing waters differently, but ideally will draw strength from one another.

Emotional ups and downs are common. Patients may face a number of fears including uncontrolled pain and/or other types of physical distress (e.g., bleeding, choking, or suffocation). Listen carefully. Encourage each one to express fears and challenges. It will be reassuring to provide good information about their condition so they can know in advance some of the symptoms they are likely to experience. Be sensitive, however, as some individuals do not want to know or discuss their condition or their impending death. It may be too scary for them. They must be supported with great dignity, compassion, and understanding. Allow them to cope in their own way.

The losses are great for the *patient, family,* and the *caregiver.* The pain increases as these losses are experienced. Encourage each one to name her losses and grieve them along the way.

- Role(s). The wife is no longer able to care for her husband and home. A mother can't parent well and must watch helplessly as others take over.
- Financial resources. Funds must be expended for medical care and the eventual funeral.
- Physical abilities. She is unable to do what she once did, due to less energy and strength.
- Mobility, which may be gradual or sudden. This may be a gradual weakening of the body so she can no longer get out of bed, feed herself, or turn and reposition her body.
- Relationships. Others may rally around at first, but slowly drift away. Some family members don't even want to come and see the patient. "I just can't see my mom like that."
- Plans and dreams. The long-awaited cruise will never be. Her illness cheats her from seeing the children grow up and get married. She won't be able to hold her grandchildren.
- Physical being. Body parts are removed with disfiguring surgeries such as colostomy, mastectomy, amputation.
- Intimacy. Holding hands, that knowing look, or talking about things in common are gone.
- Control and independence. She becomes more dependent on others.

On the next page is a chart that may provide caregivers a glimpse into the needs of the patient. Some patients may be spiritually healthy while others may be struggling.

SIGNS OF SPIRITUAL PROBLEMS AND HEALTH

NEED	SPIRITUAL PROBLEMS Behavior or Condition	SPIRITUAL HEALTH Behavior or Condition
Meaning and Purpose	Expresses despair that he/she has no reason to live Questions the meaning in suffering and death Exhibits emotional detachment from self and peers Jokes about life after death	Expresses hope in the future contentment with his/her life Desire to participate in religious rituals Lives and has lived in accordance with his/her value system

Receive Love	Expresses...
	  feelings of a loss of faith in God
	  fear of dependence
	  fear of tests and diagnosis
	  feeling a lack of support from others
	  guilt feelings
	  anger with self/others
	  ambivalent feelings toward God
	  despondency during illness/ hospitalization
	  resentment toward God
	  loss of self-value due to decreasing physical capacity
	  fear of God's anger
	Does not discuss feelings about dying with significant others
	Does not call on others for help when he/she needs it
	Behaves as he "should" by conforming to the behavior of a "good" patient or person
	Refuses to cooperate with health care regimen
	Confesses thoughts and feelings he/she is ashamed about
	Worries about how the rest of the family will manage after his/her death
		Expresses...
		  hope in life after death
		  confidence in the health care team
		  feelings of being loved by others/God
		Desires to perform religious rituals leading to salvation
		Trusts others/God with the outcome of a situation in which he/she has no control

Give Love	Worries about financial status of family Worries about separation from others through death	Expresses love for others through action Seeks the good of others

SIGNS OF SPIRITUAL PROBLEMS AND HEALTH (cont'd)

NEED	SPIRITUAL PROBLEMS Behavior or Condition	SPIRITUAL HEALTH Behavior or Condition

Hope and Creativity	Expresses...
	   fear of loss of control
	   boredom during illness and
	   hospitalization
	   anxiety about inability to pursue
	   career, marriage, and parenting
	   because of illness
	   fear of therapy
	Is unable to pursue creative
	outlets due to high level of
	physical disability
	Exhibits overly dependent behaviors
	Denies the reality of his condition
		Asks for information about his/her
		   condition realistically
		Talks about his/her condition
		   realistically
		Sets realistic personal health goals
		Uses time during illness/
		   hospitalization constructively
		Values his inner self more than his/
		   her physical self

HELPFUL THINGS TO SAY AND DO

1. **DO** listen, listen, listen, with your ears and your heart.

2. **DO** be realistic with hope and encouragement. God can perform a miracle but He may not.

3. **DO** visit but be prepared to encounter unpleasant odors, sights, or words. These often accompany the final journey of the terminally ill.

4. **DO** be comfortable with silence. It is too taxing for the dying person to stay engaged in conversation and endure continual chatter. Silence gives them opportunity to rest and even to silently work through some things with the comfort of someone nearby.

5. **DO** ask permission. Let the patient have as much control over things as she wants and is able to handle. This gives her dignity and the opportunity to make her own decisions.

6. **DO** use appropriate gentle touch, always with permission. The skin is often very sensitive so be especially gentle with massage or with patting or holding her hand.

7. **DO** allow her to talk about her funeral or memorial service if she brings it up. Don't just gloss over, deny, or postpone this opportunity. Sometimes the family can't bear to talk about it, but when the loved one expresses the desire to talk, please let her.

8. **DO** talk with encouragement but not false encouragement such as, "Oh, you can do it." Maybe she no longer has the strength, balance, or even presence of mind to please you. It may be too painful to try to get up and walk down the hall.

9. **DO** let her be open and honest. Hiding feelings takes more energy than being honest.

10. **DO** ask open-ended questions to enable her to talk about what she wants. "Tell me what yesterday was like." Then let her speak.

HURTFUL THINGS TO AVOID

1. **DON'T** have a preset agenda. Take the lead from the patient.

2. **DON'T** use words or phrases that hurt, such as, "I understand." "I know how you feel." "Well, it is for the best." "Keep a stiff upper lip." "Well, at least . . ." "You shouldn't feel that way."

3. **DON'T** give false hope or promises, such as, "You're going to beat this thing," or "You are just tired now, but soon you will be up and dancing."

4. **DON'T** tell your own stories but keep the focus on the one who is ill.

5. **DON'T** insist that the dying person talk about or face the reality of their impending death. It may be too frightening. Honor and support her with compassion and great understanding.

6. **DON'T** do a lot of talking. Constant talk is tiring. Listen more and allow periods of silence.

7. **DON'T** gloss over their remarks or use denial. In compassion,

give them a hearing so they can express their wishes, fears or feelings, pain or loss.

8. **DON'T** judge family members or friends who are unable to be present, especially at the time of death. Grieving is an individualized experience and each person needs to make his or her own decision since many variables can affect decisions.

As strength fails and the organs no longer function well, measures can be taken to promote comfort and reduce adverse symptoms. Propping a loved one up on pillows or turning her onto her side may ease breathing difficulties and provide greater comfort. Oxygen may also be ordered by the doctor to enable her to breathe easier. She may have delusions or hallucinations. Don't discount or argue with her. She may also pick at things, which may not make sense to the observer but might to the patient. Although some of these symptoms can be distressing for the family to observe, it is often just part of the process. Help make this final passage as easy as possible with great understanding and patience. Express love to her by supplying as much comfort as possible while protecting her from falls or other dangers.

Touch can also be important, but remember that the skin is very sensitive; be gentle. Please ask permission: "Would you like a gentle massage?" "May I hold your hand?" Rubbing her arm gently is often helpful near death. She may not want anything to cover her but a sheet. Ask permission: "Would you like the light on/off . . . the window open a little bit . . . the blinds up/down?" Perhaps she may enjoy nice fresh air, to be sung to, or to have Scripture read. Often dim or low light as opposed to bright illumination is preferred by those near the end of life. Give assurance such as, "I am here with you; anything you want, just let me know." Have all the items she needs handy at the bedside, such as tissues, water or ice chips, and call bell.

1. *Preparation for the end of life.* It is often highly beneficial for the ailing person and the family who will be left behind to actively prepare for the end of life. If possible, and while the patient is still alert, has energy,

and is interested, involve her in a discussion about her final wishes and the business aspects of her departure. Who will handle the checkbook for paying the medical expenses and doctors? Where are the important documents—life insurance policy, military discharge papers, social security card/info, birth certificate? Is there anyone they want to see or to inform about their condition or death? What type of funeral arrangements (e.g., casket, cremation, minister, music)? It is very helpful to let her help set her affairs in order.

A new widow said her husband's death from cancer was sudden. They both thought he had more time, so they had not taken care of the important details of the business of dying. She lamented, "There are so many things that I wish we would have prepared for had I known." As a result, a few older adults in their church collected several "end of life" plans. They compiled them into a booklet that they give as a "love gift" to their church families.[5]

2. *Caregiver classes.* Many communities and organizations offer classes to assist caregivers in this difficult season of life. It can be a rewarding time to comfort and minister to their loved one. But it can also be a challenging time as they deal not only with the impending death of the ailing patient but also with their own fears, grief, and loss. Caregiver classes prepare the caregiver for what to expect.

Sometimes spiritual problems arise within the patient. Strong Christians begin to doubt and wonder why God is allowing this. They may question God or become angry or fearful. Sometimes they have guilt. "If only I had never smoked," or "What did I do to deserve this?"

The patient often feels like she is a burden, which she doesn't want to be. Two of the main fears of the terminally ill are the fear of becoming more and more incapacitated and the fear of the pain they may experience. They don't want to lose control. They also don't want to be alone. They wrestle to accept the fact that they will not be here much longer. They think, *What is going to happen to my family? To my kids? I will miss out on all the weddings, celebrations, births . . .* They fear uncontrollable, endless physical and emotional pain. The list of fears and loss is long.

Caregivers will learn how to respond appropriately to these common concerns.

Caregivers will also experience many of the same emotions, fears, and losses that the patient does. Likewise, they need to learn to grieve the losses along the way. Many people caring for Alzheimer's or other dementia patients say, "It is like one long funeral. I watch my loved one die slowly in front of my eyes . . ." Another caregiver may question, "Why didn't they take better care of themselves? Why am I stuck with this situation?" Classes for caregivers will help them understand that these are normal feelings as well as offer helpful suggestions. The classes encourage good self-care, including how/where to get respite care. Being well prepared for this compassionate role will enable the caregiver to have greater confidence and be more effective while staying healthy in the process.

3. *Survivor or grief recovery class.* For all who have lost a loved one, the pain is very real. Survivors also face many types of losses such as: loss of a spouse, parent, or child; financial loss due to large medical bills and funeral expenses; loss of intimacy and relationship. It is important for the survivors to receive help to work through their own grief. It is important to grieve every loss, especially if they were unable to do so along the way. Participating in a survivor or grief recovery class will help prevent the compounding of losses. They need to work through the grief, to walk through that dark valley, to cry, to hit a pillow, to tell their story, or whatever way they best express the pain.

Encourage and give permission to those who have suffered to grieve their losses. So many times when a mutual friend dies, I ask people, "How are they doing?" "Oh, real well; the widow didn't even shed a tear at the funeral," they reply back. The impact of the loss may not be truly felt until the second or third month. And then the grieving survivor may realize the loss more acutely, feeling the painful emptiness of the house and the loneliness of their aching heart.

A woman attending a grief recovery group for the first time angrily declared, "I am here but I am not going to do any of that sharing stuff." At the fifth class she began to tell her story. "I went home after the last class and a few days later the smoke alarm went off. I thought to myself, 'If my husband was here, he would fix that. But he's not here.' Do you know what I did? I went into the closet where all his clothes were. I picked up one of his shoes, got a ladder, and knocked that thing off the ceiling. Screws scattered all over the floor surrounding the smoke alarm. I stomped on it and stomped on it. And then, I sat down in the middle of the mess and cried for two hours."

Grieving cannot be hurried nor can it be cut short. We all grieve in our own way and at our own pace. However, to remain healthy, the grieving process must take place before healing can occur. With healthy shepherding, the dying and those left behind can assist each other during this final journey, whether into His loving presence or into His comforting arms and tender keeping.

> Even though I walk
>   through the darkest valley,
> I will fear no evil,
>   for you are with me;
> your rod and your staff,
>   they comfort me. . . .
> Surely your goodness and love will follow me
>   all the days of my life,
> and I will dwell in the house of the LORD
>   forever.
> (Psalm 23:4, 6)

Resources

Websites

www.carepartnersor.org: Care Partners Hospice and Palliative Care
www.legacyhealth.org: Legacy Caregiver Services
www.hospicefoundation.org: Hospice Foundation of America
www.griefshare.org: GriefShare

Books

Callanan, Maggie, and Patricia Kelley. *Final Gifts: Understanding the Special Awareness, Needs, and Communications of the Dying.* 1992. Reprint, New York: Simon & Schuster, 2012.

GriefShare (Grief Recovery Support Groups). *Your Journey from Mourning to Joy.* Wake Forest, NC: Church Initiative, 2006.

Piper, Don. *90 Minutes in Heaven.* 2004. Anniversary ed. Grand Rapids: Revell, 2014.

Rawlings, Maurice S., MD. *Beyond Death's Door.* Nashville: Thomas Nelson Publishers, 2008.

Related Scriptures

Psalms 23; 27; 145:18
John 14:1–4; 16:22, 33
Romans 10:9–10
2 Corinthians 1:3–4

AUTHOR BIO

KAY KIRKBRIDE, BSN, is a retired registered nurse residing in Hillsboro, Oregon. In 1982, she helped start Hospice and Palliative Care in Washington County, serving as the first nursing director. A member of the board of directors, Kay continues to serve in an advisory capacity as well as to train volunteers. Kay has facilitated grief recovery groups and cancer support groups, and is currently active in teaching and training leaders throughout the United States to facilitate classes for family caregivers. She is a health minister on the Parish Nurse Council at her church and chairs the Older Adult Ministry Team.

Chapter 9

Physical Disabilities, Chronic Pain, and the Aging Process

Ev Waldon, RN

Aging and Disability Services, State of Oregon

*H*eidi had always been the picture of health. She travels, is active, and is independent. At age twenty-four, two months after her wedding, she began experiencing vaginal and perineal burning sensation and pain. It took two years to finally get the diagnosis of vulvodynia.[1] She has had five years of doctor visits, numerous treatments, medications, and therapies with no real improvement in the pain.

The ramifications of this diagnosis affect every area of her life:

physical, emotional, social, and financial. She has spent an inordinate amount of time and energy on doctor appointments, phoning her insurance companies, and visiting pharmacies. This syndrome dictates where she can sit and what she can wear. This newly married woman is faced with the constant challenge of sexual intimacy.

Heidi's pain is constant and shouts loudly, but very few people know about it. She hates that the pain zaps her energy and that she has to curtail her involvement at church, work, and activities with friends. She feels that she is not using the gifts and abilities God has given her. Heidi for the most part suffers silently, yet the pain is intense and real.

Understand the Issues

The issues of physical disability, chronic pain, and the aging process are closely aligned, often overlapping. Yet certain aspects are distinct so all three will be considered separately in this chapter.

Physical Disability

The term *disability* refers to permanent physical or mental incapacity. It is the absence or impairment of some function, activity, or skill that *will not* return with time, and covers a wide range. The chart on the following page gives some causes and types of disabilities.

Although most disabilities have a known cause(s), others may be of unknown or undetermined origin. However, the disabling effects are very real and apparent even when the cause is not clearly understood, such as in chronic fatigue syndrome or Alzheimer's.

It is important to remember that disabled or handicapped people are first *individuals*, who happen to have a disability, but who have the same basic needs as everyone else. These needs may actually be intensified by the particular loss of function, age, personality structure, and the capacity of the individual to adapt to her situation. With proper instruction, prosthetic devices or other aids, and ingenuity, many disabled people manage activities of daily living and are gainfully employed. Others require periodic help, while still others require assistive help or custodial care throughout their lives.

CAUSES AND TYPES OF DISABILITIES[2]

CAUSES OF DISABILITIES	TYPES OF DISABILITIES (not all inclusive)
Birth and genetic defects	Cerebral palsy, muscular dystrophy, complications at conception or during pregnancy or delivery
Injury: accident, fall, assault, war, etc.	Brain or spinal cord damage; harm to organs or body parts, amputations, traumatic arthritis
Illness/disease processes	Multiple sclerosis, diabetes, stroke, heart and lung involvement, blindness, deafness, degenerative diseases, fibromyalgia, cancer, circulation and nerve dysfunctions
Aging process	Arthritis, osteoporosis, poor circulation, stroke, heart disease
Obesity	Ramifications on joints, heart, and other organs
Drug and alcohol abuse	Brain damage, liver dysfunction, impaired judgment, injury, and impaired social skills
Possible chemical imbalance	Mental retardation, some psychological disorders
Unknown or little understood	Schizophrenia, Alzheimer's, dementia, chronic fatigue syndrome
Many types of disabilities	Chronic pain

Not everything that the disabled person is coping with is obvious. Some people can deal with one loss or challenge at a time, but when there are several to cope with all at once, it can be overpowering. For instance, a woman who has gone blind due to diabetes has many challenges thrust upon her, including loss of independence, easy mobility, driving, employment, friendships, reading, watching movies/plays/ball games, viewing sunsets or the ocean, and seeing the faces of her loved ones. She faces fears of further medical complications, dangers she cannot see, and financial concerns. She is excluded from many activities, bringing emotional pain and loneliness. Depression threatens as she has to learn new ways of doing *virtually everything*, including shopping, cleaning, cooking, getting dressed appropriately, and paying bills. If she is a wife or mother, there are additional concerns.

Chronic Pain

Acute pain is a normal sensation triggered in the nervous system to alert a woman[3] to possible injury and the need to take care of herself. Chronic pain is far different in that it persists. Pain signals keep firing in the nervous system for weeks, months, even years. There may have been an initial mishap, such as a sprained back, serious infection, or another ongoing cause of pain like arthritis or cancer, but some people suffer chronic pain with no known injury or cause.

Chronic pain affects 76.2 million Americans and is often difficult to treat. An estimated 50 percent of those suffer chronic pain on a daily basis; in 42 percent of those, the pain lasted longer than one year. Chronic pain is undertreated and has significant personal, economic, and social impact. Patients experience decreased function, productivity, and socialization. Psychological complications such as depression and anxiety are often present. The difficulty in determining the exact cause of chronic pain makes it difficult to treat.[4] Attitudes toward chronic pain can hinder diagnosis and treatment. The chart on the next page shows examples of physical, emotional, social, and spiritual changes that can occur with chronic pain.

EFFECTS AND CHANGES OF
THOSE DEALING WITH CHRONIC PAIN [5]

TYPE OF EFFECTS	PHYSICAL CHANGES
Pain drains energy	Short fuse, too exhausted to get ready to go anywhere
Sleep deprivation from pain	Batteries not recharged, many effects on work and driving
Limited activities	Difficulty opening jars, lifting grandchildren; recreation, hobbies
Weight issues	Weight loss from poor appetite. Weight gain when activity hurts and inability to exercise. Pain meds and antidepressants can have side effects of weight gain, constipation, nausea, vomiting. May need meds to counteract side effects.
Medication side effects	Anti-inflammatory drugs for arthritis/joint pain are very hard on the stomach. Diuretics not taken because it is too hard/painful to go to the bathroom often
Loss of touch and intimacy	Even hugs may be painful. Diminished sexual intimacy

	EMOTIONAL AND PSYCHOLOGICAL CHANGES
Loss of independence	Loss of driver's license, housing; requiring help to complete simple tasks
Pain rules	Pain dictates what you can and cannot do, hard to concentrate or think clearly (driving, decision making)
Depression	Almost always accompanies chronic pain. Depletes endorphins and causes chemical changes.
Fears and anxieties	There is a different set of worries with doctor appointments and responses, insurance benefits, medication issues, fear of losing everything, fear of not getting off the toilet or sofa due to pain.
Sense of hopelessness	"It will never get better," no pill to fix it. Suicide is high when pain is not well-managed.
Letting go of expectations	Letting go of dreams of what we are going to do, be, or become. Holidays, vacations, and hobbies may have to change.

EFFECTS AND CHANGES OF THOSE DEALING WITH CHRONIC PAIN (cont'd)

TYPE OF EFFECTS	EMOTIONAL AND PSYCHOLOGICAL CHANGES (cont'd)
Self-worth, self-image, and self-esteem	Maybe loss of job when that was defining who she was. Deformities due to arthritis, stroke, aging, weight gain affect self-image
Loneliness	Pain can keep them home, so isolation occurs. Loneliness often occurs with deafness.
Sense of failure	Not being able to be ideal mom or grandmother, housekeeper or gardener, etc.
Grieving over losses	Pain is constant reminder of losses
Anger	Usually directed at caregivers, family, friends, doctor, even God. Anger is expected, look at how it is affecting their lives.

	SOCIAL CHANGES
Isolated and withdrawn	Fear of crowds with cane/walker, steps, bathroom availability. Do not want to be a burden or drag on others so they do not ask for help.
PPS (Party pooper syndrome)	Plan to go on outing but pain or weakness prevents it. Tires quickly and wants to leave early. Tired of seeing others doing what they would like to do.
Family dynamics change	Kids take on more responsibility. Role changes (daughter helps mother with meds, making doctor appointments, clothes and food shopping, etc.). Chronic pain is a real drag on a marriage. High divorce rate.

	SPIRITUAL CHANGES
Time of questioning, even God	"Why me, what am I to learn in all this?" Giants in history questioned God about their health (Job, Paul).
Limited fellowship and corporate worship	Too painful, hard to get to church. Standing for songs is hard but cannot see words or screen when seated.
Hard to concentrate on Bible studies and prayer due to pain	Challenged spiritual vitality

Chronic pain is thought to have a greater economic and social impact than any other single disease entity.[6] Many disabilities may cause or involve chronic pain that in itself may be debilitating.

Chronic physical pain almost always involves emotional pain. A woman with chronic pain wants to be active. Pain keeps her from many of the activities she would like to do. She feels isolated and is often unable to get out of the house. In her mind, she wants to get dressed but often just the act of dressing can leave her exhausted and in distress. The pain saps her energy and prohibits her from going out. It is frustrating, especially if someone comes to take her to church or the store and then is told she cannot go. Eventually, they may stop offering to help, contributing further to her loneliness and separation. Some churches offer transportation but often the woman is too shy or will not ask for help. She does not want to be a burden. Others may need to take the initiative on her behalf and be proactive, expressing the needs appropriately and trying to help meet those needs.

A lot of work is required simply to function day to day for a woman with chronic pain. Many of the things that people without chronic pain take for granted are major challenges or impossibilities for the woman in chronic pain. It can be depressing and hard to deal with every day. My aging mother-in-law would drive to church only to find all of the handicapped parking spaces full. She would then turn around and go home because her arthritis was too painful to walk any distance. Women with chronic pain, as well as the elderly and people with disabilities, are affected socially and spiritually. They miss out on a lot because they are unable to have consistent fellowship.

A major challenge for a woman with chronic physical pain is in knowing that it may not get better. She may find ways to help ease the pain somewhat but there is no way to heal or escape it. So emotional pain remains, continuing to impact the physical pain. It is a vicious, never-ending cycle. Helping her grieve her losses will enable her to accept her condition and come to terms with it.

Aging Process

The entire body is affected with the aging process. The body gradually slows and systems actually shut down. As we age, we are more prone to heart and circulation problems, stroke, osteoporosis, and arthritis. An example of decline is also in the sensory systems of smell, taste, vision, hearing, and touch. The quality of life is reduced if a woman cannot smell or taste the food she eats. She might add salt and sugar for flavor, but these need to be limited because of heart disease, high blood pressure, or the growing potential for diabetes. Vision and hearing deficits are the greatest loss as they lead to isolation and loneliness. Loss of touch and numbness at fingers and toes may not seem serious until she finds she cannot button her blouse, tie her shoes, or open a jar. She may not notice that boiling water has splashed on her hand and caused serious burns or that her new slip-on shoes have caused a blister (that could easily lead to infection due to poor circulation).

Chronic pain and disabilities plague the aging body. It can require major effort to complete routine tasks. Activities and independence are reduced. She may become tired of all the pain and suffering and want to die. It is hard to linger on as the body fails and life seems to lose meaning and purpose.

Many women who are aging can embrace the changes and shift their focus to see the needs of others. They can model a life of joy and praise in spite of a declining body. They can be supportive to the pastor and others through prayer. Praying for others may diminish the focus on their own pain while advancing the kingdom of God.

Personal time with the aging is itself encouraging. Daily contact in person may be unrealistic but phone calls or a note in the mail can lift their spirit. It encourages them to know others care and they have not been forgotten. Depending on their health, outings can bring a lot of joy and enrich their life. Bringing them some special homemade dish or a favorite treat can brighten their day.

Shepherding Insights

It is important to remember that people in pain or with disabling conditions are usually dealing with multiple and often complex issues. Generally a person can deal with one loss at a time but many losses may be overwhelming.

Disability and chronic conditions can lead to irritability, anger, and bitterness, which further isolate and destroy. Or these conditions can gradually be met with acceptance and peace that enables a person to grow, move forward with her life, and be used of God. Loving, supportive friends can be a great encouragement bearing some of the burden and lightening her heavy load.

Even standing in church services for singing can be a challenge or obstacle for the aging, disabled, or those dealing with chronic pain or illness. They may feel conspicuous when they stay seated, and then visibility becomes an issue since the screen is blocked by those standing. The aging usually do not like to sit up front because they may need to get up to use the bathroom. They may also be concerned with losing their balance when walking (especially with walkers or walking sticks), plus the risk of being bumped by little children running in the church halls or foyers. Attendance at gatherings such as church may become more and more challenging.

Good communication is critical. Tone of voice, appropriate openness, and honesty contribute to meaningful encouragement by shepherds. Expressions of understanding and compassion interjected with humor, when appropriate, can be a pleasant relief from the heaviness of their situation. Scripture declares that a joyful heart is good medicine.[7] Laughter is disarming and good for the soul.

A shepherd also needs to take good care of herself. Involving others helps avoid burnout. Let family members know what specifically needs to be done and involve them as much as possible. Many people are not sensitive to what needs to be done but they are more than willing to help when asked. Assemble a team to share the load. Coordinating the enlistment of others to help will also provide good social interaction and fellowship.

Utilize other resources in the church and community. Involve a care team, if possible. Perhaps a small group can take on a project or task such as painting a room, providing thorough housecleaning, hauling large items or debris to the dump, or initiating a yard cleanup day. Keep in mind that the person is not a project and does not want to be thought of in that way.

The Healing Community

People with chronic pain, disabilities, or limitations due to the aging process need a safe, healing community filled with grace and understanding. Groups or classes may be formed for people experiencing pain or with special needs. Groups may focus on support, special topics, or Bible study. Nursing or care teams may provide specific services. Aids to spiritual growth, such as sermon CDs, books, or DVDs, may be made available.

Church care teams may assist those in need with practical helps, such as transportation, visitation, and meals. Small groups may take on a project to build a ramp, install rails, or other aids. Some churches may be able to offer transportation for the elderly or physically challenged people. Consider adding hearing devices or signing for those with limited or diminished hearing. Know the resources available in the area through other churches, parachurch organizations, and community resources. Acquire contact information for local Meals-on-Wheels, clinics, hospitals, and senior centers. Refer those in need to help outside of the church as appropriate.

Begin with one person or one segment of the population in need. Learn from her/them. Ask questions, show loving concern, and get involved. Pray. Ask the Lord where to start. It is possible to get started with one small group or Bible study. Network with other healing communities such as churches or parachurch organizations. Learn from their experiences. Explore key elements involved. Make a difference by becoming a healing community.

HELPING PEOPLE WITH DISABILITIES [8]

HEARING IMPAIRED	VISUALLY IMPAIRED	IMPAIRED MOBILITY (CANE OR WALKER)	PEOPLE IN WHEELCHAIRS
Social withdrawal and isolation is common.	Always explain what you are doing, either before or while you are doing it.	Walk beside her slowly.	Express love and help without being intrusive.
When speaking, face the listener directly, don't turn away.	Walk one step ahead of her, allowing her to hold your arm— do not grasp hers.	Avoid distractions and talking if she needs to concentrate on walking.	A person in a wheelchair is not helpless.
Remove obstacles (gum, food).	Ask, "What help do you need?"	Avoid busy hallways and foyers.	Ask if you can assist her by opening the door or in any other way.
Speak naturally, clearly, and distinctly.	Don't assume she can do nothing.	Allow her to sit in aisle seat near an exit.	Avoid pushing the wheelchair without her permission.
Do not shout (it distorts).	Be alert for hazards (tree limbs, trunk lids, holes in the sidewalk, etc.).	Ask if she would like to leave early to avoid the rush.	Allow her to do the things she is able to do.
Keep your hands away from your mouth.	If she has a "Seeing Eye" dog, do not pet or distract it while in harness and working.	Ask if she needs the restroom before the end of a program or intermission.	Sit or kneel down to her level to speak or converse.
Get listener's attention before speaking.	Always ask permission before petting.	In church, stay seated with her while others stand.	Treat her with respect and dignity, as you would want to be treated.
Avoid noisy backgrounds or close to walls.	Be her eyes.	Ask if you can help her stand—slowly. Joints stiffen so allow extra time.	Ask if she would like help with her plate or beverage at a potluck.
Pay attention, a puzzled look may indicate confusion.	Describe scenes, clothes, surroundings, etc.		It is usually her body that doesn't work, not her mind.
Ask questions as needed.	Include in activities, trips, or outings. She may not be able to see but she can still live and have fun.		Talk directly to the person, not to someone assisting her.
Avoid distractions.			Consider alternatives if accessibility is an issue.
Seek good lighting and a quiet place to speak.			

HELPFUL THINGS TO SAY AND DO

1. **DO** make an effort to help. Be proactive in asking how to help.

2. **DO** allow and encourage her to do the things she can do. Many people in wheelchairs are otherwise physically able. Affirm her and acknowledge all that she does for herself, helping her retain a sense of worth.

3. **DO** encourage her to talk especially about fears and feelings. These feelings can grow out of proportion if kept inside. Pray for sensitivity.

4. **DO** support and validate her pain. A fibromyalgia patient may have vague symptoms she cannot really describe, but this condition is still painful and limits her activities.

5. **DO** visit and offer opportunities to take her on outings, if she's not confined to her bed. Be sensitive to her needs. Provide a meal but stay and eat with her, and/or take her out to a restaurant. Take her to visit others or to church. Do not wait for her to ask. Make a specific time to pick her up but remain flexible. Sometimes she may not be up to it once you get there.

6. **DO** provide and encourage diversions. This can dilute the pain. Diversions may include games, crossword puzzles, Sudoku, DVDs, or audio books if reading is difficult.

7. **DO** make sure she has a support system. Perhaps a Bible study or small group could meet in her home if traveling is a hardship. Encourage others to visit, send cards, call, or email (if appropriate). Develop a care team to help with needs such as transportation, meals, and visits.

8. **DO** review medication management. Is the doctor aware of her pain level? Is she taking medications appropriately? Can she open the bottle? Does she understand the prescription? Does she watch the clock to know when she can take the next pain

medication? Write down the time. Is cost an issue? Are there side effects? Does she fear addiction?

9. **DO** offer help when rising or walking. Allow her to rise slowly as joints may be painful and may not work well. Walk beside her slowly. She may need to concentrate on each step and not talk. Offer an arm if she seems unsteady. If she is visually impaired, allow her to hold your arm and walk a step ahead. Ask, "What help do you need?" In church stay seated with her if worship involves a lot of standing. Be sensitive to such needs as bathrooms, seating, leaving early, and avoiding crowds or stairs.

10. **DO** take good care of yourself as a caregiver. No matter how much commitment the caregiver has, she has little to offer if good self-care is neglected.

HURTFUL THINGS TO AVOID

1. **DON'T** label or typecast her. Each person has different pain thresholds and coping abilities. Each person also has a different response and tolerance to pain medication.

2. **DON'T** try to be a fixer.

3. **DON'T** dictate to her what needs to be done, such as housework. What is important to her may not be to you.

4. **DON'T** ask sensitive questions that might cause her embarrassment, especially in a group setting. To gain more understanding of her illness or condition, gather information from organizations, brochures, and Internet. Demonstrate you care by being more informed of her particular disabilities.[9]

5. **DON'T** push her. She knows her limits better than you. She may be too tired or in pain.

6. **DON'T** wait for her to ask. Invite her along or offer your help. Take the initiative.

7. **DON'T** insist on your own agenda or timetable. Respect hers.

8. **DON'T** ignore warning signs of depression, uncontrolled pain, despondency, or even suicidal thoughts. Get professional help immediately by accessing your list of emergency resources. These warning signs are serious and need immediate attention.

9. **DON'T** use insensitive verbiage. Say someone "uses a wheelchair" or is a "wheelchair user." Don't say "confined to a wheelchair" or "wheelchair bound." Referring to a group, say "disabled people"; this treats them as individuals. Don't say "the disabled," which implies that they are all the same.

10. **DON'T** just assume. Ask if you have questions. Give her opportunities to participate as much as possible or desired. Ask how you or others can help.

Resources

Websites

www.webmd.com: Web MD is a site with good information on medications, including definition of the illness or disability and resources, newsletters, support groups, and online communities.

http://www.unitedspinal.org: United Spinal Association was created to help spinal cord injury patients and their families and friends with up-to-date information about spinal cord injuries.

https://www.dol.gov/general/topic/disability: US Department of Labor, Disability Resources. This site provides critical information on a variety of topics, including benefits, civil rights, community life, education, emergency preparedness, employment, housing, health, technology, and transportation.

Books

Copen, Lisa J. *Beyond Casseroles: 505 Ways to Encourage a Chronically Ill Friend.* San Diego: Rest Ministries, 2008.

————. *So You Want to Start a Chronic Illness-Pain Ministry*. San Diego: Rest Ministries, 2002.

————. *How to Start a Chronic Illness Small Group Ministry*. San Diego: Rest Ministries, 2010.

Harvey, Greg. *Grieving for Dummies*. Hoboken, NJ: Wiley Publishing, 2007.

Ieron, Julie. *The Overwhelmed Woman's Guide to Caring for Aging Parents*. Chicago: Moody, 2008.

Kassan, Stuart S., Charles Vierck Jr., and Elizabeth Vierck. *Chronic Pain for Dummies*. Hoboken, NJ: Wiley Publishing, 2008.

Koestler, Angela J., and Ann Myers. *Understanding Chronic Pain*. Jackson, MS: University Press of Mississippi, 2002.

James, John W. and Russell Friedman. *The Grief Recovery Handbook: The Action Program for Moving Beyond Death, Divorce, and Other Losses, including Health, Career, and Faith*. 20th Anniversary Exp. Ed. New York: HarperCollins, 2009.

Wells, Susan Milstrey. *A Delicate Balance: Living Successfully with Chronic Illness*. Cambridge, MA: Da Capo Press, 2000.

Disabilities

Alpert, Michelle J., Saul Wisnia, and Ted Purcell. *Spinal Cord Injury and the Family: A New Guide*. Cambridge: Harvard University Press, 2008.

Crabb, Larry. *Shattered Dreams: God's Unexpected Pathway to Joy*. Colorado Springs: WaterBrook, 2001.

Tada, Joni Eareckson, and Steve Estes. *When God Weeps*. Grand Rapids: Zondervan, 2000.

Related Scriptures

Psalms 23; 27:13–14; 31:14–15; 56:3–4; 139:14–17
Isaiah 26:3; 46:4
2 Corinthians 4:16–18

AUTHOR BIO

EV WALDON is a registered nurse who has worked in hospitals and in-home settings. She has provided both acute and rehabilitation care to patients with head and spinal cord injuries. For the past sixteen years, she has contracted with the State of Oregon, Aging and Disability Services. Ev goes into homes to assess the physical, mental, and emotional needs of adults who are dealing with multiple issues. In her church, Ev developed a care team ministry and was involved in a shepherding ministry. Besides her training and experience with aging and disabled people, she has also gained personal insight from a daughter who has painful chronic health issues as well as caring for both her and her husband's elderly parents.

Chapter 10

Addictions

Mary Anne Fifield, D.M.F.T., Licensed Marriage and Family Therapist
Founder and Clinical Director of the Addiction Recovery Center

Sylvia, age thirty-five, made an appointment with me at her mother's insistence because of her rapid weight gain. She was fifty pounds overweight, had been diagnosed with adult-onset diabetes, and was quite anxious about the situation. She said that she craved ice cream and could not stop eating chocolate sundaes. She had not been overweight in the past and was perplexed by her inability to say no to food. When pressed, she outlined her history with chocolate sundaes.

Three years ago, she would occasionally choose to have a sundae after a meal in a restaurant because she liked it. Over time, she would always choose a vanilla ice cream sundae with chocolate sauce when given the opportunity to have a dessert. She quickly determined that she did not like pecans on the sundae, but preferred walnuts. She learned which restaurants in town served sundaes with walnuts, and would only go to those restaurants for dinner. It was her family's custom to eat out after work on Friday nights. If her husband was traveling on business, she would take their son and go. If the son had soccer practice, she would go alone. She began to look forward to the sundae earlier and earlier in the week. By Fridays, it was all she thought about all day at her job. "It got me through the week," she said.

A little over a year ago, her son was at soccer practice and she was on her way to her favorite restaurant. Her cell phone rang. It was the coach informing her that her son had been injured, requesting she meet him at the emergency room. She was upset at the thought of missing her sundae. She was angry with her son for getting hurt and causing her to miss out on her weekly treat. She said, "I had to have my sundae." So after her son was released, she drove to the store, bought some ice cream, chocolate sauce, and walnuts, and ate it all at home that night.

Six months ago, her son was injured again and she had to meet him in the emergency room. This time she stopped at a store first, picked up ice cream and chocolate sauce, and ate her treat in the car on the way.

Since that time, she has been buying the ingredients for the sundaes and eating them every night at home after dinner. She also has found herself angry if her husband or son asks for some of "her" treat. She admits, "I love them. And I don't understand why I get so angry and why I can't stop having my sundae."

Understanding Addictions

Helping someone like Sylvia who has problematic compulsive behavior is a challenge—one worth the effort—that can be successful if undertaken correctly. The first task is to understand just what is going on, and second, decide what type of help is appropriate. This information is not gender specific, but for the purposes of this book, feminine pronouns will be used.

For our discussion, it would be helpful to keep in mind the old saying, "The woman takes a drink, the drink takes a drink, the drink takes the woman." *A choice of certain behaviors can lead over time to loss of choice.* Often there is so much confusion from all the presenting issues that it is hard to know where to start to offer care. It is helpful, then, to examine how a behavior that begins as a pattern can lead to an addiction, using the 3 C's[1] as a guide. Notice that some problematic compulsive patterns might be overlooked because they are "celebrated," not condemned. For example,

- Religion: church work, rescuing professions, martyrdom
- Service: volunteerism, charity, causes
- Perfectionism: cosmetic surgery, appearance, organization, list making, housekeeping
- Cleaning: preoccupation with structures, rules, rituals
- Money: investing, hoarding, risk-taking, collecting or acquiring valuables, binge shopping
- Health: bodybuilding, exercise, diet and weight management, medical treatments, tests, personal hygiene, megavitamins, suntanning
- Relationships: hero worship, superparenting, people-pleasing
- Work: overachievement, pursuit of academic degrees, overworking
- Play: music, TV, videos, games, sports, Internet

Some problematic compulsive patterns might cause problems for others as they veer over to the "condoned" area:

- Sexual: sex with consent, masturbation, adult pornography
- Alcohol: underage drinking at college
- Drugs: overuse of prescription drugs, illegal drugs
- Food: eating contests
- Gambling: casinos, online

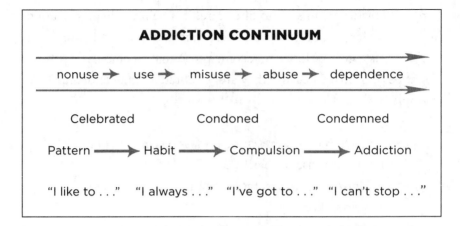

Movement across the Addiction Continuum indicates *increasing*:

- Tolerance: need for increased amounts
- Continued use despite adverse circumstances
- Preoccupation: more time obtaining, using, recovering
- Unmanageability: efforts to cut down use are unsuccessful
- Loss of control
- Loss of choice: activities reduced because of substance use; can no longer just say no
- Important social, occupational, or recreational activities are given up or reduced because of substance use.

The harm done over time to individuals by their excessive use of condoned, but damaging, chemicals and/or behaviors ultimately condemns the using or doing of sex, alcohol, drugs, food, gambling, and others. Now there is a victim, and therefore law, society, medicine, and/or religion condemns such actions. Looking back at the continuum, there is a distinction between a pattern, a habit, a compulsion, and an addiction.

Sylvia's progressive problem victimized herself, her family, marriage, health, and self-esteem. This illustrates the impact of movement across the continuum. What began as a pattern became a habit, evolved into a compulsion, and finally into an addiction. What was applauded behavior, a family time around a meal, became a condoned behavior that was tolerated by her family until her weight gain and anger became problematic to her family. Finally, her doctor condemned the addiction as she now has adult onset diabetes and needs aggressive treatment to protect against further harm.

Origins of Addiction

There are four reasons an addiction might develop: learned behavior, environment, biology (nature), and biography (nurture). Each offers a specific challenge to the caregiver as well as to the person trying to find help. The unique obstacles need to be identified and targeted tools designed and implemented. Ask questions to get as clear a picture as possible of the critical aspects of her past and present, such as the cultural, racial, religious background of her family of origin with its customs and rules, her growing-up experiences, and extended family members with compulsive or addictive behaviors.

1. Learned Behavior

Referring to the Addiction Continuum and applying "The woman takes a drink, the drink takes a drink, the drink takes the woman," one can begin to sort out what is happening. With the first phase, the woman takes a drink and it is her choice. A person who tries chemicals and behaviors are at that point—the experimentation stage when she is learning about the chemical or the behavior by using or doing again and again. With positive reward, the experimentation continues but she retains control.

But in the next stage, something different is happening in her body and brain. Tolerance is beginning and with it withdrawal. She retains the ability to not begin to use or do, but once she starts she loses the ability to stop. Harmful dependence is beginning. Her body is adjusting to the chronic presence of the effects of the chemical or the behavior and she is changing. She is developing defenses to protect what is happening. Remorse, guilt, shame, and fear are growing. And finally, the drink (or other substance or behavior) takes the woman, and addiction is now in charge, in about 7–10 percent of users and doers. The addict is living in an altered state of reality. There is a continued drive to use or do as an attempt to feel "normal." Powerlessness, unmanageability, irrational thinking, and loss of self now define her. She continues to seek the original good feeling, but can never get it back. She will keep chasing that feeling all the while feeling worse and worse, but never giving up the chase until she has to.

2. Environment

Growing up in certain environments that have risk factors can shape the pattern of a person's life. For example, certain cultures endorse the use of specific chemicals and/or behaviors as "normal." Within a large city, there can be cultures of beer, hard liquor, marijuana, crack, et cetera. There are cultures that view women as sex objects to be used at will. There are cultures driven by the need for power, success, money. The list of possibilities is long. If the culture allows solitary drinking versus the social or the religious use of alcohol only, then the incidence of alcoholism is much higher. If the culture supports the use of chemicals (food, alcohol, drugs—legal and illegal) for the reduction of stress and anxiety, there is a higher likelihood of addiction.

3. Biology or Nature

Research has given us concrete results that give understanding not only of the biological origins of addiction but also what happens to the individual suffering as an organism in the addiction. This information is de-shaming for the person seeking help and gives specific direction on how to help her. Genetic studies and extensive family histories allow us to say that an addict is born with a predisposition to becoming an addict if other factors collude. The limbic system, the brain's pleasure/reward structure, has been altered by the addiction. The brain responds to stress by pressing the person to use or to do in order to lower the awareness of the stress and to create a sense of safety. The brain's chemical messengers/

neurotransmitters have also been hijacked and the production of them has been significantly impacted. The addict's brain was wired toward addiction to begin with and then has been negatively changed by the chronic using.

4. Biography or Nurture

For the development of a healthy adult personality structure, the process of attaching and separating must proceed through certain developmental stages. If not, then there is room for addiction to be used as an attempt at repair. Attachment or connection is the first task of a child after birth.

What is attachment? It is bonding between the child and mother, and then father. It is a two-way reciprocal process created over time by both the child and the caregiver, an experience that creates safety and protection. It is a secure base from which the child can move into autonomy and it creates the basic trust that is the primary building block of the child's personality. Moreover, it is an instinctual biologically based process that supports a healthy developing brain.

When the nurture process proceeds well, the child has a secure attachment that enables her to function effectively when stressed. But when there is early trauma, the child will flee, fight, or freeze when stressed and carry her coping pattern into adulthood. Addiction can be used to facilitate these defensive responses. The using and doing addictions are ways to flee or escape, to fight by allowing the anger to create conflict, or to freeze into immobility. *Addiction can be understood as a way to manage the stresses of life when healthy functioning is not an option.* This person enters adulthood with faulty coping skills, with an adult attachment disorder.

This adult attachment disorder is called *codependency. Codependency is an identity disorder, not knowing who they are but finding identity outside of themselves.* This problem is basic to all addiction. The using or doing are attempts to offset physical, emotional, or spiritual deprivation stemming from childhood. If self-medication of internal pain is the goal of using or doing, then identifying codependency as a defensive response to childhood trauma is important when offering help.

Shepherding Insights

Dr. Patrick Carnes[2] has worked in the field of sexual addiction, but with some modifications, his conclusions apply to all addictions and to codependency.

Carnes Addiction System

- *Core Beliefs*: what a person believes about herself and reality at the present moment. These core beliefs are created by the four reasons an addiction develops—learned behavior, environment, nature, and nurture. Some of these beliefs are accurate and some are faulty.
- *Unmanageability*: the consequences of the addiction in all areas of the person's life. Because these consequences motivate her to seek help, they are to be welcomed and not eliminated. Pain drives people to change.
- *Impaired Thinking*: denial, blame, rationalization, justification
- *The Addiction Cycle*: Most addicts include more than one way of using or doing. It is important that all the ways are identified and addressed.
- *Preoccupation*: Once the addict has been triggered, awareness begins with a single thought and continues to grow until there is an obsession of the mind about the chemical and/or the behavior.
- *Rituals*: unique to the person and to the manner of acting out
- *Acting Out*: the event of using or doing
- *Pain*: After the acting out, there is pain and despair, even fear
- *Shame*: believing she is hopelessly broken and defective
- *Guilt*: knowing that the behavior(s) were very wrong

During recovery, the addict begins over time to identify her patterns of impaired thinking. This can happen because someone, such as a sponsor or a helper, points them out and suggests recovery-thinking choices. Given time, the cognitive distortions can help the person identify, accept, and then change the faulty core beliefs carried from childhood. A Christian-based program such as Celebrate Recovery can show a person her worth to God, take her back to forgive and repair trauma done to her in "nurturing," and give her hope for a future based on Christ rather than on substances or addictive behavior. It is not an easy process or a speedy one, but with understanding and information, a shepherd can walk alongside her as she goes through it.

HELPFUL THINGS TO SAY AND DO

Being a shepherd to an addict—recovering or not—is a challenge.

1. **DO** know that the first task is to understand just what is going on and from that information decide what type of help is appropriate.
2. **DO** realize that an addict is never "recovered." Just as sanctification or growing up in Christ is never finished, neither is recovery. The disease of addiction lurks waiting to re-ensnare the victim. Learned young as a coping strategy, those automatic responses dim over time and with the practice of recovery rituals and thinking. But it never really goes away. Just as Paul embraced his "thorn" as the opportunity to live in Christ's strength and to accept his weakness,[3] so the addict is always in recovery, always completely dependent on Christ's power. The good news is that Christ's power is greater than the power of the addiction, so the recovery addict can rest safely in His care.
3. **DO** understand that it takes awhile for her change from impaired thinking to recovery thinking and replacing addiction rituals with recovery rituals.
4. **DO** continually share the truth of Christ's empowerment and be ready to point out each time it is experienced. The addict most

likely will not recognize Christ's work in the beginning. For example, "Hey, Anne, did you realize that God prompted you to call me when you were thinking of getting some beer? That's terrific! Thank You, God, for helping Anne."

5. **DO** make a statement of the truth of Christ's love, rather than a question. For example, "God loves you and you will come to know that" is more helpful than saying, "Don't you know that God loves you?" God is very capable of getting the message she needs to her in a way she will be able to receive it.

6. **DO** be *very* careful to use word statements of encouragement and support when failure happens (and it will) rather than a statement that would come across as guilting or shaming. Chances are she got enough of that growing up. You may say something like this: "It is really true that relapse is part of recovery. You don't know what you don't know and now you have learned something very important. Get back to your meetings and call me tomorrow and let me know how you are doing. I'll be praying for you."

7. **DO** know that helping in the early stages is a hand-holding relationship. People who are barely in recovery still have a very foggy brain. They cannot retain information or do problem solving.

8. **DO** include her in a loving community as much as she is willing to participate. Remember that at the heart of addiction is a pervasive, deeply felt sense of detachment and alienation. The core beliefs of the addict are based on an impaired capacity to trust—others and herself. Offer her the opportunity to experience such a community.

HURTFUL THINGS TO AVOID

1. **DON'T** *under any conditions* tell someone to stop any chemical use, because abrupt withdrawal can be fatal and/or without an

existing support system the person is more apt to continue and feel more defeated than ever. Instead refer her to a local hospital for help. The first consideration must be safety. If the person has any obvious active addiction(s), then getting the person detoxed is the first step. This requires professional referral.

2. **DON'T** assume the presenting problem is *the* problem. People will ask for help believing that a certain problem(s) is *the* problem, when often it is the result of an undiagnosed and untreated addiction. It is helpful to have an addiction guideline to use when evaluating what might be addiction rather than problematic behaviors.

3. **DON'T** make it your goal to eliminate her pain. Often it is pain that will motivate her to seek help. Instead, help her find the appropriate help she needs. Walk with her in this search.

4. **DON'T** mistake a pattern for an addiction. Understanding the difference will give greater clarity for referral and define the shepherd's role. A shepherd wants to make sure she does not enable the addict to continue in her negative behaviors, but rather motivate the addict to move toward more positive life patterns.

5. **DON'T** assume that an addict who has been referred to a therapist has all the help she needs. She will benefit from additional encouragement and support from those who are available to her and understand the addiction process. Expressing support within healthy boundaries by consistently extending the love of Christ in the power of His Spirit is a key aspect of effective shepherding.

6. **DON'T** underestimate the spiritual component in her recovery process. The truth of who God says she is and who God is will be of critical importance in replacing core beliefs gained in childhood that have so negatively impacted her addiction.

7. **DON'T** expect quick recovery time. Know it is a process.

Finally, the shepherd needs support and a prayer team. The enemy uses addiction as one tool to capture good people into bondage. He will never give up trying to hold on. The battle becomes fierce at times and the helper will need support. Your team approach of resource people must include intercessors for you. Fatigue, discouragement, illness, confusion, and just not understanding what is going on are common. But don't turn from the challenge! Helping someone find freedom in Christ is the most rewarding service we can offer the kingdom of God on earth.

Resources

Referrals and resources are absolutely necessary; no one can do this alone. It is important to think "team" rather than super shepherd. Develop a ready file of local hospitals with treatment programs, doctors who can help, church programs such as Celebrate Recovery, 12-Step programs, and schedules. Compile a list of therapists who specialize in the needed treatment, and other women in recovery who are willing to come alongside. The traditional 12-Step programs such as AA are filled with Christian men and women who will help. One common mistake is to only refer people to church programs; participants in church programs most likely will not have the depth of recovery of those in other addiction groups. Include information for the family members such as Al-Anon and Alateen. The yellow pages and online sites will give local information. Each community is different and offers different resources. The job of the helper is to take as much time as needed to collect helpful information. It is better not to wait until the person is in crisis. The time to develop a resource file is now!

Websites
>   https://www.aa.org/: Alcoholics Anonymous (AA): local meeting places and times are available online.
>   https://al-anon.org: Al-Anon Family Groups: Help and hope for families and friends of alcoholics

http://www.12step.org: Twelve-Step programs are well known for use in recovery from addictive or dysfunctional behaviors.

https://saddleback.com/connect/ministry/celebrate-recovery: Celebrate Recovery. The purpose of Saddleback Valley Community Church's Celebrate Recovery ministry is to fellowship and celebrate God's healing power in our lives through the "8 Recovery Principles."

http://www.christiancounselingcenters.org: Christian Counseling Centers

https://iitap.com: The International Institute of Trauma and Addiction Professionals (IITAP)

https://www.sash.net: The Society for the Advancement of Sexual Health (SASH)

Books

Carnes, Patrick J. *Out of the Shadows: Understanding Sexual Addiction.* 3rd ed. Center City, MN: Hazelden, 2001.

Carnes, Patrick J., and Joseph Moriarity. *Sexual Anorexia: Overcoming Sexual Self-Hatred.* Center City, MN: Hazelden, 1997.

Coombs, R. H., ed. *Handbook of Addictive Disorders: A Practical Guide to Diagnosis and Treatment.* Hoboken, NJ: Wiley, 2004.

Fifield, Mary Anne, D.M.F.T., *The Serenity Prayer Workbook: Making it Personal.* Foundation for Addiction Specialist Training (FAST), 2013.

May, Gerald G., MD. Addiction and Grace. New York: HarperOne, 2007.

———. *Care of Mind/Care of Spirit.* New York: HarperOne, 1992.

Mellody, Pia. *Facing Love Addiction: Giving Yourself the Power to Change the Way You Love.* New York: HarperOne, 2003.

Minirth, Frank. *Love Hunger.* Nashville: Thomas Nelson, 2004.

Reid, Rory C. and Dan Gray. *Discussing Pornography Problems with a Spouse: Confronting and Disclosing Secret Behaviors.* 2002.

Roberts, Ted. *Pure Desire: Helping People Break Free from Sexual Struggles*. Delight, AZ: Gospel Light, 1999.

Wilson, Sandra D., PhD. *Released from Shame: Moving Beyond the Pain of the Past*. Downers Grove, IL: IVP, 2002.

Related Scriptures

Jeremiah 2:13

John 8:44b

Romans 7:15–25

2 Corinthians 12:7–10

Ephesians 5:18

Philippians 2:12–13

AUTHOR BIO

MARY ANNE FIFIELD is the founder and clinical director of the Addiction Recovery Center, a nonprofit treatment program for addicts and their partners. Mary Anne is a licensed marriage and family therapist who holds a doctorate degree from Fuller Theological Seminary and a master's degree in marriage and family therapy from Mennonite Brethren Biblical Seminary. She is certified as an addiction specialist and sex addiction therapist. Mary Anne brings a commitment to individuals and families who have been impacted by the bondage of addiction. She specializes in working with all types of addiction issues including alcohol, drugs, and sex. She was formerly an adjunct professor at three seminaries and is a trainer, lecturer, and consultant.

Chapter 11

Abortion Recovery

Mindy Johnson
Director, HEART, a ministry of First Image

*A*t last! With high school graduation concluded and college beckoning, I fully embraced adulthood. At eighteen, life was good. A summer romance blossomed, ending my years of childhood innocence. I was eager to move away from home and begin college life.

Although challenging, college started off well. That is, until I took one important test. The results confirmed my growing fears. *Oh no! I'm pregnant? How is this going to fit into my life? I just started college. This just can't be . . .* Still in a state of shock, I called my boyfriend. It was settled. While he made the arrangements, I secretly traveled back to my hometown to have the "procedure." Women had said, "It is no big deal," and "It isn't a baby; it is just a blob of tissue." *Plenty of people are doing it,* I thought. *It must be okay.*

I woke up lying on a cart in a room lined with other recovering women. *Okay, it's done. Get me out of here. I'm so thankful it is done. I don't want to think about it again.* I pushed my guilty thoughts down, out of my mind. Only weeks later, the relationship with my boyfriend ended. Devastated, I began drinking to forget and drown my pain. Since I was unable to focus on studies, my grades plummeted. By the end of the first semester, I begged my parents to let me come home. Never once did I connect any of this fallout to my abortion.

Once home, I tried to move on and not think about the abortion. I stuffed the hurt and guilt down deeper. Then, to ease my conscience, I began justifying my behavior. *After all, I was a grown woman and that was a mature decision,* I reasoned. The confused months dragged along until the day I met a special man, my husband-to-be. During our engagement I became pregnant for the second time. With memories of my previous abortion still fresh, we faced this unexpected news together. Considering all the options and challenges ahead, we chose life for our developing baby. Admittedly some of the pain of the past surfaced during the pregnancy, yet the full extent of emotions and the process of healing did not come until much later.

It came after we moved to Oregon eleven years after the birth of my second child. For over two decades I had struggled each October with a heaviness that I could not understand. Feelings of sadness, guilt, shame, and anger would surface. Eventually through my church's bulletin announcements about a local Pregnancy Resource Center, I learned about H.E.A.R.T.[1] (Healing Encouragement for Abortion-Related Trauma). I soon began attending HEART's Bible study support group for post-abortive women. It was then that I began to understand the source of the heaviness, shame, denial, and grief that I experienced over my abortion. I learned those feelings were especially strong during the anniversary month of my abortion. Although the study at HEART was an emotional time, it was incredibly life changing. God's love, grace, and mercy became real as I faced the sin of my abortion, embraced truth, accepted His forgiveness, and was set free from my past.

Understand the Issue

In the United States, one out of every four pregnancies is terminated by abortion (excluding miscarriages).[2] Nearly half of those pregnancies are unintended. Women younger than twenty-five account for 50 percent of all US abortions.[3] Forty-three percent of the women who have had abortions claimed to be Protestant and 27 percent Catholic.[4] Since the 1973 *Roe v. Wade* decision, nearly 50,000,000 babies have lost their lives due to abortion.[5] These figures are sobering and reveal the prevalence of post-abortive pain. The collateral damage is also staggering. Countless lives, marriages, and relationships have been damaged as a further consequence. Women have suffered much and are experiencing guilt, fear, and deep shame.[6] In order to help these women find forgiveness and healing, we need to have better understanding and bring this long covered-up issue out into the open.

We can no longer assume there are no abortive women in *our church*. The intent of this chapter is to increase our awareness, strengthen our understanding, and provide tools to shepherd women to a place of grace-filled healing. (Please note that the purpose of this chapter is *not* to provide an ethical or theological discussion surrounding the initial decision to abort. There are other valuable resources for that important discussion. Our focus is on the woman who has made a decision *in her past* to abort.)

Post-Abortion Stress (PAS)[7] is the chronic inability to: (1) process the painful emotions that surround the abortion decision and experience (guilt, fear, anger, nightmares, anniversary reaction), (2) identify and/or grieve for the child and the loss that was incurred, and (3) come to peace with God, self, and others involved in the pregnancy and abortion decision.[8]

Women are primarily dealing with emotional trauma when they contact HEART. They believed the lies prevalent in our culture, such as, "Abortion's fine. There are not any psychological or emotional consequences. It isn't a baby; it is just a glob of tissue." The truth is that abortion takes an innocent human life and carries with it consequences, some immediate and others long-term. Some possible symptoms are listed below.

Post-Abortion Symptoms[9]

Physical
- Immediate possibilities: hemorrhaging, perforation of uterus, intense cramping
- Ongoing possibilities: scar tissue, cancer (cervical or breast), infertility, tubal pregnancy, miscarriage

Emotional
- Anxiety—headaches, dizziness, pounding heart, abdominal cramps, muscle tightness, difficulty sleeping, etc.
- Avoidance behaviors—of anything remindful of pregnancy and children
- Depression—sad mood, sudden and uncontrollable crying episodes, deterioration of self-concept, sleep and appetite disturbances, reduced motivation, loss of normal sources of pleasure, thoughts of suicide
- Guilt and shame—results from violating one's own sense of right and wrong
- Self-abuse or self-destructive behaviors—eating disorders, alcohol and/or substance abuse, abusive relationships, promiscuity, failure to take care of one's self medically
- Anger at self and others
- Fear of never getting pregnant
- Preoccupation with becoming pregnant again—representing an unconscious hope that a new pregnancy will replace the baby who was aborted
- Re-experiencing events related to the abortion(s)—persistent thoughts and flashback memories or nightmares

- Anniversary reaction—an increase in symptoms around the time of the anniversary of the abortion, the due date of the aborted child, or both
- Brief psychotic disorder—a psychotic break with reality lasting for a short period of time
- Eating disorders; drug and alcohol use; sexual promiscuity

Relationships

- Psychological numbing—the unconscious vow to never let anything hurt this badly again can hamper the ability to enter fully into an emotional, intimate relationship
- Break up with boyfriend or girlfriend
- Marital difficulties
- Secrecy and/or wedge in the family
- Inability to trust men, women, and/or doctors
- Abusive and unhealthy relationships

The *anniversary date reaction* is often manifested each year with heaviness, depression, or a deep sadness around the time the abortion was performed or when the baby would have been born. Mother's Day is an especially difficult and painful day for many post-abortive women. The person with PAS suffers from *impacted grieving*, similar to an impacted wisdom tooth. This grief is fully formed but below the surface and difficult to extract.

In her book *Helping People Get through Grief*, Deloris Kuenning states that grief suffered as a result of abortion is unlike any other loss. She identifies the following nine problems that arise in grieving the loss of an aborted child.[10]

1. There is no external evidence that a baby ever existed. The baby exists not even as a memory of a baby but as a memory of a pregnancy.
2. There is no formal ritual such as a funeral where friends and family can acknowledge her loss and grieve with her.

3. The woman has little support because few people are told about the abortion. For those who do know, it usually becomes "the elephant in the living room" that no one talks about.

4. Abortion may be legal but it is still socially unacceptable, so the woman has no permission to grieve openly. She suffers in secret, feeling like she is strange for having feelings of grief.

5. The grief is complicated by the guilt of responsibility for ending her baby's life. Many women find it difficult to forgive themselves. They live in pain and isolation.

6. If she tells someone, she may experience rejection, disapproval, or judgment, which is devastating and causes her to retreat further into secrecy and isolation. Or, because of her fear, she may never tell anyone.

7. Few professional counselors are knowledgeable about how to help women work through the steps necessary to find healing and reconciliation with God.

8. Because those who advocate abortion provide no information about PAS to prepare the woman, she is surprised by her feelings of grief and loss, and feels she is abnormal.

9. Because of the heavy denial involved, the grief cycle and the timing are different from those experienced with other types of loss. We have seen women whose abortions were even thirty-five years earlier. The postponement of the grief creates a unique dynamic.

Shepherding Insights

Two-thirds of all women having abortions in the US have never been married.[11] Abortion is often a decision to cover up sexual activity or as a quick fix for an unintended pregnancy. Because there is so much guilt, secrecy, and shame involved, it is not easy to generate conversation about the abortion. Hurting women need to know they are not alone in their pain. Most have never heard of PAS and do not realize that much of the pain they are experiencing is a result of their abortion.

The faith community is in a strategic position to help promote healing by bringing this issue out into the open. Pastors can raise the topic in a noncondemning way and spur the church on to offer love, compassion, and redemptive care for these hurting individuals. Ask a post-abortive woman (or couple) to share her experience with a small group, or to the entire congregation. Ask her to include the resources and influences she has received that have been most helpful in her journey toward healing. Ask her to explain how repentance, forgiveness, and the incredible loving grace of Jesus Christ were catalysts for her healing. Look for other opportunities to bring understanding to the church, such as Bible studies, small groups, or one-on-one conversations. Abortion is not just a political issue. It is an experience that often leaves women with lifelong woundedness. God values all life as well as people who make wrong choices. Speaking truth in love, not with a judgmental attitude, can open hearts to receive healing and reconciliation. Many men and women sitting in our churches have experienced abortion trauma and need the love, hope, and forgiveness that Christ offers.

When speaking to a woman who has had an abortion, let her know that *she is not alone*. Carefully consider your body language and the words you speak. She needs compassion, not judgment, as she works through multiple layers of guilt for sin, shame, and pain on the pathway to healing. Your friendship and continued shepherding can help greatly as you listen and walk with her on her healing journey. Give her appropriate resources.

Be sensitive to her readiness for a post-abortive support group. At HEART, each woman is prescreened to make sure she is ready to begin a Bible study for post-abortive women. The leader and coleader meet with each woman one-on-one and also have her fill out a questionnaire. We pray for God's wisdom and discernment: "Lord, is this a good time for her to be going through this?" Occasionally we will advise a woman to wait a little longer. Many women are not ready for HEART the first year after the abortion because it is so traumatic. It is an emotionally raw and fragile time. However, they still need to be helped. Be aware of suicidal ideations or extreme depression. If appropriate, recommend a medical clinician. It may be helpful for her to probe deeper into the issues that preceded the abortion(s). In this case, recommend a therapist. Some women find it is helpful to participate in both therapy and a support group at the same time.

Various factors bring women to a point of readiness to go through a post-abortion Bible study. Making that first call to a crisis pregnancy resource center is really a breakthrough. When women call our confidential voice mail at HEART, they often say, "This is the first time that I've told anyone about my abortion." It is very important to let these women know this is a safe place and this conversation will be kept confidential. Gently guide a post-abortive woman one step at a time, reassuring her that God will help her through.

Generally speaking, women come to HEART five to thirty years *after* they have had an abortion. These support groups break through the shame and the guilt much better than personal reading or study. Nearly all of our trained leaders are post-abortive. They understand the work involved and the need for a safe and confidential environment during this process. The women are encouraged to simplify their lives during this healing journey since it will be hard work and emotionally draining. Each participant must agree that everything shared within the group stays in the group. In this safe environment, women are free to share their abortion experiences. Incredible bonding develops as they listen to one another's stories and quickly relate to their commonalities. As women learn that they are not alone, the group experience becomes very precious to them.

What People Get from Joining Support Groups[12]

1. Emotional Outlet	*I'm angry, hurt, scared. I want someone to listen and care.*
2. Emotional Support	*I'm not sure if what I'm doing, feeling, etc., is normal. I need to hear that I am a good, lovable, valuable person.*

3. Sense of Community	*I need to know there are people who understand what I am going through, people who care about me and for whom I care.*
4. Personal Growth	*I want to understand who I am, what I am going through.*
5. Guidance	*How can I feel better and learn how to deal with my situation?*
6. Social	*I need time for friends, fellowship, and fun.*
7. Giving Opportunity	*I want to help others and this group. It helps me feel worthwhile.*
8. Public Education	*I want others to know, understand, and help.*
9. Spiritual Growth	*I want to know more about God and how He can help me.*

Each person's healing journey is unique and should not be compared with other women's. The small group experience is affirming and helps each woman begin to see God's healing hand. The group helps a woman process her own past, especially when she hears and sees she is not alone. Although reasons for having an abortion vary, there is always hope and healing in the Lord.

The Bible documents the first death of a human by the hand of another as early as Genesis 4:8. One could compile a long list of others in subsequent chapters. Eventually God gave a message directly to Moses for the people that was later reiterated by Jesus, "You shall not murder" (Exodus 20:13 and Matthew 5:21). The directness of this message increases our ability to grasp the enormity of the graciousness of Jesus Christ in offering full forgiveness to one who seeks it. Jesus suffered indescribable abuse and suffering on the cross in order to provide forgiveness.

Our forgiveness is available at Jesus' expense. "If we confess our sins, he is faithful and just and will forgive us our sins and purify us from all unrighteousness" (1 John 1:9). "If we confess" is the one requirement in this Scripture. Jesus is faithful, and He promises to forgive and purify us. This is indeed good news for a woman who is weighed down with the excruciating painfulness of a past decision. Not only is forgiveness available in the immediate, but the psalmist gives great hope for the future: "Put your hope in the LORD, for with the LORD is unfailing love and with him is *full redemption*" (Psalm 130:7, emphasis added). The Lord will fully redeem those who come to Him. Jesus told observing critics that "her many sins have been forgiven—as her great love has shown. But whoever has been forgiven little loves little" (Luke 7:47). Our gracious God provides forgiveness and healing, resulting in greater love.

Healing is typically a lifelong journey. As women receive healing, they are more willing to share their story. Women come to support groups with open wounds and sometimes self-condemnation. Being real with others in the support group enables them to dig deep, allowing healing to come. Wounds will become less like an open abrasion and more like a bruise after a study and group experience. It will still hurt to think and talk about the abortion but God's grace brings healing and peace.

Another challenge some women face is the need to share their story with their children; this can also be part of the healing process. Wisdom and discernment are needed. Mothers need to seek God's counsel to determine what the children need to know and when. This experience was part of my healing process. I had been through HEART and could not imagine telling my children. However, one day when I knew the time was right, I sat down with our kids and said, "I need to talk to you about something." They were young, eleven and fifteen, but they needed to know the age-appropriate story. When they were a few years older, I expanded the original version. Now I am free to share my story publicly in hopes of helping others find God's healing grace.

HELPFUL THINGS TO SAY AND DO[13]

1. **DO** be trustworthy. You may be the only person she has ever told about her abortion.

2. **DO** keep things confidential—with one exception: if she is suicidal, get help.

3. **DO** support her with words and actions, not judgment. Offer compassion and sensitivity by willingly listening to her story. Express God's graciousness and forgiveness. Read Psalm 103:1–18 with her.

4. **DO** refer her to a post-abortion support group, a clinician, a therapist, or a local pregnancy resource center.

5. **DO** pray with and for her often. Offer grace and forgiveness. She may feel *this* sin is unforgivable.

6. **DO** understand that the symptoms she is experiencing are common to post-abortion stress.

7. **DO** walk alongside her during her healing journey.

HURTFUL THINGS TO NOT SAY OR DO[14]

1. **DON'T** assume that she has shared with others her abortion experience.

2. **DON'T** share with anyone else, not even your spouse.

3. **DON'T** forget that your facial expression and body language speak volumes.

4. **DON'T** feel like you have to have all the answers or be her counselor. God has all the answers. He has equipped you to share His truth and love with her.

5. **DON'T** forget about her. After she shares her story, she may feel a certain weight has been lifted. But that is just the beginning of the long journey toward healing.

6. **DON'T** assume she is "abnormal" or even crazy by some of the things that are said. Reassure her that the symptoms she has are normal after an abortion. There is hope.

7. **DON'T** assume she believes that this sin can be forgiven. Women typically live with incredible shame that can blur truth.

After a woman shares her story, she often feels much better. That is just the start of a long, slow process as she peels off layer after layer of pain. Each layer is important and needs sufficient time to process and resource. Each small step forward is reason for affirmation and celebration. Walking with a woman on this journey is an honor, a message of trust. Life-changing transformation is a gift to be cherished. Shepherding friends are blessed to walk alongside a woman traveling her abortion recovery journey.

Resources

Websites

    www.first-image.org/heart: HEART has been the post-abortion reconciliation ministry of First Image since 1988. HEART's confidential voicemail is: 503-22-HEART or 503-224-3278

    https://first-image.org/heart: Heart at First Image

    http://prcofportland.com: Pregnancy Resource Centers of Portland, Oregon

    https://first-image.org/pregnancy-resource-centers

    www.abortionchangesyou.com

    www.standupgirl.com

    www.care-net.org

    www.optionline.org

Men and Abortion
http://www.mistymtn.org
https://www.lifeissues.org

Books

Cochrane, Linda. *Forgiven and Set Free: A Post-Abortion Bible Study for Women.* Grand Rapids: Baker, 1986, 1991, 1996 by CareNet. (Previously published in 1986 under the title *Women in Ramah* by Christian Action Council.)

Cochrane, Linda, and Kathy Jones. *Healing a Father's Heart: A Post-Abortion Bible Study for Men.* Grand Rapids: Baker, 1993, 1996 by CareNet. (Previously published in 1993 under the title *Turning a Father's Heart* by CareNet.)

Everhart, Gayle. *Never the Same.* Pleasant Word Publishing, a division of WinePress Group, 2010. "*Never the Same* follows Gayle's life journey from desperation to the joy of experiencing God's amazing grace and Jesus' precious blood. In spite of hardships and obstacles, God is faithful to bring His plan for Gayle's life to fruition."

Hayford, Jack. *I'll Hold You in Heaven: Healings and Hope for the Parent of a Miscarried, Aborted or Stillborn Child.* Oakland: Regal Books, 2003.

Hislop-White, Beverly. *Shepherding a Woman's Heart: A New Model for Effective Ministry to Women.* Chicago: Moody Publishers, 2002.

Lafranchi, Angela, Prof. Ian Gentles, Elizabeth Ring-Cassidy. *Complications: Abortion's Impact on Women.* North York, ON: The deVerber Institute for Bioethics and Social Research, 2013.

Nykiel, Connie. *No One Told Me I Could Cry: A Teen's Guide to Hope and Healing after an Abortion.* Available from Young Family Press, PO Box 962, Frankfort, IL 60423 or Life Cycle Books at (800) 214-5849. Published in *Post Abortion Review* 7, no. 1 (Jan.–March 1999).

Reisser, Teri. *A Solitary Sorrow: Finding Healing & Wholeness after Abortion.* Colorado Springs: Shaw Books, 2000.

Reisser, Teri and Paul Reisser MD. *Help for the Post-Abortive Woman.* Niagara Falls: Life Cycle Books, 1994.

Schweibert, Pat, Chuck DeKlyen, and Taylor Bills. *Tear Soup: A Recipe for Healing after Loss.* 3rd rev. ed. Portland: Grief Watch, 2005. DVD also available.

Related Scriptures

Psalm 103:12

Isaiah 43:25; 61:1–3

Matthew 5:4

Romans 12:15

2 Corinthians 1:3–4

Ephesians 1:7–8

Philippians 4:6–7

1 John 1:9

AUTHOR BIO

MINDY JOHNSON is Director of HEART (Healing Encouragement for Abortion Related Trauma), a ministry of First Image in Portland, Oregon. As director, Mindy enjoys coleading HEART Bible study/support groups and training new leaders to facilitate post-abortion recovery groups. Mindy also speaks at churches, conferences, and schools about PAS-related issues.

Chapter 12

Eating Disorders

Kimberly Davidson, M.A.
Olive Branch Outreach

I *look in the mirror. I incessantly see an unattractive, unfit, fat person. I* *purge in the restroom after eating dinner with friends. I starve myself* *by eating only a couple hundred calories a day. I think constantly about my* *body and diet regimen.* This is my life—it's the life of a woman struggling with an eating disorder.

Eating disorders destroy lives. Most eating disorders start with a diet. Since I was a little overweight when I entered my senior year in high school, my father told me I couldn't have seconds anymore at dinnertime because I was getting fat. To spite his attempt to control me, I ate more. I put on more weight. Then he started daring me to get on the scale and started taking bets on how much I weighed. That made me angry, so I ate more. Then I saw a photograph of myself—I was mortified! That is when I reluctantly decided to go on a diet. My goal was to lose ten to fifteen pounds.

Mom called our family doctor, who recommended I lose two pounds a week and no more, to ensure I kept the weight off. The diet was successful and I started losing the two pounds a week. Soon, it started to become an obsession. Instead of merely planning the next day's diet, I started to plan two days ahead, then three, then a month ahead—calculating out all these calories.

I eventually reached my weight goal. But my mind couldn't wrap around how to maintain that goal. All I knew was dieting. Something else pretty incredible happened—I received attention and praise. When you are not used to it, you begin to associate praise and compliments with being thin. You think, *Why not lose a couple more pounds?*

About a month later I was at a friend's house. Her parents had a dinner party and we overate. We were sick and miserable. My friend said, "I know how we can feel better." She continued, "Stick your finger down your throat until you throw up the food. Keep doing it until you get all the food up." This practice is called bulimia.

This was it! Perfect! Now I could eat anything I wanted and remain thin. From that point on, my life spiraled out of control. My primary focus was my weight and food, thinking I must get thinner . . . and thinner. I set a new goal: 99 pounds. When I reached that goal, I thought, *Why not 96 pounds?* But I could never get that low as a lot of women do. This meant I had failed.

When asked why I went down this self-destructive road, I say it is a combination of the culture and my upbringing.[1] Our family moved around quite a bit while I was growing up. The first major move came when I was seven, when our family moved to London, England. I was teased by schoolmates because I didn't fit into the culture. I had an accent. My clothes were different. The message was, *You don't belong.*

You never get used to other kids being mean, but in time you learn how not to feel the sting of rejection so much because of a deep-seated desire for acceptance. We moved back to America when I was twelve. Again I was different, but now I was entering adolescence—the hurricane years. Further rejection and teasing from schoolmates only made the previous strongholds deeper. The pain of rejection became part of my normal thought process.

Rejection is one of our most powerful and destructive emotions. It may cause as much distress in the pain center of the brain as an actual physical injury. Perhaps this is why we use the term "hurt feelings." Physical pain and the result of social pain are actually similar.[2]

I expected people to not like me so I worked tirelessly trying to conform to the way I thought my peer group and teachers wanted me to be. We moved several more times. Moving can be painful. It stresses both parents and children, especially if the move is resented, as it was in my case.

Then I began to gravitate into a new world of worshiping celebrities and models. I believed the lie that to be accepted and popular you have to look like a model. The message I received from teen magazines was *Don't worry about being good; think about looking good and being socially accepted!* Girls will react to cultural pressures by abandoning who they really are. "Fat talk" flourishes. It did with me and my girlfriends.[3]

As a bulimic, there was no joy, no hope, only fear and self-condemnation. The shame kept feeding every destructive behavior. I was not only a bulimic but a binge drinker and promiscuous, all of which continued to feed the shame, paralyzing my soul in a never-ending battle. I hated myself and tried to cover up with success, gossip, and materialism. Asking for help meant admitting I was a failure.

Then I realized I was afraid. I was afraid of gaining weight, relapsing, not being perfect, disapproval, a strict new regime, being judged, change, a whole new lifestyle—afraid of achieving recovery or success, a not uncommon reaction.

By this time, my life was turning into a no-win situation. The psalmist's cry became my own: "In my distress I called to the LORD; I cried to my God for help. From his temple he heard my voice; my cry came before him, into his ears" (Psalm 18:6). Jesus walked into my messed-up life and I accepted His gracious love and forgiveness and became His follower.[4]

Although we usually see the more traditional path of lots of hard work and therapy, God can set someone free instantaneously if He so chooses. That's what happened in my case. Actually, many addicts who fail traditional treatment programs are able to free themselves from their addictions when they develop a connection with God.[5]

Once I met Him, I took a journey through the Bible and started to mend emotionally. God gradually started changing me from the inside out. I had previously been an average businessperson with low-self esteem, struggling to fit in. I *slowly* emerged a leader because God opened my eyes to the internal gifts He had created in me—gifts I had not known I had.

I knew I could not succeed without being empowered by God Himself to give me consistent strength, graciousness, love, and truthfulness. I just could not do it alone. I also came to understand that God was not going to intrude on my choices. He gave me free will, and if I wanted His power in my life, I had to ask for it and really want it. I became dependent on God. As God helped me overcome my fearfulness, my self-image and worth began to improve.

Understand the Issue

The numbers of women adversely affected by eating disorders are appalling. In the United States, as many as ten million females[6] are fighting a life-and-death battle with an eating disorder such as anorexia or bulimia.[7] Some suspect the number is even higher, given the secretive nature of bulimia and the unknown number of very young and older women who suffer from eating disorders.[8]

Anorexia, compulsive overeating (or Binge Eating Disorder), and bulimia are the three most common eating disorders. Each is an addictive process in which food is the "drug of choice." These disorders may overlap or occur sequentially in a person's life. For example, a compulsive eater may become overweight in early teenage years and then diet rigorously, leading to anorexia, followed at a later stage by bulimia (adopted as an easier way of coping).

Definitions

Anorexia Nervosa is a serious, potentially life-threatening eating disorder characterized by self-starvation and excessive weight loss.[9]

Binge Eating Disorder is a type of eating disorder not otherwise specified and is characterized by recurrent binge eating without the regular use of compensatory measures to counter the binge eating.[10]

Bulimia Nervosa is a serious, potentially life-threatening eating disorder characterized by a cycle of bingeing and compensatory behaviors such as self-induced vomiting designed to undo or compensate for the effects of binge eating.[11]

Individuals suffering from anorexia and/or bulimia generally feel that they have little in common with those suffering from compulsive overeating, which is why support groups exist for one or the other. An eating disorder is the physical expression of emotional distress, and is becoming a more frequent response to the external and internal pressures experienced by young people today. It is an addictive behavior pattern in which the person compulsively uses the "drug" of her choice, either excessive food intake or starvation, as a means of repressing or suppressing her feelings rather than facing and feeling them. Preoccupation with food and weight is a means of coping with unresolved stress and the difficulties of everyday living. The eating disorder becomes the substitute for the underlying problems. The first critical need for a person recovering from food addiction is to establish a healthy pattern of eating behavior.

No matter why some people fall victim to eating disorders, there is no denying the long-term effects. Overeating, anorexia, and bulimia are mental health diseases and are recognized as such among the medical community. Like all diseases, they are progressive and considered fatal. If left unchecked, the result is death, either from heart failure or a medical condition brought on by continued neglect.[12]

Disordered Eating is a term used by some to describe a wide variety of irregularities in a person's eating behavior but does not warrant a diagnosis of a specific clinical eating disorder. This is the person who is a "yo-yo" dieter, the person who exercises for two hours a day after eating a donut, the person who diets four days of the week, and then takes two days off. Their focus is still on their body and on their diet but they do not meet the medical criteria for bulimia, anorexia, or binge eating. There are many women who are not anorexic or bulimic or a compulsive overeater, but they eat for emotional reasons. In other words, their eating is disordered.[13]

According to the DSM-IV (Diagnostic and Statistical Manual of Mental Disorders), there is a classification of disordered eating that falls outside of the criteria for anorexia, binge eating, and bulimia. This category is referred to as EDNOS, Eating Disorders Not Otherwise Specified. These are also sometimes referred to as "sub-clinical" or "sub-threshold" disorders.[14] Somewhere between one-third and one-half of eating disorders are classified as EDNOS. That is a great number. EDNOS does not meet criteria of full-blown anorexia or bulimia but is a serious psychological condition that can be fatal if not diagnosed and treated.[15]

Use of a new brain imaging technique has revealed that abnormalities in brain circuitry may be a cause of anorexia nervosa. The imaging studies suggest that people who have anorexia also have an imbalance in brain circuitry that regulates emotions and rewards. The authors of this research note that predisposing factors, such as anxiety, perfectionism, and obsessive-compulsive tendencies, may precede the onset of anorexia, and need to be considered as well. These are characteristics often seen among adolescents and young adults as they make their transition into adulthood. This is the same age group that is most affected by anorexia.[16]

The good news is we have a huge God. Both secular and faith-based medical and mental health professionals agree that if someone's faith and hope are high, then the recovery process will most likely be successful. A number of research studies have demonstrated that people of faith suffer less from anxiety disorders and depression and they recover 70 percent faster from these illnesses than those without a strong religious faith. The suicide rate and even mortality rate is lower for religious people than the nonreligious.[17] Healers have been aware of the power of faith and hope and have long recognized that hope and faith are important elements of change.[18]

Common factors leading to an eating disorder

- Societal and cultural values that promote being thin as a part of one's identity
- History of physical, emotional, verbal, or sexual abuse
- Distorted body image and denial of it
- Use of food as a reward or punishment
- Irrational thinking and distorted thinking
- Drive for perfection
- Low self-esteem
- Depression
- Control
- Dependency
- Distorted sexual identity
- Hereditary, genetic factors
- Dysfunctional family system
- Pressure from family to perform
- Involvement in activities or athletics that promote thinness: dance, swimming, cheerleading, field and track, gymnastics, ice-skating, modeling and pageants

A woman with an eating disorder has an intense fear of being overweight. She complains constantly of being overweight when she is not. She is obsessed with clothing size, scales, and mirrors. She may also ingest a variety of diet products, talk constantly about calories, fat grams, and read a lot about nutrition, dieting, and exercise.

Some outward signs that a woman may be bulimic are (this list is not exhaustive): puffy face and eyes, "chipmunk cheeks," swollen salivary glands, a distended bruised or bloody knuckle—the hand she uses to purge is "beat up." She may have broken blood vessels in her eyes and frequent dental problems because of stomach acid erosion on the teeth. She will disappear into the bathroom during or after meals.

To the observer, an anorexic is extremely thin. She has skin and hair problems, such as pasty-looking skin, thin and dry hair, hair loss, and fine hair growth on the face and arms like a baby—all indicating malnourishment. She wears baggy clothes or long sleeves, pants, and coats during summer months to hide excessive thinness.

An eating disorder is a family issue. In some families, the parents seek to be controlling, or the young person perceives that one or the other parent is too controlling. She may develop an eating disorder to regain control over her own life.

On the other side, we know some functional families with great dads and moms. So why do their kids suffer with an eating disorder? Kids face many other pressures: to do well in school or sports, and the cultural mandate to be thin. If one pursues ballet or gymnastics or modeling, the pressure to be thin is especially strong. Some parents say to me, "I have never expected her to be perfect. That is just the way she is." And she will agree. One seventeen-year-old said, "No, I am not getting pressure from my parents, but if I don't get straight A's, I'll just die."

A disturbing trend are the "pro-ana" and "pro-mia" websites, which represent eating disorders as lifestyle *choices* rather than life-threatening *disorders*.[19] If that were so, some who made the "choice" to have an eating disorder would change their choice and simply move away from it. Not so. Eating disorders are not something one can shake off like a bad rash.[20]

Shepherding Insights

It is difficult to find release from the restraints of an eating disorder. The more quickly a caregiver can act, the better. However, be careful not to rush in and take control. Recovery demands a very fine balance of intervention.

Recovery from alcohol or drug addiction demands eventual removal of alcohol or drugs. But for the woman battling an eating disorder, removal of food is not possible. This is why a holistic approach to treating eating disorders is imperative. We know there is a mind (brain), heart, body, and spirit connection. Multiple studies suggest patients view spirituality as an important dimension in their recovery.[21] Spirituality is a powerful healing tool and can sometimes do what no psychotherapist or formal treatment can do. Eating disorders are serious and require a team of professionals. More often than not, it is the combination of spirituality, psychological therapy, and a solid medical, nutritional, and exercise plan that comprise a winning combination.

The shepherd's role is to give spiritual guidance, encouragement, and support. Approach cautiously, but don't allow too much time to go by. If Mom comes to you and says, "I think my daughter has an eating disorder. Will you talk to her?" A good response is, "Yes . . . *if* she is willing to come in on her own." Typically, if she is forced to come in, it will be difficult to move forward.

In John 5:6, Jesus saw an invalid and knew he had been in this condition for a long time.[22] Jesus asked him, "Do you want to get well?" Ask the young woman, "If Jesus said that to you, how would you respond? As you look at everything you've lost because of an eating disorder (health, friends, respect for yourself), are you ready to make a decision to accept God's guidance?"

If she is resisting or in denial, you will need to confront her. I believe, most often, she wants to be confronted, even though she will not allow you to see that. For many, once that secret has been broken, there is a great release.

Prayer is essential

Pray for her ahead of time. Pray with her. Assure her you will be praying for her all week. Every meeting must be bathed in prayer. "Give me wisdom and knowledge, that I may lead this people" (2 Chronicles 1:10). Without addressing a person's distorted perception of God, her understanding of her own identity, the work of the Holy Spirit, and how she can truly resolve anger and forgive others, there is no real freedom. She may learn interesting facts, even get in touch with various emotions, but at best she will find herself exchanging one obsessive behavior for another, often referred to as musical addictions.

God has specific processes for setting people free. Anybody suffering from unhealthy eating patterns and low self-esteem needs unconditional love, acceptance, and forgiveness. She may need to learn how to confront anger and then truly forgive others who may have abused or harmed her.

Planning is important

Plan to begin your conversation on personal issues rather than food and body image. You need to establish trust and intimacy. Open the conversation with "How is school going?" or "What's going on at home?" or "How is your relationship with your husband?" All conversations must be confidential. Do not initiate a conversation if she is tired, hungry, defensive, or distracted—or if you are. Have appropriate resources available for her.

The shepherd/caregiver should not be the one doing all of the talking. So plan ahead; generate good questions. I always start off telling my story with eating disorders. Her guard usually goes down at that point. If you have not experienced an eating disorder, you might share your own story of a different struggle. Empathy often opens the door.

What is her motivation for being there? Did she come because she wants to be there or because her husband or her parents made her come in? If she is made to come in, it is going to be tough. Ask her, "On a scale of one to ten, one being least ready, and ten being most ready, how ready are you to make changes? How ready are you to go into battle to turn things around?" She must be very honest. It is not going to be an easy struggle to win.

If she rates herself between one and four, I would be reluctant to work with her. I will tell her why but still give her the necessary referrals. If she rates herself five or higher, I know she has some motivation to do the work. I am willing to meet with a woman for thirteen weeks if she is willing to make that commitment to work through the book *I'm Beautiful? Why Can't I See It?* I preview the chapters and show her what it takes to do the work. In our sessions we will talk about the material and the reflective questions and any issues that came up that week.

I tell her, "Nobody can make you change. You are going to have to work hard to change your thinking, your habits, everything about you. And you can only do that with the help of God. Nobody else can do it for you. But, I'll walk alongside of you." I want to give each woman the benefit of the doubt, because most often many people have let her down. I do not want to contribute to her feelings of rejection.

Keep in mind some women need to bring their eating disorder out in the open. God is nudging them to do so. If you do not have experience or do not feel adequately qualified, then refer her to a professional *immediately*. Women with eating disorders are isolated from their friends and families.

Chances are she also feels isolated from God and is not reading her Bible. A shepherd's help to influence her to begin practicing spiritual disciplines can be valuable. Other women in the church can invite her to a Bible study or other gatherings of women. Include her with informal connections with people who might encourage her and reflect Christ to her. Communicating God's healing power is critical to breaking the bonds of this woundedness. A shepherd who has knowledge in the area of spiritual warfare will also be helpful. This is a spiritual battle for her soul. The enemy intends to avert or destroy her allegiance to God. The enemy wants her to remain immobilized and self-destruct. God loves her and wants to see her fulfill the purpose for which He created her.[23] Expose her to the love of Christ as often as possible.

Good questions to ask are, "What has to happen in order for you to go on with life in a meaningful way? What do you need to do?" Since there may be a physical issue that needs attention, ask, "How long has it been since you have had a medical exam? Could this be a biochemical disorder?" It is important to get an exam to rule out any sort of causative biochemical issues. Also, if she has had an eating disorder for a while, her health is most likely compromised.

Mary Anne Cohen, director of the New York Center for Eating Disorders, said, "In my eating disorder practice, 40 to 60 percent of the men and women who come to therapy for an eating problem have been sexually or physically abused. . . . People who have been sexually abused may turn to food to relieve a wide range of different states of tension that have nothing to do with hunger. It is their confusion and uncertainty about their inner perceptions that leads them to focus on the food."[24]

The eating disorder is a symptom. An abused woman, an addict, or one who is promiscuous will need to confront and process these wounds. Usually when there is an eating disorder, there are other issues in play too. Professional intervention is critical.

In conclusion, a shepherd needs to convey that the responsibility to move forward is the woman's. Most likely, she will need a team of people to help her—a counselor, a dietician, a physician, a shepherd, and the church family.

Look for RED FLAGS

1. Does she seem to have an intense fear of gaining weight or becoming fat, especially if she is underweight or average?
2. Does she talk about her body negatively?
3. Does she talk about being teased or scolded by parents or friends about her weight?
4. Does she think that if she was skinny instead of fat, then she wouldn't be teased anymore? Or she'll be "happy"?
5. At snack time, have her eating habits changed? Does she pick at her food, or nibble at it, or tear or cut the food into small pieces?
6. Is she preoccupied with dieting, diet products, calories, food grams, nutrition, and exercise?
7. Has she taken up smoking to suppress appetite and relieve stress?
8. Is there evidence of a large amount of empty food packages or laxative packages, or excessive caffeine use?
9. Has she been overexercising? Is she no longer menstruating?
10. Has she suddenly isolated herself? Is she more withdrawn than usual?

HELPFUL THINGS TO SAY AND DO

1. **DO** in a loving way, confront the person. Continue to show love throughout the whole process.

2. **DO** encourage her to seek professional help (counselor, pastor, support group) and recognize that the problem isn't "food."

3. **DO** require her to be accountable to herself and someone else.

HURTFUL RESPONSES TO AVOID

1. **DON'T** think you're the expert and have the answer.

2. **DON'T** get into a power struggle over food with her.

3. **DON'T** blame yourself or someone else (his/her "insensitive" remarks are often made the culprit).

4. **DON'T** make her feel guilty, angry, or bad for the choices she or he has made.

Resources

Websites

http://www.olivebranchoutreach.com: Olive Branch Outreach

http://www.caringonline.com: Caring Online

http://www.findingbalance.com: Finding Balance. Christ-centered Inpatient Treatment Programs

www.aplaceofhope.com/eating.html: The Center, Edmonds, WA

www.remuda-ranch.com: Remuda Ranch Treatment Center.Christ-based Support Groups and Christian Therapists. Look for support groups that are eating disorder specific.

https://www.celebraterecovery.com: Celebrate Recovery is a Christ-centered, 12 step recovery program for anyone struggling with hurt, pain or addiction of any kind. CR is a safe place to find community and freedom from the issues that are controlling our lives.

www.aacc.net: American Association of Christian Counselors (AACC). Find individual Christian counselors.

Books

Davidson, Kimberly. *I'm Beautiful? Why Can't I See It? Daily Encouragement to Promote Healthy Eating & Positive Self-Esteem.* Mustang, OK: Tate Publishing & Enterprises, 2006.

Davis, Erin. *Graffiti: Learning to See the Art in Ourselves.* Chicago: Moody, 2008.

Hersh, Sharon. *Mom, I Feel Fat! Becoming Your Daughter's Ally in Developing a Healthy Body Image.* Colorado Springs: Shaw Books, 2001.

Jantz, Gregory. *Hope, Help, and Healing for Eating Disorders: A New Approach to Treating Anorexia, Bulimia, and Overeating,* 1st ed. Colorado Springs: Shaw Books, 2002.

Morrow, Jena. *Hollow: An Unpolished Tale.* Chicago: Moody, 2010.

Pettit, Christie. *Empty: A Story of Anorexia,* rev. ed. Grand Rapids: Revell, 2006.

Rhodes, Constance. *Life Inside the Thin Cage: A Personal Look into the Hidden World of the Chronic Dieter,* 1st ed. Colorado Springs: Shaw Books, 2003.

Related Scriptures

1 Samuel 16:7
Ecclesiastes 9:7
Joel 2:25–26
Ephesians 4:14

AUTHOR BIO

KIMBERLY DAVIDSON received her MA in Specialized Ministry, Pastoral Care to Women Track, from Western Seminary. She is a board-certified pastoral counselor to women. She founded Olive Branch Outreach, www.olivebranchoutreach.com, an online ministry dedicated to bringing hope and restoration to those struggling with body image and eating disorders. Kimberly is the author of *Eyes Wide Open: Love Yourself* and *Love Your Body in 9 Weeks*. She has authored or contributed to 18 books. Contact Kimberly at www.kim-davidson.com.

Chapter 13

Incarceration

Fran Howard, MS in Guidance and Counseling
Founder of Freedom in the Son International (FITS)[1]

Laurie grew up in an alcoholic family. She was the oldest of five siblings. They lived with her mother in her grandmother's house. Their father was in and out of prison; he was rarely home. Their mother was often depressed. So Laurie raised her little brothers and sisters until she became a teenager when she ran away. She entered a series of abusive relationships, which seemed normal for her. No one in her family had taught her right from wrong, so her focus in life was simply survival. Her role models were friends on dope, prostitutes, pimps, and pushers.

It was during her third term in prison that she began to think about her life and realized she was simply hitting her head against the same wall over and over again. It was during the seven months in isolation that she began calling out to God, "Don't kill me, Lord, but get me away from this. I'm sick of it."[2] She cried about her past, couldn't sleep, and eventually asked the chaplain for a Bible. She soon realized that having the Bible in the room was not all she needed. She began to read it, asking God what He was trying to tell her. When she did not get an answer, she told the Lord she was not going to ever read the Bible again after this one last time. As she flipped to the Psalms, her eyes landed on "The LORD is a shelter for the oppressed."[3] It was as if the Lord said to her directly, "I hear you in this time of trouble." She responded by telling God she wanted Him to change her. It was from that point on that she would say she changed from the inside out.

Laurie made a decision to stop using people and stop smoking. She began attending the FITS (Freedom in the Son) services in prison. What amazed Laurie was how the FITS team "didn't preach at us or throw God in our face. *They just loved people*."[4] Laurie continued growing in her faith.

After Laurie was released from prison in 1993, she found life to be even more challenging. But she had a new desire, a determination to follow Christ. She realized that temptations, rejections, and betrayals were all part of the spiritual battle raging within. She repeatedly cried out to God at each challenge point. Eventually the Lord provided the money for her to get an apartment, and she soon discovered that the church across the street had a Jesus Against Drugs and Alcohol (JADA) program. People in the church helped her move and settle in.

Today, Laurie is the housing specialist for Central City Concern Recuperative Care Program in Portland. She is also a certified drug and alcohol counselor and a qualified mental health assistant. Laurie is a member of the FITS speaking team and mentoring program.

Understanding the Issue

Ninety-eight percent of incarcerated women have been abused.[5] Most have never had the security of a family, no healthy role models for a man-woman relationship. Nearly two-thirds of the women are mothers.[6] One of the greatest losses the women experience when they come to prison is the loss of their children.[7] If a woman arrives in prison pregnant, she will face childbirth by being restrained with one leg cuffed to the bed, except during delivery. If no provision can be made with a family member, the baby will be placed in a foster home immediately after birth.[8] Some will never see or have their children returned and some will work hard when they are released trying to prove they have the ability to parent.

Although every resident is unique, there are certain patterns of behavior that brought these women to prison. It is through observing these that you will have a better understanding of the resident without stereotyping her.

Most of the women, if not all, have a very poor sense of their value and worth. Because of the high number of women in prison who have experienced severe abuse (over 98 percent) and because in prison the sense of self-respect is further ripped away by the constant reminder that the person is a criminal, nearly everything in her life at that point drives her deeper into the pit of self-rejection. As a child, the woman may have experienced abuse resulting from a family member or friend's involvement with pornography. Because it was familiar, she chose a mate or boyfriend also in bondage to pornography. She may end up killing her abuser when she does not feel she can protect herself or her children any longer. She may abuse her children in the process.

Incarcerated women give two main reasons they come to prison. The first is because of their involvement with men. A man introduced her to abusing drugs, selling drugs, and prostitution. The woman collects the money (from drugs or prostitution), gives it to him, and he spends the money. Typically, if she gets arrested, the pimp goes free. He may abuse the woman's children. She might go to prison for not intervening to stop the abuse. Or she gets angry and attacks or kills him.

Second, women go to prison because of their involvement with drugs. The woman participates in prostitution to pay for drugs. Drugs cause the woman to abandon her children so she loses them to the state while she's in prison. She commits crimes to pay for drugs.

Many of the women we meet grew up in church. Some are preacher's kids, a few pastor's wives. They have experienced many types of abuse: incest, physical, spiritual, sexual, verbal, and emotional. One woman remembers that at age thirteen her father, a pastor, gave her to the men of the church for sexual favors, which continued until she was sent to a juvenile detention home. Today she continues to use drugs and frequently comes back to prison to "get well," then goes back to the streets and prostitution. This is her life.

Shepherding Insights

Often because of her choices, the woman does not believe that God can forgive her nor can she accept forgiveness from a loving God. The truth of Romans 8:1, "There is now NO condemnation for those who are in Christ Jesus" (emphasis added), becomes an opening to let her know she is loved and accepted where she is right now. It is important for those who connect with her to reflect that kind of love and acceptance. As the Holy Spirit reveals the truth to her, she may choose to accept Jesus into her life by repenting of her sins and receiving the forgiveness He so freely offers her. She needs to know that "The Lord is . . . not willing that any should perish but that all should come to repentance" (2 Peter 3:9 NKJV).

There are two things that are helpful to pray each day before you spend time with an incarcerated woman. One is for wisdom, out of which come knowledge and understanding. The other is for discernment, a keen sensitivity to the Holy Spirit as He works in your life and in the lives of the women in prison. Remember, "we are not fighting against flesh-and-blood enemies, but against evil rulers and authorities of the unseen world, against mighty powers in this dark world, and against evil spirits in the heavenly places."[9]

"But you belong to God, my dear children. You have already won a victory, because the Spirit who lives in you is greater than the spirit who lives in the world."[10]

We must trust the Holy Spirit to give us discernment in how to speak, share, pray, and love these women. If we verbally batter them with the Scriptures or seek to control their attitudes and behavior, they will see our efforts as abuse. Instead, we should seek to love them unconditionally, devoid of criticism and judgment, realizing that God is the One who brings about true life change.

The women's stories of how God met them are as varied as the women themselves. Janice, a thirty-year heroin addict, met Jesus while working in the kitchen. Jesus came to Patricia while she was playing on the softball field. Jesus spoke to Cass as she was playing her guitar in lockup. Jesus revealed Himself to Leslie, a college graduate and schoolteacher, as her Messiah as she walked the track wondering what in the world had happened to her life. Catherine met Jesus during a yoga class where He spoke audibly and said, "Come to Me, all you who are weary and heavy of heart, and I will give you rest." Catherine heard, she answered the call, and she followed her Lord. Two weeks after Tammy arrived at the prison, Jesus came to her while she was sleeping and let her know that He was there so she could get to know Him and experience His love. These women and many more have come to know Jesus as they are locked up and awaiting release back into their communities.

Once a woman has been released from prison, the presence of a Christian woman mentor is critical for her success on the outside. Mentoring is a relational experience in which one person empowers another by sharing God-given resources.[11] This mentor begins by meeting and building a relationship with her mentee four to six months prior to release, then continues to be there for her for a year while she is in transition. This mentoring should focus on relationships, first centering on the relationship with Christ and then with others. Mentoring is less about instruction and more about relationship, taking initiative to bring young women into maturity.[12]

Characteristics of Effective Mentors

1. Positive Christian role models
2. Covered by a church or Christ-centered organization
3. Sensitive to the needs of women in prison and in transition
4. Able to relate well to the disadvantaged population
5. Committed to be a support person as the woman seeks to live a constructive, independent life outside the institution

6. Caring, dedicated women who understand commitment and the volunteer ethic

Topics Addressed by Effective Mentors
1. Goal setting
2. Life planning
3. Spiritual enrichment
4. Career choices
5. Educational pursuits
6. Support systems
7. Financial responsibility
8. Search for significance
9. Overcoming barriers and setting boundaries

Most women transitioning out of prison have an unrealistic view of life. Some have no plans for when they are released, no short- or long-term goals. The woman released will likely have almost no possessions, so she will need the basics of living, and she will need help in finding a job, a place to live, food, and a support group. Offer to bring her to church. Perhaps others from your church will join you in giving her a "coming out" party with kitchen or household gifts. Spend time with her.

If you are able to meet her at the gate on the day she is released, plan how you will spend those first hours. Take her to breakfast (have some real coffee). Take her to get food stamps and a bus pass, and help her get clothes. You may want to take her to the parole office for her to sign in.

Once you have built a trusting relationship, by spending time with her before she is released as well as after, you may be able to help her make and carry out a realistic life plan. As you continue in relationship with her, you will earn the right to appropriately challenge her behavior and choices. She may have difficulty making decisions. You can help her by suggesting she take small steps to gain confidence and experience in healthy living patterns.[13]

HELPFUL THINGS TO SAY AND DO

Here are some guidelines that we have found helpful when ministering to women in prison.

1. **DO** always pray for wisdom, discernment, and guidance. Put on the whole armor of God in prayer each day before entering the prison gates. You will encounter spiritual warfare; be aware of the forces of evil. Know how to enter into prayer for victory and deliverance. Spend much time in prayer as preparation for the visit.

2. **DO** seek prayer support from others. The prayers of others will give you the strength and confidence to continue when you encounter difficulties.

3. **DO** prayerfully seek God's direction in regard to where and with whom you may serve most effectively using the tools and talents with which God has equipped you. If you find you are in the wrong spot, speak to the head of your organization and ask for reassignment.

4. **DO** be yourself. A phony is easily spotted and the word gets around.

5. **DO** be a good listener and slow to offer advice. Be patient. You are making a difference in someone's life.

6. **DO** talk about things and people on the outside, such as everyday activities, families, or church. Allow the woman to share her life, failures, and dreams for the future with you.

7. **DO** love unconditionally and accept the women where they are, not where you wish they were. Be compassionate, sensitive, and willing to meet people at their point of need while standing for the absolute standards put forth by a holy God. Respect the incarcerated woman as your equal at the foot of the cross.

8. **DO** call on members of your church/fellowship for help and support. You need them, and it will benefit the incarcerated woman to have others praying for her and supporting her in practical ways.

9. **DO** check out present programs already in place at the institution and see how you can complement them without competing. There is plenty of work to be done. Check with the facility chaplain.

10. **DO** obey all of the institution's rules even though they may not make sense to you. Pray for favor with the administrative staff of the facility and work to earn their respect and confidence. If you err in judgment or make a mistake, own up to it and then move on. Maintain good communication. Love the volunteers with whom you work. Love covers a multitude of disagreements.

HURTFUL RESPONSES TO AVOID

1. **DON'T** make promises you cannot keep. Don't promise to write or visit if you cannot follow through. The women have been disappointed all their lives by empty promises.

2. **DON'T** make excuses when you blow it. Confess your failure and ask forgiveness. Honesty and humility will build a person's respect for you. Excuses will tear it down.

3. **DON'T** expect instant results or success immediately. Change takes time. Remember how long you have been in process. We are not being called to fail or succeed, but we are called to be faithful! Preaching and then leaving will not bring instant results. You must take time to build relationships. You cannot get to know someone when you spend a limited time once a month with them. Don't become discouraged or disappointed when things do not go as you planned. Remember Galatians 6:9:

"Let us not become weary in doing good, for at the proper time we will reap a harvest if we do not give up."

4. **DON'T** give pat answers for the person's struggles or problems. The person needs love and understanding, and sometimes just wants to talk. You do not have to have an answer for every question that comes up. Do not play mind games or allow the woman to play mind games with you. Do not automatically believe or disbelieve her words. Simply listen. Time and the Holy Spirit will reveal the truth. "My dear brothers and sisters: You must all be quick to listen, slow to speak, and slow to get angry" (James 1:19 NLT).

5. **DON'T** try to rescue the person. She is not your spiritual project. Seek to love and serve her as Jesus would. Look for Jesus in the face of each woman you meet.

6. **DON'T** ask a woman why she is in prison. She will tell you when you have earned her respect and she knows she can trust you. It may take awhile. One incarcerated woman checked me out for two years before confiding in me and now we are good friends.

7. **DON'T** overreact or take personally any emotion, particularly anger. Women in prison have a lot of anger/rage, depression, guilt, and fear. Their emotional growth stopped when they began using drugs, so some are emotionally thirteen or fourteen years old. Don't expect them to act like mature adults. In fact, do not have expectations for them. God will grow them up in His time, not yours. Be careful not to blame yourself if the woman relapses and returns to prison after you have invested much time and resource in her. Claim Philippians 1:6: "Being confident of this, that he who began a good work in you will carry it on to completion until the day of Christ Jesus." My mentor Kathryn Grant says, "Prison ministry is not easy—just remember to give the discouragements to God, and live on the excitement of watching God at work in the lives of the women."

8. **DON'T** preach, condemn, judge motives, or evaluate behavior. These women need to be loved and see Jesus in you. Be careful not to force your convictions or theological doctrines on others. Jesus does not force Himself on anyone and neither should we. The women have a God-given right to make their own choices. We offer them Jesus whom we love and serve. They alone can make the decision to choose to follow Jesus.

9. **DON'T** talk down to the women; some may be more educated than you. Their self-esteem is at rock bottom and they need to be built up and learn who they are in Christ. They may prefer to be called by name, or referred to as "residents" rather than inmates or prisoners.

10. **DON'T** allow hard feelings with the administration or other volunteers to hinder the work of the gospel. Christian community is confession, forgiveness, and restoration. The enemy must always be cut off at the pass!

Our mission has always been to reach out to hurting women with the life and love of Jesus Christ. Our desire is to "Continue to remember those in prison as if you were together with them in prison, and those who are mistreated as if you yourselves were suffering" (Hebrews 13:3).

Weekly FITS volunteers sponsor groups, requested and organized by the women in prison. Following the prayer times each week, Bible studies are held in treatment, minimum general population, and medium units. On any given night around 120 women gather to study the Word of God with FITS volunteers. Around these Bible studies, volunteers are also mentoring, counseling, and praying with individual women.

Situations warrant special classes requested of us by programs inside the prison. Classes are taught on subjects such as forgiveness, grief recovery, and building healthy relationships. These classes are not mandatory and the women sign up to attend knowing they are faith-based and Christ-centered. We use the Bible as our textbook.

Questions for Prospective Volunteers

1. Am I answering the call of the Father to a life of intimacy with Him?
2. Has the Father given me the assignment to carry the life and love of Jesus to women inside prison walls?
3. Do I understand that only Jesus can meet the needs of women and heal their wounds? I am only a conduit of His grace.
4. Do I understand that we are all equal at the foot of the cross—sinners saved by grace—so we show respect for the individual the Father is sending to us.
5. Are my needs being met by Jesus so that I am not expecting ministry to meet them?
6. Do I know who I am in Christ—that I am complete in Him?
7. Can I learn to see the women through the eyes of Jesus and love them with His heart?

Prison ministry[14] has been full of excitement, challenges, miracles of God's grace, difficulties, heartache, and oh so much learning and receiving through the faithfulness of our heavenly Father. I love the women, and I have never been disappointed in Jesus Christ or His ability to heal their broken hearts, change their lives, and give them a purpose for wanting to live again.

Resources

Websites

> Freedom in the Son, Inc., founded by Fran Howard, is a ministry that shares the life and love of Jesus Christ in a practical way with hurting women—primarily to women in prison and women in transition and their children.
>
> www.speakupforhope.org: Speak up for Hope
>
> www.pfi.org: Prison Fellowship International
>
> www.kairosprisonministry.org: Kairos Prison Ministry International, Inc.

Books

Arthur, Kay. *Lord, Heal My Hurts: A Devotional Study on God's Care and Deliverance.* Colorado Springs: WaterBrook, 2000.

———. *Lord, Is It Warfare? Teach Me to Stand: A Devotional Study on Spiritual Victory.* Colorado Springs: WaterBrook, 2000.

Christensen, Monty, and Roberta Kehle. *70 x 7 and Beyond: Mystery of the Second Chance.* Prison Impact Ministries, 1987.

Christenson, Evelyn. *Lord, Change Me.* Evelyn Christenson Ministry, 2008.

Dobson, James. *Love Must Be Tough.* Carol Stream, IL: Tyndale House, 2007.

Logan, Jim. *Reclaiming Surrendered Ground.* Chicago: Moody, 1995, 2016.

McGee, Robert S. *Search for Significance: Seeing Your True Worth through God's Eyes.* Rev. ed. Nashville: Thomas Nelson, 2003.

Minirth, Frank, and Randy Reese. *Growing into Wholeness: Putting Body, Mind and Spirit Back Together.* Chicago: Moody, 1993.

Referrals

Local sources such as St. Vincent de Paul or Goodwill for getting clothing, kitchenware, and furniture

Salvation Army may provide housing assistance

Local food banks will supplement food stamps and they are free

Locate support groups such as Celebrate Recovery

Related Scriptures

Isaiah 42:6–10; 61:1–3

Jeremiah 17:14; 29:11–13

Matthew 25:31–40

Galatians 5:1, 13

Hebrews 13:3

AUTHOR BIO

FRAN HOWARD earned a BS in health and physical education from Lewis & Clark College in Portland, Oregon, and an MS in guidance and counseling from Creighton University. She worked as assistant professor at George Fox University and Mt. St. Scholastica College, followed by women's athletic director and associate professor at Willamette University. She received honors from the NAIA, Coaches Hall of Fame and Willamette University Coaches Hall of Fame. Fran was founder and president of Freedom in the Son, Inc., beginning in 1985. She received the Christian Servant Award, the Corrections Volunteer of the Year Award, and the Department of Corrections Outstanding Citizen Award. Fran was a member of the American Correctional Chaplain's Association.

Chapter 14

Homelessness

Jan Marshall, Founding Director of Shepherd's Door,
a ministry of Portland Rescue Mission

*I*t was a cold, damp evening as I stood alone in the reception area of the Portland Rescue Mission. My team couldn't make it that night, so I was the only woman to join the men's staff. I was as uncomfortable, as though I'd been standing up to my knees in murky, cold water.

Misty rain was falling as the long line of hungry, chilly, and cranky homeless men and women waited outside for the doors to open. I knew the crowd would be entering soon and planned to get behind the serving line to avoid having to talk with anyone. My obedience to "show up" seemed unneeded. "I feel this is a waste of my time, Father," I prayed. The smell was overwhelming. All I could think about was doing my bit and going home to warmth and familiarity.

I heard her before I saw her. A short, angry, disturbed woman had made her way in. She babbled and raged, dominating everyone's attention. They knew her as Tye. The men's staff tried to reason with her, but to no avail. I desperately prayed they could solve the problem. Time stood still as they turned and looked at me; I knew I had to do something. As I left the safety of the reception office, my mind raced. *I don't know what to do, Lord.* I felt Him smile at me. He seemed to enjoy my discomfort. Did my cry for help go unheeded? I could feel all eyes on me. *What do I do, Lord?*

The woman looked at me and began sputtering unintelligible words. Noticing her thin wet jacket, I had a thought. "Do you want me to find you a coat?" She glared for a moment. I thought she was going to hit me but instead she yelled "Yes!" Welcoming the escape, I found my way downstairs to the clothing area where choices were slim. I found a reasonably warm jacket, but it looked too small. I picked a mauve sweatshirt; it looked too big. When I arrived back upstairs, she was still rambling. Holding up both, I asked her which she wanted. Angrily she grabbed both.

Now what, Lord? I could feel myself sinking deeper into that murky water again. Tye didn't seem to notice me but instead was preoccupied with the coat; it was too tight. Out of the corner of my eye, I saw her slip on the sweatshirt. What happened next was unforeseen. Only God could have planned the next moment.

As Tye slipped the sweatshirt over her head pulling it down over her small frame, a thought crossed my mind and came out of my mouth before I could stop it. "Why, Tye, it's beautiful. I believe that's your color!" She stopped babbling and looked right at me. Her mouth curled up in a small smile. "Will you be my foster mom?" she asked. As quickly as the lucid moment had come, it was over. She resumed her crazy behavior as she made her way out the door.

In that moment the waters parted and I stood on dry ground. It may seem insignificant to some but for me it was profound. God had asked me to show up. That is all. My plans were made out of duty but God was about to "ambush" my heart. I had not expected God would meet me there, though He loved me enough to ask me to come. Had I not been willing to go to the place of discomfort, I would never have experienced Him. Oh yes, I had dragged my feet and nothing in me saw His hand. Yet, in that moment I saw Tye through His eyes and I loved her. Tye and I connected in a circle of three. He stood with us.

Now each week I travel downtown and look women in the eye, ask their names, serve them food, and pray for them.

One would think having been in rescue mission work for many years, I would be comfortable and eager to serve the women on the streets. The truth is I was not initially comfortable in the culture of the street homeless. I wanted to avoid facing these dirty, mentally ill, and addicted street women. When a woman hits the streets, she quickly deteriorates both physically and emotionally on entering street culture. But God gave me a love for these women.

Today I am ministering at Shepherd's Door, the women's ministry of the Portland Rescue Mission, in a brand-new 42,000-square-foot facility offering long-term programming for homeless women and their children. Our target population is the "couch homeless," homeless women who move from shelter to shelter, home to home.

What does "homeless" mean? Simply, without a home. The dictionary defines home as "one's principal place of residence."[1] Loris Sheets, who writes about homeless women in America,[2] describes *home* as a

> place where one belongs . . . where a woman can be herself, and if lucky accepted as she is. It is a place where she can grow, can discover who she is and learn to like herself . . . and give thanks for the blessing of having a home and all that's in it. A home is a refuge from the world. . . . It is a place where, hopefully, we can feel loved.[3]

Homeless women find themselves without such a place. Instead of having a refuge to return to at the end of each day, a homeless woman finds herself in a vulnerable, dangerous place. Granted, some women live in a house but it is not a place of refuge, acceptance, or love. *Home* brings a variety of images to women. Some painful, some warm.

Understand the Issue

Who are the women found in homeless shelters? This is not an easy target group. Don't expect them to show gratitude for your efforts. Rather, because they are comfortable with rejection, they will likely set you up to reject them. They will likely test, lie, manipulate, argue, and compete. They may be depressed, suicidal, angry, even kicking and screaming. There are typically five issues that homeless women are likely to be experiencing: a false belief system, emotional immaturity, survival behaviors, grief, and addictions.

During the early years of life, while the brain is developing, the *belief system* is cemented into a woman. This belief system is cast upon a woman by her caregivers. In many cases, she as a child was reared in a culture of cruelty and crudeness. That is the "normal" in which she lived and survived. In this culture lies developed within the belief system of this child, such as

- *You'll never amount to anything*
- *It's all your fault Daddy did that to you*
- *You're stupid, slow, and ugly*
- *I wish you had never been born*

These are called *projected lies.* They are projected onto a child by the caregiver initiating within that child's belief system survival lies. Examples of survival lies may be

- *If I love someone, they will hurt me; therefore, I cannot love at all.*
- *If I don't know all the answers, I'm a failure.*
- *Since I can't trust adults, I will need to take care of myself.*
- *I don't need anyone.*
- *Fathers always hurt so I can't trust him.*

These are only a few of hundreds of lies a child grows up believing. Sometimes the lies are unarticulated. The homeless person believes them as truth and will fulfill the prophecy of these lies if there is no intervention.

When a child is traumatized, she will not grow emotionally more than three years beyond the trauma of her childhood. In most cases, the homeless person's *emotional growth* is stunted. Most of the women who have come to the shelters in my thirty-nine years of experience are between the ages of five and thirteen years old emotionally.

To survive in a traumatic childhood, the homeless person had to create *survival behaviors.*

To survive, a child might learn or adapt roles early in life allowing her to fit into the family of origin, such as Scapegoat, Princess, Hero, Lost Child, or Enabler. Actually these coping skills worked and kept the child safe at times, but for adults they are destructive, isolating, and annoying. The homeless person finds she is then avoided, feared, and criticized. When the homeless woman comes into our facilities, she actually believes she *is* her behavior. She has not asked, "Who am I without my behavior?" She knows nothing else. It is imperative she participate in long-term residential processing to help break down the walls of the lies and survival behaviors. It takes time to make such immense changes.

The homeless woman is a *grieving* person. When most of us lose someone to death, a healthy grief process is typically two to four years. However, the homeless woman does not know she is grieving as she enters into the process of catastrophic loss. She has experienced loss of childhood, innocence, relationships, dignity—the list of losses is long. She has nothing with which to measure what is normal or to understand the grief of loss.

She has spent most of her life trying to fill the empty void of intimacy and the pain of loss with a temporary fix. It is never enough. Nearly all of those entering our shelters today are *addicted* to alcohol, drugs, and/or unhealthy relationships in an attempt to dull the pain of abandonment (loss) and lack of intimate love.

In summary, it is important to understand the profile of the homeless person. She functions within a *false belief system* (lies from childhood), is *emotionally* a child, has created *survival behaviors*, is in *grief process*, and usually comes with multiple *addictions*. This understanding leads us to create processing that will help her choose recovery in an environment that is safe and healing.

Shepherding Insights

Shepherding must include creating an environment in which we can equip her with tools to "go through the pain to get to the other side," rather than avoid, bury, and/or sedate her emotional pain. At Shepherd's Door, we tell the residents that we can help them remember the pain but we can't go through the pain with them to get to the other side. However, we can hold them while they bleed and cry. It is important for each woman to be willing to initiate the pain, feel it, and courageously forgive. Our role is to stand with her and watch God transform her pain and brokenness into the oil of gladness and healing as she forgives her past and embraces her future. This is the deep rich blessing of true shepherding.

God creates the heart for intimacy. We are all created for relationship. If a person believes the lie "If I love someone, they will hurt me, therefore I cannot love at all," she will hold others at arm's length. Nearly all the women who come to the shelter had no healthy father image in their home. Most of the women were molested by a father, stepfather, grandfather, brother, or uncle. So from early childhood these women do not have the concept of a father's tender, healthy touch or love.

Edina (not her real name) hates Valentine's Day because to her "love" meant having forced sex with her father. Imagine how difficult it is to help a woman die to the grief of that horrid childhood and embrace the heavenly Father's unfailing intimate love for her. She starves for it but is repulsed by it at the same time. So women like Edina will choose something they think they can control to sedate the pain caused by the lies they believe, instead of understanding God's great love for them.

At Shepherd's Door, intentional programming is designed to assist a resident to move from her old belief system into the transformational power of Jesus Christ. Without surrender to the love of Jesus Christ, there is no true deliverance in her life. Salvation is the first "ambush" experience. Though there are many important components of a long-term program for the homeless woman, therapeutic programming alone will not transform a person's life. Only the transformational power of Jesus

Christ can break through the above five established patterns and bring lasting freedom.

Carefully chosen curriculum is vital in addressing addictions. Shepherd's Door uses *Genesis Process*,[4] which includes processes through which the resident is lead to understand her

- false belief system
- need to find identity with Christ
- need to measure her relapse pattern
- need to set up accountability in her life . . . and more.

This biblical approach enables the resident to release the pain of her childhood and risk walking into the arms of a loving God who called her before the creation of the world[5] to belong to Him. This is what God wanted to do and it *gave Him great pleasure.*[6] Imagine that! Could it be that our homeless hurting woman was called before the world was even created? Could it be we would look differently at the homeless if we really believed this? This truth as delineated in the curriculum equips us to understand, shepherd, and evangelize this dear, hurting woman.

These truths cannot be embraced with effective outcome outside of relationship. Authentic relationship is vital in assisting these precious women in pain. Early in life they became sharp discerners of authenticity. Our challenge is to see them through God's eyes and love as God loves. As the homeless woman works through these difficult processes with staff, she will be equipped to realize that truth is a person . . . Jesus. When truth is spoken against her childhood lies, then addiction slows and stops. The pain begins to fade as Christ replaces the deep vacuum caused by the past. *Then* Christ will be more and more at home in their hearts as they trust in Him.[7]

A shepherd *must* have a personal disciplined walk with the Lord in order to establish an ongoing authentic relationship that fosters healing in others. If a shepherd is not daily dying to self-centeredness and exercising the disciplines of the faith[8] in her own life, she will by default fall into the therapeutic side of recovery. A shepherd will be most effective as she lives in the power of the death and resurrection of Jesus Christ and imparts the tools to help homeless women embrace a full recovery. Simply put, we walk in the standard of Christlikeness as we evangelize and disciple. What draws a person to Christ is His presence in our lives. That comes through our authentic walk with Him.

My story of Tye reveals how God "ambushed" my heart. As a shepherd offers authentic relationship, accountability, teaching tools, and a willingness to honestly speak into a person's life, she will discover open and teachable hearts among homeless women. The heart of a homeless woman "ambushed" by God will reflect fresh gratefulness, childlikeness, humility, and teachability. God transforms miraculously. I see this every day at Shepherd's Door.

HELPFUL THINGS TO SAY AND DO

What is our challenge to help these pain-ridden women?

1. **DO** gain an understanding of their profile and the five issues they will likely be experiencing. Your understanding will be critical in helping you shepherd effectively. It will keep you from enabling the homeless woman to continually make poor choices.

2. **DO** begin building an authentic relationship. Know this takes time and commit to the long haul. Remember, many of these women have had many people walk in and out of their lives. Someone committed to stay, no matter what their responses, will certainly challenge their false beliefs.

3. **DO** ask questions that are very specific and begin with "how," "what," and "where." Questions that begin with "why" can be shaming.

4. **DO** probe for feelings after a person has responded to your question. "Tell me what you were feeling then. What are you feeling right now as you share this with me?"

5. **DO** be quick to tell her how sorry you are that she had to experience such terrible acts against her (particularly if she was an abused child).

6. **DO** educate yourself on the behaviors of an addict. This will keep you from becoming an enabler, rather than a shepherd who effectively affirms positive though difficult decisions.

HURTFUL RESPONSES TO AVOID

1. **DON'T** minister alone. Work within a team made up of various strengths. There are many aspects to this woman's life, and not only is it more effective to have her observe community love and acceptance, but it will be less likely the shepherd will burn out. It is beneficial to both the shepherd and the homeless woman to work in teams.

2. **DON'T** ask questions that can be answered by yes or no. For example, rather than asking, "Have you been using?" Ask, "When was the last time you used?" or "What did you use?" These questions require answers that will help you speak into her life.

3. **DON'T** assume the past experiences of a homeless woman are so completely different from your own. You may be surprised to find emotionally painful experiences in her childhood, adolescence, and adulthood that resonate with your own. Even if you have not experienced the same kinds of pain, you may be able to relate to the universal pain of feeling unloved or abandoned. The God-given desire of all humans is to be loved unconditionally.

4. **DON'T** hesitate when establishing authentic relationships to share appropriately out of your own life struggles. Homeless women are often much the same as you or me; if we had experienced the same set of circumstances and made similar

choices in our lives, we too might well share their situation. Each woman usually realizes she is down, but she doesn't know quite how or where to turn for support. She can feel like she is falling without a safety net. Many feel worthless and incapable of escaping their situation.

5. **DON'T** underestimate the power of the Spirit of God to transform the homeless woman, and you as a shepherd in the process.

After Gloria (not her real name) "graduated" from a local homeless shelter, she found herself exclaiming repeatedly the initial surprise when everyone on staff and volunteers at the shelter all treated her with love, not "like something on the bottom of your shoe." This was a new experience for her—being genuinely loved. And it opened the door for her to begin a new way of living.

Resources

Websites

www.genesisprocess.org: This website will help you understand the addict and the process information from the writer, Michael Dye.

https://www.familyshelter.org: My Father's House—a nonprofit shelter ministry that opened to meet the needs of homeless families, with an amazing success rate of getting families "back on their feet."

https://www.citygatenetwork.org/agrm: Association of Gospel Rescue Missions.. This will tell you where to find missions and resources nationally for referral.

https://www.portlandrescuemission.org/recovery-programs/shepherdsdoor: Shepherd's Door.

Books

Allender, Dan. *The Wounded Heart: Hope for Adult Victims of Childhood Sexual Abuse*. Colorado Springs: NavPress, 2008, 2018.

Amen, Daniel G. *Change Your Brain, Change Your Life: The Breakthrough Program for Conquering Anxiety, Depression, Obsessiveness, Anger, and Impulsiveness*. Easton, PA: Harmony, revised and expanded 2015.

Augsberger, David. *The Freedom of Forgiveness*. 3rd ed. Chicago: Moody, 2000.

Beattie, Melody. *Codependent No More: How to Stop Controlling Others and Start Caring for Yourself*. Center City, MN: Hazelden, 1992.

Foster, Richard. *Celebration of Discipline*. Hachette, UK: Hodder & Stoughton Ltd., 2008.

Hemfelt, Robert, Frank Minirth, and Paul Meier. *Love Is a Choice: The Definitive Book on Letting Go of Unhealthy Relationships*. Nashville: Thomas Nelson, 2003.

Manning, Brennan. *Abba's Child*. Enlarged ed. Colorado Springs: NavPress, 2015.

McGee, Robert S. *The Search for Significance: Seeing Your True Worth through God's Eyes*. Nashville: Thomas Nelson, 2003.

Seamands, David. *Healing for Damaged Emotions*, new ed. Elgin: David C. Cook, 1991, 2015.

Thompson, Curt. *The Soul of Shame: Retelling the Stories We Believe about Ourselves*. Downers Grove, IL: IVP, 2015.

Yankoski, Mike. *Under the Overpass: A Journey of Faith on the Streets of America*. Sisters, OR: Multnomah, 2005.

Related Scriptures

Matthew 8:20

1 Corinthians 4:11

Ephesians 1:4–6; 3:17–18

AUTHOR BIO

JAN MARSHALL became the director of women's ministries for the Portland Rescue Mission in 2000. She designed the overall building project for the new Shepherd's Door women and children's shelter in Portland, Oregon. She established and trained staff and developed the long-term program for women and their children at Shepherd's Door. Previously, Jan served as founder of the Evergreen Training Center for women and their children in Erie, Pennsylvania. She sat on the national board of the Association of Gospel Rescue Missions, as the chairperson of the Women and Family track of the AGRM. Jan reconstructed the Moriah House Shelter program for women and their children in Memphis, Tennessee. She established aftercare programs for bereaved women and children in New Castle, Pennsylvania. In 1998 she established her consulting business to assist missions across the country in management of leadership programs for women and family shelters.

Chapter 15

Suicide

Kay C. Bruce, Psy. D.
Certified Trainer for QPR-T Suicide Intervention Workshops
Professor of Counseling at Western Seminary

*H*er erratic driving attracted the attention of a Portland police officer, whose siren and lights brought the weaving vehicle to a stop. The driver, a female in her twenties, was quite obviously intoxicated as indicated by the pungent odor and her slurred speech. On the seat next to her lay a handgun and a red blanket. Her stated plan was to drive to a nearby cemetery, lie down on the ground, cover her head with the blanket, and fire the gun aimed at her forehead. She reasoned that the red blanket would mask the blood and thereby reduce the traumatization to whoever found her. She had given much thought to immediate reactions of friends and family, but had no awareness of the permanent abyss that such an act would create in the hearts of those who knew and loved her. By arresting her, the police officer saved her life and prevented untold grief to the community. Follow-up support helped her to rediscover meaning in life and reconnect with family and friends. Today she would tell you she is grateful to be alive.

Understand the Issue

Although this young woman's plan was unique, the skewed logic is quite common. People who are contemplating suicide often create detailed plans, which include provisions for those they are leaving behind. They write letters to loved ones, purchase life insurance, attempt to stage "an accident," and give prized possessions away. They imagine how much better off people would be without them.

On average, one person in the United States kills himself or herself every sixteen minutes, over 30,000 per year.[1] Guesstimates are that at least six close friends and family members are significantly impacted by each suicide. This means that every sixteen minutes there are six additional people in deep mourning and at greater risk for suicide. Surveys of students have found that approximately 14.5 percent of high school–aged students have seriously considered suicide as an option during any given year.[2]

Suicide is a serious issue for women in pain. Three times more women attempt suicide than do men.[3] Men, however, often choose more deadly methods and are therefore more likely to die from their attempt.

People kill themselves when the pain of living seems greater than the pain of dying and they can see no hope of improvement. Most people contemplating suicide do not really want to die, they just want the emotional psychache in their life to stop.[4] It is often true that when a person takes action to kill herself/himself but survives, she/he has a sense of regret and develops a desire to live, especially if she/he receives healthy support from friends and loved ones.

Kirk Jones of Canton, Michigan, went over Niagara Falls headfirst because he was "driven by depression" after the family business was shut down. By God's grace, he survived the fall and now wants to live again. In an interview Jones stated, "I honestly thought that it wasn't worth going on. But I can tell you now after hitting the falls, I feel that life is worth living."[5] His comments are consistent with interviews of others who have been stopped during attempted jumps from the Golden Gate Bridge in San Francisco.[6]

The majority of completed suicides (both male and female) in this country are committed with a firearm. While ingesting poison can be deadly, often time permits one to have a change of heart, seek medical assistance, and live. On the other hand, once the trigger of a gun is pulled, a newfound desire to live does not typically alter the outcome.

Although there are some people who use suicide in a manipulative fashion with friends and family members, the majority of those who attempt are very serious about their action. Just because one has a change of heart after taking some form of action does not negate the seriousness of their initial intent. A woman[7] who overdoses on pills and then seeks help should be considered a serious risk. To presume otherwise is dangerous. One who repeatedly threatens suicide needs to be in treatment with a professional who is experienced and competent to maintain appropriate boundaries and monitor risk assessment.[8]

Shepherding Insights

A good strategy for shepherding a woman who struggles with ongoing suicide ideation[9] would be to ensure that the woman has a good relationship with a competent therapist. The shepherd should discuss with the therapist appropriate boundaries to maintain as well as red flags to observe. This could be accomplished either by attending a counseling session with the woman or by obtaining a signed authorization from her permitting contact with the therapist. A coordinated team approach to helping can be most beneficial and help to minimize any manipulative tendencies, while easing the burden of the shepherd.

The first step in helping a woman at risk for suicide is accepting the woman's emotional pain as genuine and valid, though not insurmountable. A pastoral caregiver must be willing to clearly hear a woman's distress before trying to rebuild hope. At the same time, a caregiver must maintain her own internal hope and optimism while genuinely sympathizing with the woman's pain. It is important to communicate genuine care about the woman's plight when listening to her story. When the woman in pain no longer feels alone in her distress, it frees her to discover hope.

Suicide can be a double-edged sword for Christians who have the conviction that a blissful eternal life in heaven awaits their death. Some see suicide as a route to immediate and permanent relief from pain. Others worry they might not be accepted into heaven if they choose suicide, so their belief becomes preventative. Yet other Christians cannot understand why anyone who claims to love the Lord would even seriously consider suicide as an option. The reality is that many people of deep faith have killed themselves—among them are pastors, missionaries, and seminary professors.

As a young woman, Kristina became deeply depressed over a period of several months. Her mother had also struggled with depression during Kristina's childhood and during later years her mother became a withdrawn, bitter, and hostile woman. Kristina knew that her mother had survived physical abuse as a child and domestic violence as an adult. Though Kristina felt sympathy for her mother's pain, she was often the target of her mother's lashing tongue. Kristina held a deep resolve to never become like her mother. Over several months, when her own depression began to drain energy and life from her, Kristina began to compare herself to mental images of her mother. She became concerned that she was a burden to her family and feared that they would soon come to despise her. All of her efforts to improve her own outlook had failed. Though she believed killing herself was wrong, Kristina also concluded that God would understand her desire to protect her family and still grant her eternal life.

The story of Elijah, as recorded in 1 Kings 19 (NKJV), graphically illustrates God's response to a man of faith who came to the point of wanting to die. In the previous chapter, God had dramatically answered Elijah's prayer before "all of the children of Israel" and the prophets by sending fire down to consume a water-soaked sacrifice. Shortly thereafter, the evil queen Jezebel threatened Elijah's life, so he escaped to the desert where he "prayed that he might die, and said, 'It is enough! Now, Lord, take my life.'"

Notice that God's response was not one of chastisement but rather of simple provision for his immediate physical needs. God sent an angel with food, water, and instruction to sleep and eat. God could have said, "Don't you remember what I just did for you in front of all who you consider important?" But, it was not until over forty days later that God began dealing with Elijah's spiritual condition. God knew Elijah was in a crisis state of temporary need and He responded accordingly. God modeled the importance of addressing very practical physical and emotional needs when one is in a place of despair. Helping a woman to survive the crisis gives time to address the spiritual and philosophical questions later when she is more stable. God's short-term plan was for support, food, rest, and exercise.

When faced with a person who is contemplating suicide, the primary agenda should be to collaboratively plan for immediate safety to sustain the person at risk during this crisis period. When the crisis passes and strength is regained, there will be time to address spiritual issues for growth and maturity.

HELP PLAN FOR SAFETY

Hear the cry for help	**P**eople
Evaluate risk	**L**ethal means
Listen to problems & possibilities	**A**lcohol and drugs
Plan for safety	**N**o harm/no suicide

1. *Hear the cry for help.* To intervene with a person who is at risk for suicide, we must first be able to identify that a person is in crisis.

A sad face is easily recognizable with no specialized training. When we observe that someone appears to be sad or depressed, the next thought should be, "Is she considering suicide?" Pay particular attention when a person has experienced a personal loss.

Loss of a close friend, family member, mentor, or loved one to death
Loss of a significant relationship due to conflict or separation

Loss of pride involving some form of humiliation

Loss of security, including loss of financial stability or employment

Loss of health, especially when diagnosed with a chronic or terminal
    illness

Loss of freedom, including severe punishment or incarceration

Loss of hope, meaning, or purpose in life

Loss of sobriety after a period of remaining clean and sober

Our fears of rejection and not knowing what to say or do often get in the way of our demonstrating love and kindness in opportune moments. When you observe a sad face, you have a choice. You can take a risk and become involved or you can turn away and pretend you did not notice. Any talk of a desire to die, depression, or expressions of hopelessness, even if said in jest, should be taken seriously. When you hear a cry for help, pay close attention. Choose to take a risk and become involved. The next step will be to evaluate the risk. Is the person so distressed that she is considering suicide?

2. *Evaluate risk.* How do we know if someone is considering suicide? Currently, there is no scientific test to accurately determine suicidal intent. The best indicator is simply to ask the person very directly if he or she has given serious thought to killing herself or himself. It is important to be very straightforward using the words "suicide" or "kill yourself."

Even if you feel nervous, you want to communicate both verbally and nonverbally that you genuinely desire to hear about their distress, no matter how disturbing it may be. "You're not thinking about killing yourself, are you?" implies that the questioner really does not want to know the truth. Simply ask, "Are you in so much pain that you've thought about killing yourself?"

If the person at risk acknowledges serious consideration of suicide, you will want to know if they have determined when, where, and how they might carry out their plan. A detailed plan of action considerably raises the level of risk. When a person has gone beyond thinking about suicide as a possibility to taking action—such as stockpiling pills, obtaining a gun and ammunition, giving away prized possessions, or writing notes to loved ones—the level of risk is high and merits a professional evaluation.

Other factors that increase the level of risk for suicide include an increased use of drugs and alcohol (particularly if this is a relapse in recovery), previous suicide attempts, a family history of suicide or violence, or serious untreated depression. Interrogation is not an effective method for suicide intervention. Rather, assessing risk involves listening to the person's story, reflecting what you hear, and asking pertinent questions along the way. "Have you ever felt this way before?" "What did you do to survive that time in your life?" "Have you known other people who have struggled with thoughts of suicide?"

3. *Listen to problems and possibilities.* Before offering any advice or sharing your perspective, listen until you understand her feelings, experiences, thoughts, and behaviors. Explore what has brought her to the point of considering suicide. Listen for what solutions she's already tried. When you allow yourself to truly hear the other person's pain and despair, then your compassion for her will come across as genuine. She will perceive that you honestly understand why she feels so hopeless.

As you hear her story, you can begin to observe possible reasons to live. "Oh, you have children. What are their ages . . . tell me about them." This takes time. During this process, you want to communicate that you are on her side and that you care.

4. *Plan for safety.* As you listen to their story and gently highlight reasons to live, you gradually shift the focus from the problems to possible strategies for getting through this time. You collaboratively develop a plan to help them cope during this crisis period. The plan should be a simple and straightforward strategy for surviving the next day or two. In most cases, you will not be able to solve all of the problems that have brought the person to this point, but you can identify some first steps toward getting help.

5. *People.* The plan begins with brainstorming a list of people she considers to be safe and helpful—friends, family, neighbors, a pastor,

a counselor, a physician, and yourself. You want to create a safety net of people who are willing to help. Write down specific names and phone numbers. Together call and schedule appointments with appropriate professionals. Together call a few people who will help support this person over the next few weeks. Make a copy of the list of names and numbers, including crisis line numbers (1-800-273-TALK or 1-800-SUICIDE are national hotlines). Make one for them to carry and one for you to keep as you facilitate the creation of a safety team.

6. *Lethal means.* When people kill themselves, they generally use means or weapons that are readily accessible to them. By removing all guns, knives, pills, etc., it becomes more difficult for the person to follow through with her plan. Buying time is always helpful when assisting someone through a crisis. Police are glad to pick up guns or knives. Pills can be left with friends, family, neighbors, or flushed down a toilet. As a shepherd, be sure to keep yourself safe in whatever preparations you make. A suicidal person can become violent with others if they are already committed to dying themselves.

7. *Alcohol and drugs.* "There is no safety without sobriety," states Paul Quinnett.[10] Alcohol is a depressant. When one is already depressed and adds alcohol into the mix, depression is exacerbated, thinking is clouded, inhibitions are lowered, and impulsive actions are common. Alcohol and drug usage significantly increase the risk of suicide for someone who is already considering the possibility, even for those who are not addicts.

A majority of people who commit suicide have some form of alcohol or drug in their system at the time of completion. Substance abuse makes it easier to follow through with lethal plans. Helping a person to remain clean and sober during a crisis period helps reduce the risk for suicide. The safety plan might include contacting a sponsor and/or attending support groups.

8. *No suicide until the next meeting.* The final but most important component of the plan is to negotiate a period of time that the person at risk agrees not to harm or kill herself or himself, accidentally or on purpose. People can genuinely promise not to harm themselves when

they have every intention to kill themselves. The two terms are not synonymous.

A person who is overwhelmed with the prospect of continued life can only commit to safety for a limited period of time. The person at risk may feel capable of making a 24- or 48-hour promise, but not a month, and certainly not a lifetime promise. You will want to schedule the next contact within the next few days and elicit a promise for safety between now and then.

The tone of the agreement should be a personal promise to you based on the relationship. You will support her in her safety plan, but she must assume the responsibility for keeping her promise. Asking them to recite their understanding of the agreement and plan will allow you to assess her understanding and sincerity. If you have any lingering doubt about her commitment to safety, it may be wise to seek an immediate evaluation by a professional. One can always call 911, go to the emergency room of a local hospital, or call the local crisis hotline for assistance. It is always better to err on the side of safety.

Helping a person to plan for safety not only allows the Lord to continue His work in that person's life, but it prevents untold grief of family and loved ones whose lives would be forever changed by an untimely tragedy. The Lord is the only One who can permanently and eternally save a life, but He sometimes gives us the privilege of helping to temporarily sustain a life here on earth, and in that there is great reward and blessing.

Carol's husband left her for another woman. Her children were grown and seemed to have such busy lives they had very little time to spare. Carol felt awkward attending church by herself and became sick to her stomach every time someone asked her where her husband was. Nancy, the director of women's ministry at church, noticed Carol's absence and called one day to check in with her. In the phone conversation, Nancy heard a somber tone in Carol's voice. As she gently and genuinely inquired as to how Carol was feeling, Nancy soon heard how discouraged Carol sounded. When she asked Carol about thoughts of suicide, Carol acknowledged that thoughts of suicide had become prominent in recent days.

Nancy listened carefully to Carol's story and then invited Carol for coffee and asked permission to invite a few of the trusted members from their women's group to join them. Nancy let Carol know how much she cared about her and that Nancy wanted to walk through this tough time together with her. Nancy wanted to help Carol get reconnected with some friends and family and share her story with those she trusted. With Nancy's help, Carol regained the courage she needed to reshape her life as a single woman. Over time, Carol began leading a support group for other single women. God used her experience to bring comfort and healing to others. Nancy's willingness to reach out to Carol resulted in help for many.

Working with people who are contemplating suicide is emotionally draining and risky work, but often quite rewarding. Caring, supportive friends and family make a huge difference in a person's ability to cope with life. A person can often reconnect with her hope in God when she sees His love reflected through one of His children. Most efforts to help someone recover a meaningful life will be met with success. There are effective treatments for depression; both medication and counseling can make a difference. A good sleep, a healthy diet, and exercise frequently improve a person's capacity to cope. But there are times when for some, it just does not seem to be enough.

In the case of Kristina, despite the best efforts of those around her, she finally took her own life. She just could not bear the thought of becoming the bitter, nasty person she had experienced in her mother and now in herself. Her family and people who had cared for her grieved deeply and wondered what more they could have done. Ultimately, as much as we might want to, we cannot force a person to stay alive. Sometimes people choose death. To care for people who are in life or death situations requires that we be solidly anchored in our faith and hope, regardless of outcome. We need to care for ourselves and others around us when the unthinkable occurs.

After a Suicide

Losing someone to suicide creates for survivors a complicated grief that is unlike any other. When a loved one takes her own life, the feelings that follow for the survivors are typically intense and conflicted. Reactions often include grief, shock, denial, embarrassment, anger, blame, shame, relief, disorientation, and frequently thoughts of suicide themselves.

Eight years after the suicide of one young man, his mother stated, "I will never 'get over' his death." A website dedicated to the memories of those who have died by suicide stated, "The person who completes suicide dies once. Those left behind die a thousand deaths trying to relive those terrible moments and understand . . . Why?"[11] Survivors struggle with the guilt of wondering if they could have somehow prevented the tragedy. They feel tremendous grief and sadness at the loss, and at the same time they feel intense anger at the betrayal they perceive. We would expect to be angry toward the murderer of a loved one, but what happens when the murderer *is* our loved one—suicide is murder of self.[12]

When working with survivors, shepherds will need to offer care, consolation, and compassion, which will include talking about how the survivors will be supported through this time. Caregivers can normalize the feelings survivors are experiencing and talk about the possibility that suicidal thoughts may occur for them. Point out how much pain a suicide creates. The personal pain that drives a suicide is passed on to the survivors in the form of grief, and so the pain of suicide can be unending.

It is a good time to seek a commitment to safety and life from the survivors. Talk about danger signs to watch for—depression, hopelessness, substance abuse, and isolation. Brainstorm available resources for times when these danger signs might appear. Strongly suggest forming an agreement that they will call a designated friend, counselor, or shepherd when the need for support arises. Suggest joining a survivor support group of others who have lost loved ones to suicide. Helping survivors to cope is a form of suicide prevention.

HELPFUL THINGS TO SAY AND DO
after a Suicide

1. **DO** say, "I am so sorry!" Extend sympathy with open arms.

2. **DO** allow the survivors to tell their story if they wish to, even if you've heard it before. Let the family label the death a "suicide."

3. **DO** create a safety plan of self-care, including food, sleep, exercise, and crisis numbers.

4. **DO** offer to accompany on difficult tasks such as funeral arrangements.

5. **DO** send flowers, a card, handwritten note, or leave a brief phone message, alleviating pressure for the recipient to respond.

6. **DO** give practical help for everyday living. Provide transportation, food for the family, mow the lawn, or care for children and pets.

7. **DO** maintain frequent, short visits.

8. **DO** talk about memories of the deceased.

9. **DO** encourage joining a support group for survivors (see websites for local groups).

10. **DO** mark the calendar and remember the family on anniversary dates of the death.

11. **DO** suggest it is okay to express their pain to God.

12. **DO** pray regularly for the survivor.

HURTFUL THINGS TO AVOID
after a Suicide

1. **DON'T** say, "I can't believe a Christian would do this!"

2. **DON'T** say, "Didn't you see any warning signs? Did you see it coming? Couldn't you stop him/her?"

3. **DON'T** suggest that their loved one may be in hell because of the suicide.

4. **DON'T** stop the person from talking about memories of their loved one.

5. **DON'T** say, "Let me know if there's anything I can do for you." Instead, be specific, "Would you like me to help in notifying family or friends of _____'s death?" Or, "I can come tomorrow and babysit for three hours. Would that be helpful?"

6. **DON'T** tell a survivor when they should be past the grief stage. Grieving a suicide is a long and complicated bereavement that often feels endless to the survivor.

Self-Care for Shepherds

Shepherds are not immune from feelings of sadness, despair, and weariness. If we are to remain calm, hopeful, and strong in times of crisis, then we must be building strength in the in-between times. We need to practice the self-care that we encourage in others—adequate sleep, healthy diet, regular exercise, and a reasonable schedule that includes time for relaxation. Maintaining a close walk with God, knowing how to tell Him the most intimate details of our thoughts and heart, conditions us to His presence with us at all times, especially in the crises moments. It is crucial to have a support network of people we can turn to and trusted sources for consultation already in place.

If a person we have helped commits suicide, we will need time to process our personal grief. We may need to take some extra time off from work or decrease some of our responsibilities. It will be essential to consult with a safe, knowledgeable person who can help us sort out our own questions. McGlothlin notes, "It is okay to get help!"[13] The Gospels tell us that Jesus left crowds of needy people, who desperately wanted Him, to go and pray to His Father (see Luke 5:15–16). If Jesus, being God in human form, needed time away for prayer, how much more do we mere humans need to take the time away from work to be restored, commune with Him, and solicit the Father's help.

Jesus came that we might have life.[14] He values our lives so much that He laid down His own life on our behalf. As shepherds of women in pain, we are also called to view life as precious and to work toward sustaining the gift of life in those we encounter. By hearing the cry for help from those who are struggling, taking the risk to ask them if they are thinking about suicide, evaluating their risk, listening to their problems and possibilities, and then helping them to plan for safety, we can help prevent a legacy of unending pain. Preserving life gives more time for God to work a masterpiece of beauty out of otherwise tragic circumstances.

Resources

1-800-273-TALK (8255) or 1-800-SUICIDE are national hotlines.

Websites

https://afsp.org: American Foundation for Suicide Prevention

https://www.suicidology.org: American Association of Suicidology

https://www.cdc.gov: Centers for Disease Control and Prevention

https://www.dbsalliance.org: Depression and Bipolar Support Alliance

https://qprinstitute.com: QPR Institute

https://save.org: Suicide Awareness Voices of Education

https://www.suicideinfo.ca: Centre for Suicide Prevention. A branch of the Canadian Mental Health Association.

https://teenlineonline.org: Teen Education and Crisis Hotline

https://www.crisisconnections.org/get-training/schools: Crisis Connections Washington State Youth Suicide Prevention Program

Books

Bongar, B., et al. *Risk Management with Suicidal Patients.* New York: The Guilford Press, 1999.

Demy, T. J., and G. P. Stewart, eds. *Suicide: A Christian Response.* Grand Rapids: Kregel, 1998.

Hsu, A. Y. *Grieving a Suicide: A Loved One's Search for Comfort, Answers & Hope.* Rev. and exp. ed. Downer's Grove, IL: InterVarsity Press, 2017.

Maris, Berman R., and M. Silverman. *Comprehensive Textbook of Suicidology.* New York: The Guilford Press, 2000.

McGlothlin, J. M. *Developing Clinical Skills in Suicide Assessment, Prevention, and Treatment.* Alexandria, VA: American Counseling Association, 2008.

Quinnett, P. G. *Counseling Suicidal People: A Therapy of Hope,* 3rd ed. Spokane, WA: The QPR Institute, 2009.

———. *Suicide: The Forever Decision.* Spokane, WA: Classic Publishing. Available as a free download at http://www.ryanpatrickhalligan.org/documents/Forever_Decision.pdf

Shea, S. D. *The Practical Art of Suicide Assessment.* Hoboken, NJ: John Wiley & Sons, Inc., 2002, 2011.

Related Scriptures

Psalm 46:1–2
Isaiah 50:7
Lamentations 3:19–24
Hebrews 4:14–16

AUTHOR BIO

KAY BRUCE, after earning a doctorate in clinical psychology in 1996, began teaching at Western Seminary where she continues to serve as a professor of counseling and Director of the Counseling Program. During this time she has also established two nonprofit counseling centers in the community, specialized in suicide prevention and intervention work, and made trips to Africa teaching trauma healing skills to indigenous church leaders. Kay and her husband, Paul, have been married for over forty years and have three grown children and five grandchildren. She enjoys family, gardening, and travel.

Chapter 16

Domestic Abuse

Stacey Womack
Founder and Director of
Abuse Recovery Ministry & Services (A.R.M.S.)

*W*hen Deb[1] entered the room, her appearance was heartbreaking. She was thin, pale, and shriveled with a voice barely audible. She sat with her head down, avoiding eye contact. Emotionally, spiritually and physically beaten down, she was literally dying because of emotional abuse.

But Deb's friends faithfully took turns driving her each week to a domestic abuse support group. She went through the fifteen-week "Her Journey" program[2] several times, gaining herself back little by little. It was an exciting day when she felt well enough to drive herself to the meeting. Her friends rejoiced at the change in her. She had come a long way. And what a journey! She told me her story . . .

Once, during a verbal altercation, Deb had stood up to her husband. He spit in her face, grabbed her by the throat, and threw her backward. She fell, breaking her tailbone in the process. He proceeded to jeer and taunt her by reminding her she would never tell the police. Confidently, he went out to the garage, leaving her sprawled on the floor where her two sons soon found her. They walked on past to check on Dad, which was typical. It was safer to make sure Dad calmed down.

In the meantime, Deb found the strength to get up and call the police. Unfortunately, the police in this small town happened to be friends with her husband. She heard them laughing in the garage, unwilling to make an arrest. He cheerfully agreed to stay away from the house for a few days. In the past, when there had been physical abuse, he would leave for a time, supposedly for a cooling-down period. After a few days she would call and apologize to him (for his abusive behavior) and then he would return. However, this time Deb filled out a restraining order instead.

While she was at the courthouse, her husband went to their home and took their two small dogs, both cars, money she had stashed, and everything that had any value to her. When she returned home, she was shocked to discover that she had no money, no transportation—nothing. Unable to work because of her declining health, she found herself in quite a quandary. Sadly, even though the restraining order stood, she lost her kids and she lost her home. She lost everything. Since he had the kids and the restraining order stood, she could not even go to their school functions. It was heart-wrenching.

Several months later, her church family set up an apartment for her, purchased the necessities, and decorated it. She called and sounded giddy as she said, "I haven't been this happy since I was seventeen years old!"

Time passed and I did not hear from her for a couple of years. One day we had some volunteers come into the office and I walked past one woman a couple of times wondering, "Could that be Deb?" It *was*! She literally looked twenty years younger. Her health had improved. Her facial color was glowing. She was beautiful! I was so amazed. God was also restoring her relationship with her sons, who had just brought her a dozen roses.

Understand the Issue

What is *domestic abuse* and *domestic violence*? "*Domestic abuse* is a pattern of behaviors used to gain and maintain *power* and *control* over an intimate partner."[3] "*Domestic violence* is the willful intimidation, physical assault, battery, sexual assault, and/or other abusive behavior perpetrated by an intimate partner against another. It is an epidemic affecting individuals in every community, regardless of age, economic status, race, religion, nationality or educational background."[4] Harming others physically and threatening their life are both illegal. Domestic abuse is not about one specific behavior, like hitting, as most people would think. It is really about any behavior by which a person gains power and control to intimidate or coerce their partner into getting what that person wants. There are several types of abuse, including: psychological/emotional, physical, sexual, property, animal, spiritual, financial, and verbal.

TYPES OF DOMESTIC ABUSE[5]

Types of Abuse	Examples
Psychological/emotional	Mind games, mental coercion, using looks or actions to generate fear, conditional affection, manipulation, spying, going through your partner's mail, email, purse, stalking, treating your partner like a servant, using the children, isolation, depriving your partner of friends and family, frequent moves (home or church), making the victim feel crazy, public humiliation. All forms of abuse are psychological.
Physical	Hitting, shoving, grabbing, slapping, kicking, punching, pushing, biting, tripping, spitting, pinching, hair-pulling, scratching, restraining, choking, smothering, posturing to intimidate by size and strength, making someone move or not move against their will.
Sexual	Rape, unwanted sexual comments, jokes or put-downs, attacking body parts, requiring her to dress a certain way, requiring bizarre sexual acts, whining, pouting, pornography, affairs, interrupting sleep, extreme jealousy.

TYPES OF DOMESTIC ABUSE (cont'd)

Types of Abuse	Examples
Property	Punching walls or doors, kicking or hitting furniture, throwing things, destroying things, slamming doors, pounding tables, sabotaging the car, destroying a phone or pulling the phone cord out of the wall.
Animal	Kicking the dog, throwing the cat, harming or killing an animal, threatening to get rid of a family pet, neglect, not feeding or watering your pet, throwing things at an animal.
Spiritual	Misusing Scriptures or God to control or abuse, negatively affecting someone's image of self or God, demanding submission and obedience, questioning their salvation, not letting them go or making them go to church, going to the pastor to discredit their spouse.
Financial	Controlling the money, unilateral decisions, lying about finances, hidden accounts, restricting employment, not paying child or spousal support, denying basic needs, requiring an account for every penny.
Verbal	Yelling, swearing, put-downs, name-calling, sarcasm, shouting, threats, abusive jokes, the silent treatment, continual arguing, belittling, controlling conversations, countering or discounting, criticizing, questioning, blaming, constant undermining.

Most domestic violence goes unreported.[6] Domestic abuse usually does not start with physical abuse. That often happens as the abuser[7] has to ramp up his level of abuse in order to maintain control. All forms of abuse are psychological in nature and are designed to keep the victim off balance and unsure of herself. Like sand constantly shifting beneath her[8] feet, she keeps trying to find a safe place to stand but there is no safe footing. The rules are always changing. What she said one day was okay but the next day it is not. Intimidating looks and stares imply, "You go there and you are going to pay for it." Cutting off supportive relationships through isolation tactics adds to her dilemma. It may be done overtly by saying, "You can't have contact with them" or by making her pay for it afterward. Friends and family may become so uncomfortable that they stop coming over. He plays mind games continually by telling her she said or did something that she did not say or do, or saying he did not say or do something that he did say or do. He continually tells her and others that she is crazy, or implies it. All these are psychologically abusive.

Financial abuse is something that we see the majority of our abusers use even if there has been separation or divorce. He continues to exert control over her through finances.

Stalking behavior is also common and can become frightening. Over a million women are stalked annually in the United States. Fifty-nine percent of those women are stalked by an intimate partner.[9] In the past, such behavior included showing up uninvited or not leaving when asked to. However, with modern technology, stalking has become more sophisticated than ever. Computer spyware is cheap and easy to get. Cameras and audiotapes add to the problem. The misuse of the cell phone with multiple calling or multiple texting is also used to keep track of her. The GPS unit, great for keeping track of kids, can also be used for stalking.

Domestic abuse and violence are about power and control. Many women have shared with me that the first time they experienced physical violence was on their wedding night. A lot of it has to do with a sense of entitlement or male privilege, thinking he "owns" her now. He may not say it like that but it is the mentality of what is going on in their relationship.

Statistically, younger women are more likely to experience physical abuse than older women. Females between twenty to twenty-four years of age are at the greatest risk of domestic violence from an intimate partner.[10] More often the older women are more compliant. Their husbands no longer have to use physical violence to get them to comply. They are so emotionally beaten down that they just do not have any strength or confidence to go against him. Now all it takes is a look or word for them to back down. Regardless of what form the abuse comes in, it all brings death to the victims. It brings death to their soul, the mind, will, emotions, their health, their dreams—everything.

Even if there has been physical violence, it is often brushed under the rug. "Well, it hasn't happened for six months . . ." By minimizing the abuse or denying it, she may try to convince herself she should not be afraid because it is not going to happen again. Yet, domestic violence is the single major cause of injury to women in the United States.[11] Physical violence does not usually happen every day, although there are women who experience physical violence all the time, every week. One in four women (25 percent) will experience domestic violence in her lifetime.[12] More than three women are murdered by their intimate partners in the US every day.[13] This is not something to be taken lightly. Women are more at risk of fatal injury after they leave their abuser. Seventy-five percent of domestic violence victims who are killed are murdered during the separation. Death is the ultimate control.[14]

All forms of abuse, whether sexual, animal, property, financial, et cetera, are used to gain and maintain power and control. Spiritual abuse is the misuse of Scripture to gain power and control. It is not about what is right scripturally. It is about winning, about being right and getting her to comply. (See chapter 20 on spiritual abuse.) The abuse may be designed to punish her. It may come from extreme jealousy of the affection that she is giving and receiving from her pet, friends, family, coworkers, or others. Most abusers are not abusing to primarily keep her fearful, but may use fear for the ultimate goal of convincing her she is inferior or less important than he is, and to get her to behave as he wants her to. An exception is abusers who are psychopaths and sociopaths; they use fear to exert power and control.

The abuser thwarts her efforts to be successful or to think that she can do anything. He is the one who is important and she is subordinate and must comply with all his wishes. He is smart and right; she is dumb and wrong. Since being wrong is viewed as weakness, he will fight to prove that he is right. Even when he knows she is right, he cannot let her win. So he continues to argue with her until she concedes. There is a lot of confusion and brainwashing used to keep her off balance. It is that "crazy-making" piece of abuse that causes a woman to lose her equilibrium.

Clearly, we have all said or done something that is abusive. However, that does not make everyone an abuser. There is a very distinct difference between someone who does it occasionally (and we all need to work on that because abuse is never okay) and somebody who has a life pattern of abuse. An abusive personality is someone who is using a pattern of behavior over and over, usually in multiple areas, for power and control.

Signs of Possible Victimization

It is often difficult to be able to identify victims of abuse as there are no sure signs. They are sitting in our church rows every week appearing as the perfect family and we are not aware of the pain behind the smile. Women may talk about struggles in their marriages but they do not define the issues as abuse. They may say they have communication problems or anger issues without understanding the destructive dynamics at work in their relationship.

Often, low self-esteem is a precursor to walking into an abusive relationship. Women who have grown up in an abusive environment are much more likely to enter into an abusive relationship. They accept the abuse as the norm from their past experience. Generally these women, from the moment they enter into an abusive relationship, stop becoming who God has called them to be because they are conforming to their abuser's view of them. They begin to lose themselves, their confidence, and their ability to make decisions.

Characteristics of a Victim

- Very low self-esteem, although she may be good at covering it up
- Loss of self-confidence
- Inability to make decisions and want others to tell her what she needs to do
- Depression
- Hopelessness—especially in Christian women who believe there is no way out of an abusive situation. Often they are counseled

against separation in fear that it will lead to divorce, so she feels stuck.

- Suicide—about 25–35 percent of abused women consider suicide. It is a huge issue for those who have lost hope. They sometimes pray that they would die or that their abuser would die as it seems this is the only way the abuse will end in their lifetime.

- Physical problems and health issues arise due to the stress of living under abuse. In response to unrelenting stress, toxic chemicals are continually released into the brain, which eat away at vital brain functioning and can cause multiple physical and mental illnesses.[15] Unlike women who are dying every day from gunshot wounds or stabbings, many are actually dying from the inside out, dying a little bit at a time.

- Isolation

- Possible signs of physical abuse (black eyes, unexplained bruising, broken bones, etc.). But most often physical abuse is done in areas that can be concealed.

- May have a history of abuse

- Takes responsibility for abuser's behavior

- Believes if she just prays enough, submits enough, or fasts enough, the abuse will end.

- She wants to please God and feels like she has failed.

- She may have a "fix-it" mentality, meaning she focuses on helping others rather than working on her issues and may attract needy people.

In most men, abuse starts in the teen years as they discover, "When I am intimidating, I get my own way. I have some power." If they were abused as children, they may have decided, "I am not going to be weak." So they take on the persona of being abusive. We surveyed our men[16] a few years back and asked when they first started using abusive behaviors (as we define it in all the different forms). The average age was eleven. He chose to be abusive at an early age; it is not the woman's fault. There are many reasons why an abuser behaves the way he does; often he has wounds from his past. But we have a saying at A.R.M.S., "There is always a reason for the abuse but never an excuse." Abusive behavior is never justified.

Characteristics of an Abuser[17]

- The abuser is often charming and believable.
- He may have come from an abusive past.
- He may have an explosive temper.
- He blames other people or circumstances for his problems.
- He may see himself as the victim.
- Often he is jealous, excessively possessive, and controlling.
- He has unrealistic and rigid role expectations.
- He is verbally abusive and cruel.
- He claims the relationship issues are her fault.
- He states that she has mental issues.
- He claims that she has cheated on him.
- He minimizes, justifies, and denies his abuse.
- He works very hard on image management; often the public views him as a great guy.
- He controls most of his home life: the finances, her thoughts, feelings, and actions.

The Cycle of Domestic Abuse

The traditional cycle of abuse was three-pronged: (1) tension building, (2) the event when the abuse happens, and (3) the honeymoon phase. We now use a seven-pronged model. (See "The Cycle of Abuse" wheel for a description of each phase that is predictably repeated again and again.) Some abusers never enter the guilt phase where they are afraid of getting caught, apologize, cry, give gifts, or make promises. Instead, he just rationalizes how it is her fault and never feels remorse for his abuse. The abuser, after rationalizing his abuse, pretends as though the abuse never happened. In order for her to stay safe, she does not bring up the abuse either. They both pretend that everything is fine and normal but she still has the sense of walking on eggshells.

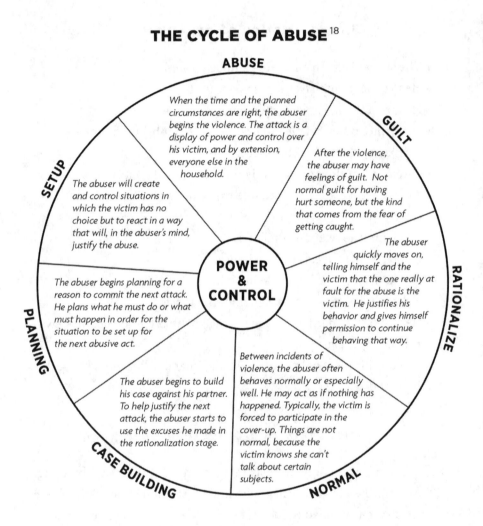

THE CYCLE OF ABUSE [18]

ABUSE

SETUP

GUILT

RATIONALIZE

PLANNING

NORMAL

CASE BUILDING

POWER & CONTROL

When the time and the planned circumstances are right, the abuser begins the violence. The attack is a display of power and control over his victim, and by extension, everyone else in the household.

The abuser will create and control situations in which the victim has no choice but to react in a way that will, in the abuser's mind, justify the abuse.

The abuser begins planning for a reason to commit the next attack. He plans what he must do or what must happen in order for the situation to be set up for the next abusive act.

The abuser begins to build his case against his partner. To help justify the next attack, the abuser starts to use the excuses he made in the rationalization stage.

After the violence, the abuser may have feelings of guilt. Not normal guilt for having hurt someone, but the kind that comes from the fear of getting caught.

The abuser quickly moves on, telling himself and the victim that the one really at fault for the abuse is the victim. He justifies his behavior and gives himself permission to continue behaving that way.

Between incidents of violence, the abuser often behaves normally or especially well. He may act as if nothing has happened. Typically, the victim is forced to participate in the cover-up. Things are not normal, because the victim knows she can't talk about certain subjects.

As he begins to build a case against her, using a lot of self-talk, he thinks about all the ways that she irritates him. She senses that his attitude toward her is changing. He is being snippier and not very nice. She can feel tension building. He begins to, subconsciously or consciously, plan the abuse. "If I get home tonight and the house is a mess, that's it. I'm just going to let her have it." Usually, the setup starts with an argument or he looks for the reason, like a mess in the house, to justify the abuse he will then do to her. Sometimes he begins questioning her about things that he knows will upset her. When she is worked up and starts yelling and screaming, he then feels justified and begins his abusive behavior or he calmly says, "You started it; it is all your fault. You are the one who is abusive. You're the one who has the anger problem." She begins to question and think, "Maybe that's true." Now he is justified to yell, scream, and throw things at her. So, the cycle plays out over and over. There might be a lot of smaller cycles that are not as overt that build on more obvious forms of abuse.

Victims and perpetrators may not recognize there is a cycle at first, but once they begin to identify it then they can begin to change. Separately, both can write the cycle out. But if they are not willing to identify it, then they can never change it.

Shepherding Insights

Women raised in abusive homes are more likely to walk into a relationship where abuse will be present. They are more likely to accept the familiar as normal, not being able to identify or label abusive behavior. After all, most victims think, "Domestic abuse is black eyes and beatings. That is not going on here—or at least not very often." We have good teachings about what healthy relationships look like but they may only see, "I need to be better and try harder." Yet, in reality, she cannot change enough to alter the behavior of an abusive partner. It is truly his problem and only he can change.

We need to be talking about what unhealthy relationships look like. Perhaps in a small group setting, like a Bible study, there will be discussion of life responses. If an abuse issue comes up, do not brush it under the rug. The woman may be minimizing it. "Well, it doesn't happen that often" or

"It wasn't like that . . . " or "He's a really good man. If I hadn't done_____,
he wouldn't have done that." An educated leader is able to say, "That is
abuse." For some women that may be the first reality check. She may be
shocked. "Oh no! No!" That might be upsetting to her, but it is good for
her to hear abuse called what it is and that it is *not* okay. Begin giving her
resources, books, and places she can go for more information. Sometimes
women call and ask, "I am not really sure if I'm in abuse or not . . ." "Okay.
Here is a book you can read. Give me a call back after you have read it."
Usually these women call back crying and say, "Oh, my gosh! Someone
wrote my life!" Another way to help a suspected abuse victim is to invite
(or take) her to a group meeting and see if she identifies with it.

Women may not talk about their abuse due to shame or feeling it is
their fault. Others may have tried to talk about it but it did not bring the
desired results. In fact, she may not have been believed, or sharing the
secret of abuse may have made it worse if the husband found out that
she had talked. Still others accept the abuse since they do not want to
displease God or they feel they need to be long-suffering.

Providing a safe environment may enable a woman to open up and
share about an incident that happened. That may be the first time you
realize there is abuse. You may need to call it abuse because she may
never have called it abuse herself. Give her resources as needed.

When a woman comes forward and admits she is in an abusive
relationship, believe her. The abuser is really the crazy one and it is not
her fault. She needs to hear that. Do not go question her husband as you
may be putting her in more danger. Women need our support to think
through a safety plan, to get into a safe place if there is physical violence,
and to begin to receive healing. She may need legal counsel. Do not give
up on her. Walk with her during this difficult journey. It is a big step for
her to admit the abuse in her home. She does not want to displease God
and may fear alienation from her faith community if she separates from
her abuser. She is likely to feel that she is failing God and failing every-
body around her when she makes the decision to stand up against the
abuse. However, you cannot rush a woman along in the process. If she is

not ready to take steps to end the abuse in her life, all you can do is say, "I love you. I am here for you. I don't believe that what your husband is doing to you is okay. I will stand with you and be here for you if you ever want to talk." God is on the side of the brokenhearted and those whose spirits have been crushed (Psalm 34:18). We should be too.

Sometimes, with physical abuse, others will try to help her move out. However, if she is not ready to move out, she will probably go back within a few days or a couple of weeks. She may not be strong enough at that point. No one works harder than an abused woman to try to save her marriage. She tries every avenue possible. Typically, she has a library of self-help books. She will go to counseling and go on retreats. She will be praying and fasting. She works so hard to try and fix it. But it does not work because he has to be the one who chooses to get the help that he needs.

On average, a woman will leave her abuser eight times before she leaves for good. Usually when a woman leaves, all she is doing is trying to make a statement to him, "This needs to change." And then he seems like he is changing. He makes promises and he is nice. He exchanges his mean controlling behavior to nice controlling behavior for a while, such as making promises, apologizing, buying gifts, or helping around the house. We view those kinds of things as showing repentance. We have been taught, as Christian women, to forgive and extend mercy. But we are often out of balance without the understanding that accountability needs to accompany mercy. An apology never lowers the risk of reoffending.

When women are in a recovery or support group, they get affirmed setting boundaries to end the abuse they are suffering and they make less back and forth moves. Often, it has taken years to get up the courage to admit that there is a problem in their relationship. They may take our number and not call us until a year later. It may take them another two to six months to attend a group after their first phone call to us. This is a very long, slow process. It is a very complicated issue, especially for Christian women because of their desire to do what is right before God and before their spiritual leaders. Unfortunately, many church leaders are misinformed about domestic abuse issues and do not have the education or experience to keep women safe. Just recently, a pastor said to a woman in one of our support groups that it was her duty to stay in the relationship. We cannot just send women back into abusive relationships to die, either literally or spiritually. The appropriate steps need to be taken to ensure the woman's safety, as well as offering the appropriate services for the abuser, but the victim's safety needs to be the first priority.

It is so important for pastors and caregivers to understand the cycle of abuse. When the husband brings her roses and says, "I'll never do it again," it is not the end. Without intervention the cycle will continue on.

Many victims ask for couples counseling. And most perpetrators ask for couples counseling when she is at the point of separation. Now he is ready to go to couples counseling because he wants the counselor to put her in her place and show her how unbiblical her responses are. That is very, very difficult. Abusive men will often call the counselor ahead of time and discredit her. *Couples counseling is NOT recommended for many reasons. Some of those reasons include:*[19]

- Focusing on the relationship assumes that each person contributes to the abusive behavior, when in truth the perpetrator is solely responsible for his abusive behavior.
- Focusing on issues other than the abusive behavior allows the abusive behavior to continue.
- Danger to the victim may increase due to the counselor's involvement in the relationship. The abuser wants to maintain control and any outside interference may lead to escalation of the abuse.
- A couple's counselor who is focused on the relationship may be hesitant to strongly confront just one of the individuals.
- Out of fear of further abuse, the victim may not be honest about the abuse in a couple's session, giving the false impression that things are better than they really are.
- On the other hand, the victim may have a false sense of security in a couple's session and disclose information she normally would

not, believing the counselor will keep her safe. Once they have left the safety of the counseling room, the husband may then retaliate.

If couples counseling is to take place, it will be well after he works through his power and control issues. He must display genuine repentance, accountability, and a new sustained pattern of relating to his wife—not powering over her. Domestic abuse is a very complicated issue. We do well to remember that abuse is not normal marital conflict. Abuse is not an anger issue (which is a feeling) but a control issue (which is a choice). Abuse is an issue of oppression, not submission. Separation may be necessary if he is unwilling to make the needed changes. In some cases the separation may last a long time, but always with a hope of future reconciliation.

God does not sacrifice a person for the sake of relationship. We must look at the whole heart of God. We need to think as a parent protecting a child. It is our responsibility to protect a powerless one. Wives are not property to be used and abused, but they are a gift from God to be nurtured, loved as Christ loves the church,[20] and protected. Laws protect citizens from assault and battery as well as slander and other forms of harm. Courts remove children from abusive homes. Even so, the law protects women from treacherous relationships. How much more should the church?

> One woman on a mission trip to Afghanistan said she felt safer in this war zone than at home. As she was praying and telling God how He was supposed to fix her abusive relationship so they could be a testimony to others, God told her, "You have tried everything you can to fix this and it's not going to work. I sent My Son to die for you and your husband and I'm not calling you to die along with Him."[21]

As shepherds to women in pain, we must keep in mind these priorities in ministering to women who are abused.

1. SAFETY for the woman and children
2. ACCOUNTABILITY for the abuser
3. RESTORATION of individuals and, IF POSSIBLE, relationships, or MOURNING the loss of the relationships

HELPFUL THINGS TO SAY AND DO[22]

The abused woman

1. **DO** believe her. Her description of the violence is only the tip of the iceberg.

2. **DO** reassure her that this is not her fault. She does not deserve this treatment. It is not God's will.

3. **DO** give her referral information: services for abused women, shelters, or the national hotline.

4. **DO** support and respect her choices. Even if she chooses initially to return to the abuser, it is her choice. She has the most information about how to survive.

5. **DO** encourage her to get a safety plan: set aside some money, copies of important documents for her and her children, a change of clothes hidden or in the care of a friend, how to exit the house if violence erupts, what to do about the children if they are in school, asleep, etc.

6. **DO** protect her confidentiality. Do not give information about her or her whereabouts to the abuser or to others who may pass information along to the abuser.

7. **DO** emphasize that the marriage covenant has been abused by the violence from her partner. The abuse is not her fault. Assure her of God's love and presence and your commitment to walk with her through this valley. Help her to see that God wants her to seek protection and safety for herself and her children. Pray with her.

HURTFUL THINGS TO NOT SAY OR DO

The abused woman

1. **DON'T** minimize her danger. Only she fully knows her situation. You can be a reality check for her. "From what you have told me, I am concerned for your safety."

2. **DON'T** react with disbelief, disgust, anger, or passivity at what she tells you. Let her know that you are concerned and that what the abuser has done to her is wrong and not deserved by her.

3. **DON'T** blame her for his violence. If she is blaming herself, try to reframe it: "Even if you had the supper late or forgot to water the lawn, that is no reason for him to be violent. This is his problem."

4. **DON'T** recommend couples counseling or approach her husband and ask for his side of the story. These actions will endanger her.

5. **DON'T** send her home with a prayer and directive to submit to her husband, bring him to church, or be a better Christian wife.

6. **DON'T** encourage her to quickly forgive and quickly take him back. An apology never lowers the risk of reoffending. He should take the necessary steps to show through his attitude and actions genuine remorse, genuine repentance, and a sustained pattern of changed behavior before she considers working toward reuniting.

7. **DON'T** encourage her dependence on you or become emotionally/sexually involved with her.

8. **DON'T** do nothing. This leaves the victim unsupported and unsafe. Consult with colleagues in the wider faith community who can assist you.

HELPFUL THINGS TO SAY AND DO

The abuser

1. **DO** approach him and express your concern and support, if possible, by holding him accountable, *once the victim is in a safe place.* Pastors have a great opportunity to encourage men to attend a domestic violence batterer intervention program. Early research shows when church leaders refer men to these programs, they are not only more likely to attend but also complete, even more so than when the courts require them to go. Also, hold him accountable to the separation agreement his wife has requested.

2. **DO** address his religious rationalizations he may be offering and questions he may have. (It is difficult if he is in a church that supports irrational positions. That can be very, very difficult. The court system has referred men to A.R.M.S. because their church supported men spanking their wives.)

3. **DO** name the violence and control as his problem, not hers. Only he can stop it, but be willing to offer your help.

4. **DO** refer him to a program that specifically addresses abusers.

5. **DO** assess him for suicide or threats of homicide. Warn the victim of any threats he makes.

6. **DO** pray with him. Ask God to help him stop his violence or use of abuse, repent, and find a new way. Assure him of your support in this endeavor and the importance of him taking responsibility.

7. **DO** find ways to collaborate with agencies and law enforcement to hold him accountable.

HURTFUL THINGS TO NOT SAY OR DO

The abuser

1. **DON'T** approach him or let him know that you know about his violence or abuse *unless all three of these are in place*: (a) You have the victim's permission; (b) She is aware that you plan to talk to him; and (c) She is in a safe place separated from him. The perpetrator should not be held accountable until after she is in a place of safety. That is *really important*.

2. **DON'T** meet him alone and in private. Meet only in a public place with other people around.

3. **DON'T** believe him easily or allow him to use religious excuses for his behavior.

4. **DON'T** pursue couples counseling if you are aware that there is violence or power and control tactics being used in the relationship.

5. **DON'T** go to him to confirm the victim's story.

6. **DON'T** give information about his partner or her whereabouts.

7. **DON'T** be taken in by his minimization, denial, or lying about his violence. Don't accept his blaming her or other rationalizations for his behavior.

8. **DON'T** be taken in by his "conversion" experience. If it is genuine, it will be a tremendous resource as he proceeds with accountability. If it is phony, it is only another way to manipulate you and the system and maintain control of the process to avoid accountability.

9. **DON'T** advocate for the abuser to avoid legal consequences for his violence. He should be encouraged to be honest and accountable. The best way to love him is to allow him to go through that.

10. **DON'T** forgive an abuser quickly and easily. Avoid confusing remorse with true repentance.

11. **DON'T** send him home with a prayer. Work with others to hold him accountable. Lay out specific agreements that he is to follow through with and check with him regularly to make sure he is.

12. **DON'T** provide character witness for purposes of legal proceedings. This is very important. Abusers are very manipulative. We always should have the victim's safety in mind above all else.

Resources

Websites

https://abuserecovery.org: Abuse Recovery Ministry & Service (A.R.M.S.) is a Christian agency that has resources available to equip pastors and other caregivers with the tools they need to be able to understand domestic abuse and violence and to deal with it effectively. ARMS National Office: 866-262-9284 or 503-846-9284. P. O. Box 663, Hillsboro, OR 97123.

https://www.theraveproject.org: RAVE is an initiative that seeks to bring knowledge and social action together to assist families of faith impacted by abuse.

https://www.faithtrustinstitute.org: Faith Trust Institute – working together to end sexual and domestic violence

https://www.lifeskillsintl.org: Life Skills International

https://www.thehotline.org: National Domestic Violence Hotline 1-800-799-7233 or 1-800-787-3224 (TDD)

Books

Alsdurf, James, and Phyllis Alsdurf. *Battered into Submission: The Tragedy of Wife Abuse in the Christian Home.* Downers Grove, IL: IVP 1989; Eugene, OR: Wipf & Stock, 1998.

Bancroft, Lundy. *Why Does He Do That?* New York: Berkley Publishing Group, 2002.

Clark, Pastor Ron. *Setting the Captives Free.* Eugene, OR: Cascade Books, 2005.

Evans, Patricia. *The Verbally Abusive Relationship: How to Recognize it and How to Respond.* Avon, MA: Adams Media Corporation, 1992, 1996, 2010.

Kroeger, Catherine Clark, and Nancy Nason-Clark. *No Place for Abuse: Biblical & Practical Resources to Counteract Domestic Violence.* Downers Grove, IL: InterVarsity Press, 2001, 2010.

Kubany, Edward, Mari McCaig, and Janet Laconsay. *Healing the Trauma of Domestic Violence: A Workbook for Women.* Oakland: New Harbinger Publications, 2004.

Miles, Reverend Al. *Domestic Violence, What Every Pastor Needs to Know.* Minneapolis: Fortress Press, 2000, 2011.

Related Scriptures

Psalms 11:5b; 17:8–9; 55:3–5, 12–13, 20–21; 72:12; 107:14–15
Proverbs 18:21
Isaiah 61:1–3
Malachi 2:16

AUTHOR BIO

STACEY WOMACK is the founder and executive director of Abuse Recovery Ministry & Services (A.R.M.S.). She has dedicated herself to building community awareness around domestic abuse issues from a faith perspective since 1997. Stacey, along with staff and volunteers, has served victims of domestic violence through victim recovery classes, prevention programs for men, and intervention programs for youth. Stacey's dedication and determination have grown a small "grassroots" endeavor into a viable organization that has done much to end the cycle of abuse for thousands of women, men, and youth. Stacey is married to Jerry, and they have six adult children.

Chapter 17

Sexual Abuse

Kathy Rodriguez, Psy.D, Psychologist

*N*orma shares her story of abuse:

> I grew up believing that I was the only one with this problem. I never told anyone, because I was afraid people would not believe me, much less understand. I remember hearing Dad say, "No one will believe you if you say anything. So don't say a word. If you do, I'll have to go to jail, our family will be destroyed, and it will be all *your* fault."
>
> I really did believe it was all my fault. In the back of my mind, I was convinced that somehow I had asked for it. I felt sure this didn't happen to other people. After all, my dad was a fine Christian man. He went to church every Sunday, sang in the choir, and looked like the clean-cut, all-American good old Joe.
>
> It started when I was five years old. When Dad tucked me in at night, he whispered, "This is our 'special time' together, and you are my precious little princess." He usually rubbed my arms and legs to help me get warm when I was between the cold sheets. Then his

hands wandered farther up my legs, until finally his fingers went inside my panties.

I remember the first time it happened. It's kind of like a snapshot in my mind. I had almost fallen asleep. But when I felt his hand inside my underwear, I jerked away, saying, "Dad, I don't like that! Don't do it anymore." He promised me he wouldn't and quietly crept out of the room. He never kept his promise. It happened again . . . and again.

When I was twelve and started developing physically, Dad became jealous. He did not let me have boys as friends. They could not call me more than once, and he made sure they didn't. Whenever I talked to a boy on the telephone, he went to the extension and rudely interrupted our conversation, saying, "I'm expecting an important call. This is not a convenient time for you to talk." Needless to say, the boys never called back.

One friend, Kevin, worked up enough courage to come to my house. Dad met him at the door and told him I wasn't home. Later, when we had our "special" time together, he said, "Boys are only after one thing. I'm just trying to protect you." Feeling confused, I remember asking, "Then, why is it all right for you to do these things to me?" That's when he told me that it is the responsibility of a good father to introduce his daughter to sex. I wanted to believe Dad really loved me and that I was his special princess. Now I realize I was just an exploited toy to him.

I often wondered if Mom knew what was happening. It always seemed as if she was sick. Most of the time she stayed in her darkened bedroom, for days on end, with migraine headaches. When she ventured outside her four walls to spend time with the rest of the family, she was quiet. Dad ruled the house, and Mom jumped to his commands. As a strict disciplinarian, Dad beat my brother whenever he did something wrong. Mom didn't say much about the beatings or about Dad's "special" times with me. She seemed like a prisoner in her own little world. I was afraid to tell. I remember curling up on my bed, in the corner of my room, crying and thinking I must be a terrible daughter for Dad to hurt me this way.

I wish all this was a bad dream and that these terrible flashbacks would disappear. It has been twenty years, but the shame is just as real as if it happened yesterday. Every day a reminder seems to cross my path. My husband thinks there's something wrong with me, because I don't enjoy sex. But the thought of it turns my stomach. I feel so guilty. When my husband holds me, it reminds me of my father touching me. I enjoy being hugged and caressed, but somehow I feel guilty, because my father did those things to me too. I have many conflicting feelings. My marriage is not the only relationship this affects. It's really hard for me to make friends and to trust people. I guess I fear that when they get to know me, they won't like me.[1]

Understand the Issue

Childhood sexual abuse is devastating. It not only traumatizes the child and destroys her innocence but it has far-reaching effects. A child, much like a sponge, is taking in everything as she tries to make sense of her world. The trauma of abuse skews her understanding as she learns about trust factors and how people relate to one another. Often the secret of the abuse is unreported and kept hidden for many, many years. But unhealthy dynamics were set in motion that continue until the pain of the abuse is exposed and dealt with. Healing is possible for women who have been sexually violated but it is a long and painful process. Many never experience that healing journey.

Some women who have been abused do not know what actually constitutes sexual victimization. Victims are usually unfamiliar with the fact that long-range effects may arise from sexual abuse. Defining the terms used will bring understanding.

Definitions

Incest describes any sexual approach, including exposure, genital fondling, oral-genital contact, and vaginal or anal intercourse between relatives by blood, marriage, or adoption.[2]

Sexual molestation refers to the inappropriate sexual stimulation of a child, when no family relationship exists.[3]

The *sexual misuse* of a child refers to situations in which a child is exposed to any type of sexual stimulation considered inappropriate for his or her age, level of development, or role in the family. Showing a child a pornographic magazine, touching a child's body inappropriately, or allowing a child to view an X-rated movie can be considered sexual misuse. Encouraging a child to be in bed with the opposite-sex parent, when the parent is naked, can also be considered sexual misuse if the child is old enough to understand that this is wrong.[4]

Touching offenses include fondling; vaginal, oral, or anal intercourse or attempted intercourse; touching of the genitals; incest; prostitution; and rape. *Non-touching offenses* refer to verbal sexual stimulation intended to arouse the child's interest, obscene telephone calls, exhibitionism, voyeurism (that is secretly viewing sexual activity between adults or children and adults when such viewing is unknown to the participants), and the general letting down of privacy so the child can watch or hear an act of sexual intercourse.[5]

SEXUAL ABUSE CHART[6]

Term	Type of Offense	Relationship
Incest	Touching Non-touching	Family
Sexual Molestation	Touching	Nonfamily
Sexual Misuse	Touching Non-touching	Nonfamily Family

Sexual assault includes all of the above.[7] One out of every six American women has been the victim of an attempted or completed rape in her lifetime. That adds up to 17.7 million women.[8] Nine out of ten rape victims are female.[9]

Victims of sexual assault are

   3 times more likely to suffer from depression.

   6 times more likely to suffer from post-traumatic stress disorder.

  13 times more likely to abuse alcohol.

  26 times more likely to abuse drugs.

   4 times more likely to contemplate suicide.[10]

Long-term Effects of Sexual Abuse[11]

- Self-defeating or acting-out behavior (self-mutilation, suicide attempts, illegitimate pregnancies, prostitution, and drug/alcohol abuse)
- Psychological problems (depression, suicidal thoughts, mind-set leading to sexual/physical victimizations, multiple personality)
- Medically unsupported physical complaints (headaches/back problems, frequent among women of incest)
- Interpersonal problems (difficulties establishing relationships and marital problems)

    Victims tend to take responsibility for others' behavior. They have difficulty achieving intimacy with others. They tend to think if they please others, they will be viewed as "perfect." Victims obsessively worry about problems and sabotage their efforts to change.

- Sexuality confusion (promiscuity, frigidity, lack of sexual enjoyment, confusion over sexual identity)
- Low self-esteem (unassertive, worthless, undeserving, and helpless). Victims minimize their own abilities and maximize others' strengths. They are overly critical of self, blame self, and become responsible for others' behavior. They lack willingness to trust, a sense of protection, and lack a desire to socially relate with others.

Additional long-term effects stem from the three basic methods offenders use to groom victims: triangulation, isolation, and power and control.[12]

Triangulation is the inappropriate inclusion of a third party in a strictly two-party relationship. In many cases of incest, the father triangulates his victim by intentionally reversing the roles of spouse and daughter. He relates to his daughter as a wife, leaving his wife to become a potential rescuer of the daughter. He is able to coerce the daughter into meeting his needs. Sadly, the mother may not know what the father is doing or, even if she suspects, she may be too afraid the family will be destroyed if she intervenes. She also stands to lose her husband and the financial support of the family. The daughter, who loves both her parents, may have many misgivings about what Dad is doing to her but is hoping Mom will rescue her. When there is no rescue, the child feels helpless to change the situation and believes this behavior must be normal for families. In actuality, healthy families form a strong parental unit that does not inappropriately include children in the middle.

One of the long-term effects of sexual abuse is victims using triangulation when they become adults. Whatever the relationship might be, whether it is at work with a boss or within the nuclear family that they have now, the relationships are often a triangle. There is always somebody that is hurting them in some way, usually emotionally. And they are appealing to a third party to help with the pain. So there is a triangle: the perpetrator, the potential rescuer, and the victim.

The victim will often move among the different elements of the triangle. It is easier for her to cross that invisible boundary from assertive or aggressive to become abusive. As a child, she learned that overpowering had an effect. She may respond abusively to her own children. It may seem to undo the trauma that was done to her if she is now the one who is stronger and can overpower another.

Another common dynamic in this triangle is the enabling and rescuing types of behavior. For instance, a woman may call her husband's boss and cover for her drunken husband's absence. Or she may finish her child's report, after he has procrastinated on it for a month, so he can turn it in to his teacher on time.

Isolation breaks the victim's ties with others who may be able to help. An abusive father limits the contacts with the outside world that his daughter and wife are allowed to make. He works hard to prevent interference from anyone who might intervene. Later the adult victim often maintains the same silence and seclusion in her few relationships. In a healthy family, expression of feelings between family members is encouraged and supported. In a dysfunctional family, members do not honestly communicate their feelings. Isolation inhibits communication with people in the outside world, unlike the healthy family, which creates an atmosphere that welcomes and encourages interrelationships and stimulation from the outside world.

Power and control is what motivates the perpetrator. In order to feel powerful and in control, he trains his victims to meet his demands. In this dysfunctional family, use of authoritarian control violates the personal space of family members. On the other hand, in a functional family, freedom and autonomy foster personal control and do not violate family rules.

An abused woman was overpowered and controlled. She was not even in control of her own personhood or safety. So in an attempt to have some control over the uncontrollable, she exerts more control in other areas of her life, like food and relationships. There is a high correlation between sexual abuse and eating disorders. An eating disorder is an attempt to have control. She may even be overly controlling with her children, especially with their safety. In an attempt to make up for the lack of safety in her own life, she can erect walls in the name of boundaries and become obsessive about safety for her children.

Boundary issues are common for sexual abuse victims. While some may set up walls instead of boundaries as mentioned above, victims can also have difficulties knowing and setting healthy boundaries as an adult. In the formative years of childhood, she should have learned what good boundaries are and what they are not. For the woman who has gone through any kind of abuse, however, boundaries become fluid and blurred. The woman can quickly be on an emotional overload. She does not feel strong enough herself to figure things out or to have the wherewithal to say, "No, that is not right, I'm not going to cross that line." She will leave gaping holes in her boundaries that result in getting abused again, while overcontrolling other boundaries.

Victim Characteristics

Hyper-responsibility is a characteristic seen in women who experience some type of childhood abuse. The perpetrator does not take any responsibility for his actions. Often the potential rescuer is not strong enough to be able to validate that child or maybe she does not even know that there has been abuse; now the child takes responsibility. The child may form a false belief or a vow that says, "It is up to me to take care of this." And so she takes care of herself. That false belief follows her through different situations in order to survive life. It might not be something as traumatic as sexual abuse when she is older but that belief is operative and she becomes hyper-responsible. Whatever the situation is, it is up to her to take care of it because that is what sexual abuse taught her. Since no one else took responsibility for the abuse, she also decides, *it must be my fault*. That false belief will follow her as she continues to try and make sense of the world. Perceptions were created and she applies them to new situations as she grows into adolescence and adulthood thinking "this is the way the world works."

Another indicator of childhood sexual abuse is anxiety disorders. Women who are high-strung, have a high level of anxiety, and demonstrate a hyper-vigilance often have been abuse victims. Although this does not always indicate abuse, it is usually evident if there has been abuse.

The trauma of sexual abuse brings a fight, flight, or freeze response in the limbic area of the brain. Once a child has experienced this kind of traumatic event, it is difficult to create normalcy. The results are what Patrick Carnes calls trauma blocking, trauma repetition, and trauma bonds.[13] All of these come out of the trauma and how the brain processes it. The executive function of the brain located in the frontal lobe tells one how to get out of unsafe situations, how to plan, and how to execute, but does not fully develop until around the age of twenty-five. A child does not have the capacity to know how to make good sense out of what is happening to her, or how to respond. Once the brain's frontal lobe is fully developed, then she can learn coping strategies as she thinks through past events. Typically this happens in therapy. She will go back and reexperience the trauma and find new tools for coping, putting a new experience into the limbic system. Essentially it says, "Okay, I can go through situations that I have no control over and I can survive."

That fight, flight, or freeze response is in every single one of us. It takes a lot of intense reprogramming to get a person healthy. Unfortunately, the limbic system is not changed with words alone. New experiences are what reprogram the mind. New experiences can change the fight, flight, or freeze response.

That is why it is really common for an adult female victim to have a misperception of touch. Her husband with good intent might come up and grab her playfully. Instead of feeling joy, she is immediately on guard, because the experience that first activated the fight, flight, or freeze response was one of trauma and terror. Her husband, of course, feels offended because his wife responded this way but she does not have any other "folder" for this experience to go into. Until they can come together and work through that, he has to be willing to acknowledge, "Hmm, she does this when I touch her there. How do I not put her in a terror state?" Sometimes the victim has to ask, "When is a hug just a hug? Or is this a hug that is going to go someplace?" She needs to have a vote in the answer. She did not get a vote when she was younger. Her response to a hug can actually change if both husband and wife are willing to process it. Gradually she can move to a place where she is experiencing safe touch. With a lot of reprogramming, it is possible for a sexual abuse victim to feel safe in a sexual relationship.

When a husband hears about his wife's childhood abuse, he may become angry, understandably so. His first response might be to go punch the lights out of the perpetrator, to tell off her father, or whomever did this to her. This is not a good idea for several reasons, but primarily because he is unintentionally taking the power away from his wife to confront in an appropriate time and place. Less often a husband will be incensed, feeling high levels of anger and rage when the victim herself is not feeling or expressing those at all. Instead, she tries to placate her husband and calm him down. That is actually called *projective identification*; the victim unconsciously projects onto the husband what she should be feeling.

Shepherding Insights

Victims need listeners. Part of the whole healing process includes a lot of grief work. Become familiar with the five progressive stages of the grief process: (1) denial, (2) anger turned outward, (3) anger turned inward, (4) genuine sorrow, and (5) resolution and acceptance.[14] When someone dies and grief work begins, the survivor needs to tell the story of the one who died, including the relationship they had. Although a sexual abuse victim can get stuck in denial for quite awhile, when the story starts coming to the surface, she needs to talk about it. Sometimes that does not feel safe because she thinks she is going to be judged or disbelieved. A shepherd, friend, or neighbor with whom she feels safe enough to talk, who will listen, not try to fix her but bring comfort, can be a great gift to her.

One of the greatest gifts this woman in pain may receive is Scripture. Encourage her with verses such as "But you, God, see the trouble of the afflicted; you consider their grief and take it in hand. The victims commit themselves to you; you are the helper of the fatherless" (Psalm 10:14). "So do not fear, for I am with you; do not be dismayed, for I am your God. I will strengthen you and help you; I will uphold you with my righteous right hand" (Isaiah 41:10). "Restore to me the joy of your salvation and grant me a willing spirit, to sustain me" (Psalm 51:12). Read Psalm 23 or 139 together.

The fear and anxiety that surface when an abuse victim revisits the pain of the past may prompt her to stay in the place of just talking about it. She may not want to get help to process it. A shepherd can be instrumental in helping her choose to get professional help. Offer to go with her to the first appointment, but insist she make the call. It is important that she be the one to ask for help by making the appointment. This is also an opportunity for her to exercise control over her life again, instead of a caregiver usurping her power of choice.

HELPFUL THINGS TO SAY AND DO[15]

1. **DO** talk with her privately rather than in front of others.

2. **DO** keep what a victim shares confidential.

3. **DO** be a good listener with your eyes and ears.

4. **DO** provide reassurance in your words and body language. Hugs from women shepherds say a lot! *(Ask permission first.)*

5. **DO** advise victims of community resources where they can receive help.

6. **DO** help victims follow through with counseling. Go to the first session with her, if she desires.

7. **DO** remind her that God loves her, wants to heal and restore her.

8. **DO** tell a victim repeatedly of your love for her, especially when she feels unlovable.

9. **DO** expect many emotional ups and downs during recovery.

HURTFUL THINGS TO AVOID[16]

1. **DON'T** display horror, shock, or disapproval.

2. **DON'T** pry into unrelated family matters.

3. **DON'T** place blame or judgment on the victim.

4. **DON'T** give advice as to how victims should solve their problems.

5. **DON'T** ask *why* questions. Practice good listening skills. When appropriate ask "what," "where" or "how" questions, such as "what happened next?" "How did you feel?"

6. **DON'T** make sexual abuse into solely a spiritual problem. The ability of the victim to move to a place of health is clearly empowered by a genuine relationship with Jesus Christ. However, there are many facets to an abusive experience and these must be included in understanding recovery.

7. **DON'T** force victims to talk about their recovery process. Let them initiate.

8. **DON'T** force victims to think positive. A period of grieving is necessary for recovery to occur.

9. **DON'T** impose your timetable for healing on victims. God is working in them at His pace.

For every one hundred people in your community, church, or organization, you can expect to find more than thirty women and about fifteen men who were molested before the age of eighteen. If sexual abuse were a biological disease, it would be declared a major epidemic of catastrophic proportions. The whole country would be mobilized toward treatment and prevention of any further outbreak.[17]

A woman who is struggling with sexual abuse should be encouraged to go to a licensed professional such as a psychologist, a clinical social worker, or a licensed professional counselor. These women have been severely traumatized and need someone who is experienced in sexual abuse trauma. Sometimes help from a well-intentioned friend with similar life experiences can actually do damage if she offers self-help advice, particularly if the friend has not processed her own past abuse. Some women may gravitate to a pastor for help because it is free. Most of the time, pastors are not the best clinically trained people to assist deeply wounded individuals. Abuse is trauma. Someone who is skilled in clinical trauma will best be able to help a traumatized individual because of the complexities of the brain and limbic system. However, in addition to a clinician, a shepherd who consistently expresses acceptance, grace, and support will be invaluable in the extensive journey the abused victim has before her.

INDICATORS OF HEALING CHART[18]

The Survivor	The Victim
Is able to cultivate intimate relationships with the opposite sex without compromising her own identity.	Experiences difficulty in forming relationships with men who don't compromise her.
Draws self-esteem from focusing on her relationship with God and her internal qualities.	Draws her self-esteem from a preoccupation with accomplishments, appearance, and other external qualities.
Experiences healing in her relationships with loved ones who were part of her abuse.	Closes out relationships with loved ones who were part of her abuse.
Is able to assertively, honestly, and directly express feelings and needs to others.	Does not express her feelings and needs directly and honestly.
Cares for herself by establishing a broad support system.	Tends to withdraw from others, rather than asking for support.
Becomes increasingly comfortable in sexual expressions with a loved one.	Is sexually inappropriate, either avoiding sexual expressions altogether or indiscriminately expressing them.
Is comfortable with expressing her personal belief system.	Holds back in expressing beliefs and opinions.
Is able to give and receive healthy expressions of love.	Has difficulty in recognizing healthy expressions of love.

Once the woman is evaluated, she may be encouraged to participate in group therapy. Healing often takes place much faster in a small group setting. She will quickly discover she is not the only person to have experienced such horrific wounding. Others know what she is feeling because they have been there too. They are all learning and challenging each other together on the pathway to healing and restored health.

Being part of a healing community[19] can also assist victims of sexual abuse to enter into that healing journey. A loving, accepting environment can be a strong support as they take steps to regain control of their lives and move on in a healthy way. Classes dealing with wounds in the family of origin offer a good starting point. Restorative ministries can do a deeper work in specific areas of need.

Resources

Books

Allender, Dr. Dan. *The Wounded Heart: Hope for Adult Victims of Childhood Sexual Abuse.* New ed. Colorado Springs: NavPress, 2018.

Bromley, Nicole Braddock. *Hush: Moving from Silence to Healing after Childhood Sexual Abuse.* Chicago: Moody, 2007.

———. *Breathe: Finding Freedom to Thrive in Relationships after Childhood Sexual Abuse.* Chicago: Moody, 2009.

Hemfelt, Dr. Robert, Dr. Frank Minirth, and Dr. Paul Meier. *Love is a Choice: The Definitive Book of Letting Go of Unhealthy Relationships.* 1989. Rev. ed. Nashville: Thomas Nelson, 2003.

Rodriguez, Kathy, and Pam Vredevelt. *Surviving the Secret: Healing the Hurts of Sexual Abuse.* Grand Rapids: Revell, 1992. Rev. 2003. 3rd ed., self-published, CreateSpace, 2013.

Rodriguez, Kathy. *Healing the Father Wound.* Enumclaw, WA: Pleasant Word, 2008.

Springle, Pat. *Untangling Relationships: A Christian Perspective on Codependency.* Nashville: LifeWay, 1993, CreateSpace, 2015.

Related Scriptures

Psalms 10:14; 18:30; 139:1–4

Isaiah 41:10, 13

Lamentations 3:22–23

Matthew 7:11

Romans 8:15; 12:19

2 Corinthians 1:3–4

Ephesians 4:31–32

AUTHOR BIO

KATHRYN RODRIGUEZ is a licensed clinical psychologist specializing in small group healing for over twenty years. Her areas of expertise revolve around healing the wounds of dysfunctional families in order for individuals to "grow up" in Christ and include specialization in sexual abuse, father-wounding, and eating disorders. She holds a master's and doctorate in clinical psychology from Western Seminary. Kathy teaches biblical foundations for family ministry, and ethical and legal issues for counselors at the seminary level. She served multiple years as the Director of Restoration Ministries at East Hill Church. Kathy and her husband have two adult children.

Chapter 18

Divorce

Welby O'Brien, MS Counseling

I was blessed to have been raised in a Christian home. I came to know the Lord at a young age and had the privilege of attending a Christian college. It was there that I met my husband-to-be and was thrilled that he was going into ministry.

We married after graduation and I taught school while he ministered. We had a good marriage, including our share of normal ups and downs. I imagine many were envious of us. Several seminary degrees later, a home of our own, and finally a little boy, we were living "happily ever after" . . . or so I thought. Then one day after twelve years of marriage, he came to me and said, "Welby, I don't want to be married anymore." And two weeks later he was off with someone else.

My world came crashing in. I collapsed physically and emotionally. This was the deepest, darkest valley I had ever known. Where was the Lord in all this? There were times I was so angry and wanted to have nothing to do with God. It wasn't fair. I had done things His way all along. And there were times when all I could do was crawl into His arms and weep. I was exhausted.

Almost two decades have passed since the excruciating pain of those seemingly endless days and nights. My experience during that time has proven the Bible's message to be true in my life: God IS GOOD.[1] His grace IS sufficient. His Word never promised a comfortable life. In fact, He tells us over and over again that this world is hard. People will hurt us. There will be pain. Yet His comfort, grace, and love, and support from those around me have carried me to the place of healing and hope I enjoy today.

Understand the Issue

A woman[2] who is in the aftermath of divorce, whether it was initiated by her or by her husband, will likely feel she is in the deepest, darkest valley she will ever experience. Hope is shattered. Trust is an illusion. Every possible emotion that can be felt pierces her soul. Every step of grieving overwhelms the survivor. Thoughts of suicide are common.

Not only was I struggling to just survive, I hardly had the strength to care for my little boy. It ripped my heart out as I held him every night when he woke up with night terrors for over a year. He was terrified that Mommy would leave like Daddy did.

Watching him drive away with his dad every weekend brought me to my knees sobbing.

No woman has childhood dreams of growing up, getting married, having children, and then getting divorced. There is a tremendous amount of shame, which is often heightened in Christian circles. The divorced woman feels like a failure. Where does she fit? She can no longer attend married couples groups. She may feel she is being treated as if she has the plague. Well-meaning Christians sometimes have trouble differentiating between God's hatred of divorce, and His love for the individual wounded from it.

The one person in the whole world who knew her best and loved her most has now rejected her. She feels totally worthless. Betrayed. Abandoned. Frightened. Terribly alone. The divorced woman needs affirmation, love, practical help, encouragement, prayer, and above all, God's grace.

Shepherding Insights

Although it may feel uncomfortable to reach out to those who are hurting, don't wait until you feel you can do it perfectly. You may never feel completely adequate in ministering to the divorced. *What do I say? How can I help?* Let me encourage you to just show up and let Jesus love her through you. God uses willing people to help others.

NOTE: The shepherding insights in this chapter are written with the assumption that a shepherd, minister, or friend has already done all that can be done to encourage the couple to reconcile, without success. The suggestions in this chapter begin at the point in which it seems clear that reconciliation is no longer an option. You do not have to condone divorce to minister to the wounded. The divorced person knows better than anyone why God hates divorce. But now more than ever, she needs the love and grace of God flowing through you. *God's grace is big enough even for the divorced . . . no matter whose fault it was.*

The divorced woman feels like a fifth wheel. Everyone seems to be part of a couple or a family. Where does she fit? She is no longer part of married groups and she has no desire to be labeled as a single yet. Include her thoughtfully. She desperately wants to be included. Continue to have her and her children over to your home, and invite them to join you when you go somewhere or have a fun activity. Be sure to convey that you *want* to be with them, rather than just extending pity on them. It is incredibly meaningful to her and her children to be part of your family or gathering. When asking her to join you, do it in a way that allows her to graciously decline without giving a reason. It is also important for her to have the freedom to decline if she is having a particularly hard day and prefers being at home.

Reach out to her children. They are hurting too. No matter how old they are, the children of divorce are deeply affected by the destruction of their family. They need all the love and encouragement you can give. And keep in mind that as you minister to the children, you also minister to the parent. Send cards, letters, or emails to the children. Occasional surprise gifts will do wonders. Have the kids overnight, or include them with your family celebrations and outings. If possible, connect the children to a godly mentor who will stay in their lives for the years to come.

Very soon after the divorce, the Lord sent such a person to us. One evening on our way to take my little boy to his father's for the weekend, we happened upon a deputy sheriff in the store parking lot. He immediately befriended us, taking a special interest in my son. Not only did he show him the patrol car and turn on the flashing lights, but let him sit in the driver's seat. Wow! Then from the trunk, he pulled out a big brown teddy bear with a sheriff's badge and handed it to my son. Upon hearing that this was a devastating time in both of our lives, this man made a commitment in his heart to be there for the long haul. For almost twenty years he has continued to pray and send cards and gifts to my son. As a result of his influence, my son graduated from the police cadet academy. Although my son is now grown and on his own, it continues to touch my heart to see that teddy bear still sitting on his bed.

Another crucial area for the divorced woman is sexual purity. The most difficult time is right at the beginning. It is extremely intense. There is a vacuum of emptiness just longing to be filled with love and affection. There is no one to hug you, touch you, love you. It's a shock to see his side of the bed and his part of the closet empty. Heather told me the ink was still drying on her divorce papers when she was already in an admittedly unhealthy relationship. Her desperate explanation was, "I just want someone to love me."

There are some things you can do to help her get through this intensely challenging time and for the long haul to stay sexually pure. It is important to help her understand the value of doing things God's way. He rewards those who stay on His path, and those who do not will suffer the consequences. The reason He tells us to save sex for marriage is because

He loves us! He knows the pain and troubles ahead. God wants instead to richly bless us.

If she is willing to be in an accountability relationship with you (or someone else), consider the following.

- Help her be aware of her own areas of vulnerability such as hormonal fluctuations, certain fragrances, places, or people.
- Channel energy into positive and fulfilling ways such as projects, music, volunteering, and hobbies.
- Encourage her to exercise regularly. This releases sexual energy, builds self-esteem, and improves outlook.
- Remind her to stay in the Word. Keep eternal perspective. Claim the promises.
- Remind her that *nothing feels as good as being right with God.*
- Pray *with* her.
- Give her hope, encouragement, and love.

Pray *for* her. Don't quit. It doesn't have to be every day, but when she crosses your mind, pause to pray. Lift her up to the Lord. Then let her know. I received a little card in the mail one day. It said, "I prayed for you today. Love, Carolyn." That note touched me deeply. It stayed on the refrigerator for three years. There were many times I could physically and emotionally feel that someone was praying for me.

Give her permission to take some time out. Most of us are too busy as it is. We are overcommitted to too many activities, and find it hard to say no. Then when you take an already overly committed person and hurl them into a crisis, something has to give. I wish someone had given me permission to just survive. It is okay. Help her know her job right now is to *just survive.* The focus is taking care of herself and her children. Everything else may have to be put on hold. Ask the question: Is this activity essential to my survival? Is it building me up or draining me? She needs to rest, heal, and rebuild.

Help her maintain the "Checklist for Survival."[3] She needs permission to just survive right now, to take care of herself and her children. Take some time to sit down with her and go through this checklist.

1. Saturate yourself with Scripture.
2. Pour out your heart to God.
3. Feel the feelings.
4. Let yourself cry.
5. Talk to someone trustworthy.
6. Laugh, giggle, play.
7. Be open to wise input.
8. Write down your feelings.
9. Make sleep a priority.
10. Fill your body with healthy things.
11. Do some physical activity every day.
12. Be your best from the inside out.
13. Treat yourself (and take time out).
14. Let go.
15. Don't rush.

Celebrate together each step she takes toward caring for herself and her children. Help her to see the good choices she makes each day.

Remember, God uses imperfect people (you and me!). Don't worry if you do not feel comfortable . . . you probably won't. Don't wait to do it perfectly. Ultimately, our job as ministers of His grace is to *show her Jesus*.

Open up your heart and let Him love her through you . . . and He will.

HELPFUL THINGS TO SAY AND DO

The following practical list of things to say and do was very helpful to me in my deep dark valley, as well as many others with whom I have worked over the years.

1. **DO** encourage and affirm her as a valuable person. Most people in crisis end up at one of two extremes: either bitter and hardened against God, or driven into His arms for comfort, strength, and hope. Show her Jesus. Encourage her to draw closer to Him in the pain. Remember her on her birthday. Give lots of hugs (women to women, men to men). Speak words of encouragement, such as "I love you," "We are praying for you," "Hang in there," "Your faith is an encouragement to me." Be a good listener.

   You don't have to fix her. Just show that *you care*. Don't say, "I know how you feel." You can never know *exactly* how she feels. You may understand and relate from your own painful divorce, but one person can never fully know how another feels. As with any crisis, this comment will devalue her painful feelings. She needs to know, above everything, that you *care*.

2. **DO** consider how you can help her with practical needs. Find out what she needs. Offer a specific service, such as cleaning her gutters, changing her oil, etc. Enlist the help of others also. It is not practical to be the one to do everything, but your help as a resource finder is invaluable (food, legal help, plumbing, financial resources, child care, etc.). The tasks of maintaining a home and family can be overwhelming. Sometimes it is a tremendous blessing just to know who to call for specific services.

3. **DO** provide a godly support system or group. Who are the people (or person) who will be with her for the immediate crisis and for the long valley of healing? Help her connect with them. Be careful not to volunteer for this assignment yourself unless you are willing to be there for her for years. Your ministry may just be to get her connected to a lifeline. It may be that a small group of church people will be what she needs. Or she may benefit from a divorce recovery group.[4]

4. **DO** know when to refer her to a professional counselor. Too many ministry leaders seem to be uninformed, biased, or too proud to know when an individual needs more help than they can provide. Scripture, prayer, and sound advice are crucial; however, when a woman is in the midst of the most intense crisis of her life, she needs more. Just as a physically sick person needs a professional physician, so an emotionally traumatized person needs a professionally trained counselor.

   It is not uncommon for abuse in some form to be part of a divorce situation. And it is also typical to see depression and suicidal tendencies. Have some resources ready. Pray for wisdom as you search out the reputable Christian counselors and psychiatrists in your community. You may save a life.[5]

5. **DO** give her Scriptures for comfort, encouragement, and hope. God's Word is supernatural. It can soothe the deepest wound. It comforts the broken heart. It pours light into the darkness. It is God Himself touching the soul. Encourage her to cling to her lifeline—the Word of God. Send notes, cards, and e-mails. Call her. Look up a verse to write out and send her. One that gave me many days of strength and comfort was Deuteronomy 33:27a, "The eternal God is your refuge, and underneath are the everlasting arms."[6]

HURTFUL RESPONSES TO AVOID

1. **DON'T** preach or give unsolicited advice. Saying "Divorce is wrong" is only hurtful. It is too late. The one who has experienced the devastation of divorce, the ripping apart of a family, knows why God hates it. The time to give this message is before marriage. Don't say, "You should . . ." or "he should . . ." Even if she has issues to work on, now is not the time. Avoid comments like an older woman spoke to a young woman still reeling from the rejection of her ex-husband, "Well, honey, maybe if you just lose some weight." *Ouch!* Even if it were true,

now is not the time! Reject giving her unfounded promises. I was told many times, "If you just keep praying, he'll come back." Guess what? I prayed. He never came back. God's Word never promised he would. That advice only set me up to be a failure.

2. **DON'T** bash her ex-husband. Check your attitude. Are you praying for him? This can be very difficult, but perhaps you may be the only one praying for him. Ask God to work in his heart. Only He knows what really goes on deep down inside. And only He can reach that heart. Also, it is important not to bash the ex-husband in front of her or the children, even if what you speak is true. Putting him down only hurts her more. Your energy is best spent on your knees.

3. **DON'T** abandon her if she is involved in processing the divorce with her church leaders. Offer to be with her when church leaders meet with her. If there is a public process, sit with her. Support her. It can be a painful and potentially embarrassing process. Bathe her and the leadership in prayer. This will minister to her more than you realize.

4. **DON'T** keep asking for updates or details. It is nice that you care, but it is draining and discouraging. Try to have all your communication with her be uplifting and encouraging.

5. **DON'T** give up on her. Track her progress and stay in touch with her. Send notes, cards, and emails. Let her know you care. Call her to see how she is doing. Ask for what you can be praying. Pray with her. Give her time. There is no timeline for healing. Every woman's situation is different, but it will get better.

Resources

Websites

www.welbyo.com: Resources for those who have experienced divorce, grief, and PTSD.

www.divorcecare.org: DivorceCare is a nationwide organization that identifies support groups meeting in local churches. Check their website for one meeting near you.

www.aacc.net: American Association of Christian Counselors is a nationwide resource for finding local Christian counselors.

Books

Aldrich, Sandra. *From One Single Mother to Another,* rev. ed. Ventura, CA: Regal Books, 2005.

Barr, Debbie. *Children of Divorce.* Grand Rapids: Zondervan, 1992.

Conway, Jim, and Sally Conway. *Moving On After He Moves Out.* Downers Grove, IL: InterVarsity Press, 1995.

Kniskern, Joseph Warren. *When the Vow Breaks: A Survival and Recovery Guide for Christians Facing Divorce.* Nashville: Broadman and Holman, 2008.

O'Brien, Welby. *Formerly a Wife.* Sisters, OR: Deep River Books, 2018.

Smoke, Jim. *Growing through Divorce.* Eugene, OR: Harvest House, 2007.

Related Scriptures

Psalms 32:7; 73:25; 145:18; 147:3

Isaiah 40:31

Jeremiah 29:11

John 14:27

Romans 8:37–39

Philippians 4:6–7, 13[7]

AUTHOR BIO

WELBY O'BRIEN holds a master's degree in counseling from Portland State University and a teaching degree from Biola University. Drawing from her own personal experience along with input from others, she has authored *Goodbye for Now* (grief support) and *Formerly a Wife* (divorce support) and *LOVE OUR VETS: Restoring Hope for Families of Veterans with PTSD*. She is also a contributing author to *Chicken Soup for the Soul: Divorce and Recovery, Chicken Soup for the Soul: The Spirit of America*. Actively involved in leadership and teaching for over 30 years, Welby has also been a welcomed guest on radio and television, as well as featured in video productions. For more information and encouragement, visit www.welbyo.com

Chapter 19

Pornography

Help for Wives Who Have Been Betrayed by Spousal Involvement in Pornography

Sandy Wilson, MA Counseling, D.Min.
Therapist and Codirector of Tuff Stuff Ministries

*S*omething's wrong, *but what*? My questions elicited a quick, emphatic, "No, no, no!" Over time, Earl's continual denials left me with an ugly feeling inside as I tried to make sense out of it. *Why have I been so suspicious of my Christian husband? Am I going crazy?* Earl's reaction to me had made me wonder, my questioning thoughts continued to linger over the next several years.

Finally! Years later my suspicions were confirmed and Earl, a professional therapist, admitted his affair with a client. Initially there was a sense of relief as the truth validated what I had been sensing. In my denial I said to him, "We'll get through this." That was Sunday night. When I went to work Monday, my mind and emotions were going wild. I woke up in the middle of that night and started writing. I was so angry. He had shown no care or concern for me or our family. He had violated the promise that he had made to me and to God. When questioned, he had lied to me over and over and over for years. Deliberately he denied the truth and covered up his activities. About six in the morning my mind was set; I wanted a divorce.

Earl cried and begged me not to go. "At least consider it over the weekend." After speaking at a women's retreat that weekend, I went down to the beach and had a long talk with God. The Lord seemed to say, "Sandy, you have My permission to go or to stay. I will be with you whatever you decide to do." After mentally wrestling with God for a while, I returned home. I informed Earl, "You have a choice to make. You can go and do those things but you don't live with me if you do. Otherwise, you have one year to turn your life around." I insisted that he get counseling, get some people to come around us (Spiritual Care Team),[1] and to totally break off the relationship with the other woman. Relieved that I was staying, he quickly agreed. With a few boundaries clearly set, our journey began.

I was numb with pain and the overwhelming magnitude of this uninvited crisis. Could I survive? I had absolutely no positive feelings for Earl. Food didn't taste like food. Small events, big events, nothing held meaning anymore. I had moments when I wanted to take him back and other moments when I pushed him away. The shame, the lies, the betrayal of the most intimate nature brought incredible pain into my life and family. Fears and uncertainties overwhelmed me as I dealt with anger and agony. The confessed adultery was just a line item on a long list of other sordid acts, including pornography. When the term "sexual addict" surfaced, I feared that he could not overcome this dreaded behavior. Thus began my own personal journey, something I had to walk through. The only guarantee was the Lord's sustaining presence.

Understand the Issue

What is pornography? Pornography is sexually explicit material: films, magazines, writings, photographs, or other materials that are sexually explicit and intended to cause sexual arousal. Those who indulge in this material and fantasy world for any length of time often go on to act out, committing sexual acts. Pornography is insidious and corrupting as it arouses and entices its prey. Lies and cover-ups are utilized to maintain this private world of fantasy and self-indulgence. Pornography ensnares participants, corrupts lives, and destroys relationships. It results in various unnatural manifestations of sexual desire, including, but not limited to: prostitution, pornographic magazines/videos/pictures/Internet sites, masturbation, topless bars, strip clubs, adultery/fornication, rape.

The *use of pornography* is entertaining sensory input from any source other than the spouse for the purpose of sexual arousal. It may involve use of stimulus material like pictures or reflecting back on words and images stored in the playpen of the mind, which is available for fantasy and masturbation any time the person chooses to escape into the playpen. Individuals who use pornography often develop compulsive rituals around their habit that begin to take over their lives: visiting pornographic websites for hour upon hour, watching late night television, establishing communication with women in chat rooms, contacting old girlfriends or lovers. This is manifest by more and more time and resources spent on pursuit of the fantasies that the use of pornography stimulates. This obsessive behavior is called sexual addiction. The payoff for the pursuit of sexual fantasy is usually the pleasure associated with masturbation. This may result in lessened sexual interest in the spouse and in less time spent with the spouse because of the guilt and shame.

These changes over time are very confusing to the spouse because most of these activities are carried out in secret. Once this secret life has been exposed, their journeys begin. They each have a very separate journey on the road to healing before the marriage can be rebuilt. They must each allow the other person to take his/her own journey.

The Unfaithful Partner

The revealing of secret sins is often a bittersweet experience for the unfaithful partner. Once the secret is out, he may initially feel a huge relief. He has lived for months or years dreading this moment of truth. He has invested immeasurable emotional energy in keeping his secret and trying not to slip up in hiding the details of his double life. Even though he still has much pain to confront, he is relieved of the burden of cover-up. He is most likely clueless about the many decisions he will have to make as he begins the healing process for himself, plus for his spouse and family. Ideally, his sorrow will lead to godly repentance and a desire to help his wife recover from the implications of his infidelity. However, this is not always the case. Here are some of the responses the shepherd may encounter:

- Relief and repentance
- Relief and continued denial of the magnitude of the problem
- Relief but unwillingness to give up the behaviors or the other woman if there has been an affair
- Anger and denial

He may also entertain a variety of perspectives on what he needs to do to deal with the issue.

- Willingness to change
- Believes he can change
- Only wants to give lip service to change
- Believes he cannot change
- Only wants it to look like he is changing

The unfaithful partner will most likely experience a great deal of anxiety and depression as he realizes the damage he has done. At this point he may become even more self-absorbed and angry.

Typically there is a lot of self-centeredness or narcissism. He may isolate himself and not have anything to do with others. Depression and hopelessness may continue to paralyze him as he experiences great shame and self-disgust. This is particularly true when he finally realizes that the repulsive things he has engaged in have caused pain and suffering to others. However, in some cases he may express a sense of entitlement to a self-focused life and not show guilt, shame, or remorse. He may become impatient with the spouse for having so many questions and may demand that she "get over it," so that his life may get back to normal. He will show little understanding for the fact that he has destroyed their "normal" and there is nowhere to which they can return. A new life in which they will honor God and each other will have to be built. Once this is realized, the unfaithful partner may choose to break free from the bondage of pornography and take steps to change and become sexually pure and a man of integrity. With hard work, honesty, and accountability, it is possible to be set free and restored. There will still be consequences for his past behavior but there is hope in the Lord and empowerment through His Spirit for healing and deliverance.

The Hurt Partner

When a wife learns that her husband has been unfaithful and has defiled the marital bed, it is extremely traumatizing. He has known of his infidelity for ages and has learned to live with it. But this is brand-new information for her and she is reeling in agony. Her vacillating feelings are all over the map: shock, revulsion, anger, hurt, confusion, uncertainty, powerlessness, multiple fears, rejection, vengeful, and wanting to forgive but not knowing if she can. Post-Traumatic Stress Disorder (PTSD) may play a big part in this betrayal and her journey of healing. She has been rejected and deceived over and over as her husband has sought sexual gratification outside of the marriage. Instead of forsaking all others, he has forsaken his wife and shattered their covenant relationship.

Intuition often alerts women that something is going on, often with an accompanying gut-ache. Most women wonder if he will act out again. It is hard to know if he is acting out since he is so good at hiding it. There is a psychological impact of an affair. She may swing from hyper-vigilance (watching everything he does) to depression. She no longer feels special to her husband and loses her self-confidence. And now, after the truth is out, she is floundering as she learns that he has been involved in all kinds of unseemly activities.

Whether the husband actually committed physical adultery, masturbation, sexual fantasy, or was heavily involved with pornography, the impact is very similar. Some may downplay it ("Well, he just looked at a few pictures"), but the impact is huge. He has shown preference to a fantasy world rather than a tender, loving relationship with his wife. He has cast aside his chosen bride to sleep with harlots (physically, mentally, and/or figuratively speaking). The pain for the wife is unspeakable. She loses trust in herself and questions, *How could I have let this happen or not been aware of it?* She begins to believe she does not know anything. She also loses a sense of her own womanhood. The intimacy and exclusivity of the marital union has been broken. When she had sexual relations with her husband in the past, she wonders, *Was he really fantasizing about others? How can an image be more desirable than my affection? Was he so dissatisfied with my lovemaking that he had to seek out liaisons with strangers? How can I compete with the voluptuous women in the sensuous photos?* These are normal responses to an acute traumatizing experience. She will experience flashbacks and will be retraumatized as she envisions her husband saying and doing indecent, unthinkable things.

When there is strong suspicion that a husband has been unfaithful, especially after the secret is out, it is wise to insist that he have a polygraph. It is important to find an experienced polygrapher who has dealt with sexual addicts. This helps expose acting out behavior. Healing does not start until everything is out. Every time there is new information, you question, "Now is this *all* the truth?" Every time there is more revelation, it is harder and harder to rebuild trust and romantic feelings. That is one of the reasons a polygraph is so helpful; many men come clean the night before the polygraph. A lot of men have sworn up and down to their wives, hundreds of times, there is nothing more. And when she asks for a polygraph, then he tells her the rest of the story. He protests disclosure—"It will hurt her too much" or "She can't stand to hear any more." It is really self-protection but he projects it onto her, saying he is helping her. In fact, he is more concerned about himself than anyone else.

Where is God in all of this? Each woman processes the betrayal experience and her faith differently. For some women there is not much hope that their husbands are going to become and stay clean. God is the only constant for these women. Some hold on to God and never seem to waver. Others are so angry with God they do not have anything to do with God for a long time.

At first, I did not have any doubts about where God was. He said He was going to walk with me through this. I spent a lot of time praying and talking with Him. However, the longer it went on, the more I began to struggle with, *How come it is taking so long? Are You sure You are here in all of this, God?* I could not always see evidence that anything was happening. The pain also weighed me down. I not only had my own pain but I had the pain of my children, my mother, his parents, the extended family, friends. I also struggled with forgiveness. What do you forgive? How do you forgive? I felt like God was asking an awful lot. There were times when I pushed away from God. But I still remember the day that it finally registered to me: God had been more hurt by this than I had been. Earl had betrayed Him as well as me. That was a huge revelation.

Boundaries are important. I established a boundary that if Earl was unfaithful again, he could not live with me anymore. That was one very firm boundary that I was able to clearly draw. But later as we began to work through some of our marriage issues, I discovered that I did not have very clear boundaries. One example is that Earl would often speed when driving. On one long-distance trip to see the therapist I had asked Earl to slow down several times with no lasting results. The therapist helped me to see that I was not holding Earl accountable for his behavior. I was letting him treat me any way he wanted. The therapist asked, "Why do you ride with him when he is going excessively fast?" I answered, "Well, he is my husband." It has been implied that in the Christian community we have to do what our husbands say. So he helped me understand that Earl can drive any speed he wants but I do not have to ride with him. He helped me begin to say those kinds of things to Earl and know that I could follow through by getting a cab or driving separately. It is very important for a healthy marital relationship to know how to set and maintain healthy boundaries.

Another significant consideration is the possibility of sexually transmitted diseases or AIDS. No matter how much he denies sexual involvement, take this possibility seriously. Remember he is a very good liar. She needs to talk to a doctor and be tested. It may be extremely embarrassing but imperative that she be checked out thoroughly. She should also insist that he be tested.

Lapses and Relapses

Some of the questions women ask are, "How much do I have to put up with him having lapses and relapses?" And, "Can he stay clean the rest of his life?" Men do not like to hear it or may have difficulty believing it but it *is* possible for them to stay clean. They need to accept the responsibility, make right choices, and get the help they need to make it happen. As long as they give themselves permission to "slip up" and act out, then they are not dealing with their own issues or their relationship with their wives in a healthy manner. It is too easy to say, "I won't, I won't, I won't . . . Oops! I did. Oh well, forgive me; take me back." This is very destructive and further traumatizes the wife. The husband can have lapses but not relapses. For example, he may walk in the park and a woman strolls in front of him. He lets his eyes follow her a few seconds, but then he says, "Oh, stop!" And he quickly pulls his eyes back and says, "I don't want to do that." The important choice here is to choose not to be entertained by what he sees. I consider that a *lapse*. But a *relapse* is an actual acting out such as getting on the Internet, masturbating, or committing adultery. Some husbands do not stop acting out. And that is very painful for their wives.

POSSIBLE WARNING SIGNS

- Intuitive sense that something is wrong. Trust your intuition!
- Changes in attentiveness
- Looking more at women
- Fighting over things they do not usually fight over to keep her off balance
- Lack of responsiveness to a request
- Withdrawal
- Lying
- Secretive behavior
- Isolation
- Shifting the focus to make it look like she is the one who has a problem: "You're bringing that up again?"
- Compulsive behavior such as: excessive attention to emails, voice, or text messages

Shepherding Insights

This is a very lengthy healing journey, usually lasting several years, and it cannot be cut short. Given the level of intensity and the length of commitment, pastors usually do not have the time or expertise to be the primary caregiver. Nor is it advisable for the male pastor to be the primary listener and help for a woman in pain. She is often in a very vulnerable and confused emotional state. Great care must be taken to guard against unhealthy emotional attachments. This would be a great opportunity for women in the church who are trained and willing to shepherd a woman in pain to meet regularly with her. A male pastor can be instrumental in identifying help by asking, "Who are your friends? Do you have someone who will just listen to you? Is there someone you know who won't try to fix things but who can hear you vent your true feelings without judgment? Who do you trust to keep your confidences?" Friends who offer practical help, such as doing laundry, housecleaning, or picking up the children from school also provide valuable support. The male pastor may also be able to recommend a woman who has successfully walked through similar trauma and found healing, to come alongside the betrayed wife. This can be a great source of encouragement and help. Meeting with an experienced counselor will be beneficial as the wife processes her pain and broken marriage. Finally, a Spiritual Care Team[2] can be a tremendous help to a hurting couple as they try to find healing and help for their shattered lives and marriage.

The best way a caregiver can help is to listen. Listen in a way you do not normally listen. Most of us listen just long enough to decide how to answer. She does not want an answer, she just needs somebody to listen and hear her pain and confusion. If she says, "I don't know what to do about _____." Engage her with a question, "What have you considered so far?" Be careful not to give advice. Asking appropriate questions will help her see her strengths and enable her to make good decisions. Be careful to put aside your own anger toward her husband or you will not be effective in helping this hurting couple. Listen to her and just hear how she is that day. Some days she is feeling good about him and you want to scream, "Caution!" And other days she is not feeling good about him and you think, "Well, he has been working really hard . . ." But you need to let her be wherever she is on her healing journey.

Some women are unable to feel any positive feelings for many months. Try to understand the strong emotion that a woman is feeling. Help her identify her emotion and let her talk. If she appears depressed, say, "You seem really down or discouraged today." And then let her talk. You cannot "fix it" for her. Try asking her, "Is there anything I could do that would be helpful for you today?" or "Is there anything you want from me?" Let her think and respond. Often she just needs a shepherd to hear her pain and love her through it. Sometimes invite her to go to a play or concert or something that is totally unrelated to her pain. This change of pace will help her to feel less consumed. Be a support person. Tell her you love her and care about her. Tell her you understand that her journey is hard and painful. Encourage her in the steps you see her taking. Remind her of concrete examples of progress that you have seen her take.

Deep Losses

Experiencing betrayal takes a deep emotional toll and results in the betrayed woman feeling many losses. Loss of:

trust

innocence

an undefiled marital bed

intimacy

respect

relationships

normal, healthy family

self-worth and confidence

dreams

finances

privacy in the most personal matters

stability

husband/father roles

Some women are so depressed they cannot begin to figure out what to do. Encourage her to see a medical doctor or mental health professional if she shows signs of extreme depression or has suicidal tendencies. Encourage her to talk about her feelings and thoughts. Offer to drive her to get medical attention, if needed. A calm caregiver may provide strength and perspective in a world that seems to be in total chaos.

Be careful not to judge. Remember that it is a huge process. You may feel that she has progressed to a certain place in her journey when actually she may have gone backward and is really struggling. One of the issues women often struggle with is that society tends to blame the wife, saying, "If you had just been _____" or "If you had just worn a different nightgown . . ." or "If you had just been nicer . . . or had sex with him more, then he wouldn't do this." However, his sexual addiction has nothing to do with the wife and is not primarily about sex either. This is about the hole in his soul and the things he has been trying to use to fill it.[3] Many pornography addicts have two seemingly satisfactory sex lives: one with their spouse and the other with self as they engage in pornography and masturbation.

Forgiveness

It takes time to work through the betrayal in a healthy manner. In the early stages of the process, it is usually *not* helpful to ask a traumatized wife, "Have you forgiven him?" When women come in for counseling after talking with their pastor, this is the one source of pain I hear most often. The woman is not even fully aware of the amount of pain that has been inflicted upon her. How can she be expected to forgive the unknown? In the beginning, it is unlikely there has even been full disclosure. Healing cannot really begin until it is all out in the open. Forgiveness is for the victim and her healing health.

Although we are commanded to forgive, we need to address some misguided notions about forgiveness. Forgiveness is a process and not a quick fix. "We often assume that a sinner who asks others for forgiveness has a *right* to be forgiven—and that forgiveness must be instantaneously offered and accepted, with little regard for the pain that has been suffered. We also assume that whenever pain resurfaces, it is an indication that forgiveness has not occurred. Both are untrue."[4] Even as the offender cannot demand forgiveness, we cannot demand it as an attempt at a quick fix. In time, and with healthy healing, the injured party will be able to work toward forgiveness.

I learned something new about forgiveness when Earl's therapist asked, "How are you doing with forgiveness?"

I replied, "Well, I think I am in the process of forgiving."

And he said, "Well, how specific are you being?"

"What do you mean?" I asked.

And he said, "You will continue to have flashbacks until you are *very specific* about what you are forgiving."

I queried, "Could you give me an example?"

"Yes. I think you need to be so specific that you would say, 'I forgive him for putting his _____,'" he told me, voicing the clinical summary of intercourse.

I had never thought of being *that* specific. I still was thinking in general terms until he used that graphic wording. But when a scene comes back to my mind, I can say, "Get behind me, Satan.[5] I have forgiven that." Probably one of the biggest things I learned about forgiveness was that I needed to name the offense and the offender, and then forgive him for that specific offense. The other thing is to keep working on forgiveness, knowing that it will take a lot of time. Each memory or flashback will feel like a new offense and you will need to forgive the new hurt. To avoid bitterness, I needed to forgive Earl even if he was to leave our relationship or if I needed to leave.[6]

It is important to make a distinction between forgiveness and trust. God asks us to forgive but He does not ask us to trust. Trust is built on honesty and changes in attitudes and behaviors on the part of the unfaithful partner. We are called on by God to forgive but trust will depend on the choices the unfaithful partner makes.

Shepherds should initially anticipate the wife feeling anger in her deep pain. Do not try to squelch those angry feelings too quickly. Shepherds may need to give her permission to feel her anger by saying, "You need to be angry. What he has done to you is wrong. He made a promise to you at the altar that he would love you and you only. He promised you and God and he has broken his promise to both of you." Even God is angry at sin, unrighteousness, and sin-hardened hearts.

Providing accountability for the woman can be a great asset and encouragement. Sometimes she may want to become vengeful and do mean things. Allow her those feelings, but also ask questions that will prompt her to think about the outcome of actions based on angry feelings. Accountability helps protect her during this very emotionally vulnerable time. Another man could come along and be very tempting because he says the right things. In an emotionally raw state, she needs appropriate male affirmation but in a safe atmosphere. Pray for her. Ask God to give you appropriate questions that will enable her to remain pure. As she strives to become more Christlike and work through her pain, she will learn to trust God. The Spiritual Care Team mentioned earlier can also be useful to provide support and balance in these issues.

Our Spiritual Care Team consisted of two mature Christian couples who held Earl accountable and encouraged him on the journey of restoration. Although it was Earl's accountability team, I benefited much from it. They asked hard questions, made tough decisions and recommendations, and supervised his journey to healing and wholeness. The wife should never be placed in the position of being her husband's accountability person. It will keep her emotionally stirred up and delay her own healing journey. If she is too involved in his journey, she will never feel like he is well. She needs him to take responsibility for his own healing. She will never feel cared about until that happens.

The betrayed and traumatized wife needs compassion and a safe environment for healing. Pastors who offer support and protection through caregivers in the church can be strategic in the healing process. Pastors who realize that sometimes separation is needed can provide space for processing and recovery. As an advocate, a pastor may need to say to the husband, "You need to show her for at least nine months that you are seriously going to work on things and you can't do that in the home. You need to find another place to stay." The unfaithful husband should be referred to a therapist trained in these types of issues, a therapist who can confront and break through the denial, and deal with some of the deeper character issues. A Spiritual Care Team should be strongly recommended for accountability and encouragement on this path to healing. Hurtful patterns will need to be broken. Eventually healthy patterns can be rebuilt. This takes time and support from others.

Rebuilding Trust, Respect, Love, and Commitment

When betrayal occurs, the marital dynamic is shattered. The four most important components of a healthy relationship—trust, respect, love, and commitment—are destroyed. Only time and appropriate changes in behaviors and attitudes can bring about healing. Words and promises have no meaning without action to back them up. At first the betrayed spouse will doubt the offender's *sincerity*. Even after he has shown some progress, she will still question his ability. She will wonder if he has the *ability* to remain pure for the rest of his life. The next stage will be *durability*. When durability has been demonstrated, then the components of trust, respect, love, and commitment can become firm. The process from ability through durability may take three to five years.

HELPFUL THINGS TO SAY AND DO

1. **DO** be willing to listen. However, in listening you may lose some of your innocence. You will hear about things you never imagined. A lot of listening is crucial to understand what she is going through.

2. **DO** set appropriate boundaries. Listening is very important but not at the expense that you end up stumbling or struggling with it. Some things may be best addressed with a therapist.

3. **DO** consider, "What is she *not* thinking about?" and gently help her address those. What are they going to do with their kids? What about going to a doctor to have herself tested, etc.

4. **DO** let her feel and express anger. Give her permission to feel the feelings.

5. **DO** be compassionate, understanding, and patient as she struggles to regain steady footing.

6. **DO** let her express anger toward God . . . Hard things can shake even the godliest of saints. Ask, "How are you doing with God?" Let her speak. Offer support. Help carry her burden.

7. **DO** pray for her and the family. It is a painful, embarrassing, and difficult time.

8. **DO** consider bringing a Spiritual Care Team alongside the repentant sinner and his hurting family.

9. **DO** encourage the pastor to continue making contact. A phone call every few weeks, asking, "How is it going?" can be an encouragement during this difficult season.

10. **DO** consider a professional referral to a counselor experienced with these types of issues.

HURTFUL THINGS TO AVOID

1. **DON'T** put the blame for the husband's moral failure and sin on the wife: "If you had only . . ." Remember, he made the choices to forsake his wife and defile their marital bed, she didn't.

2. **DON'T** expect instant forgiveness. It is a process that takes time to work through.

3. **DON'T** expect the male pastor to be the primary listener for the traumatized wife.

4. **DON'T** expect all friends to be supportive in the same way. Not all can bear the emotional pain.

5. **DON'T** judge her walk with God. Working through trauma, she may be angry with God. "Why didn't You prevent this?" God is patient and understanding with her, so we should be too.

6. **DON'T** expect his journey to look like her journey. They will be quite different.

7. **DON'T** expect this journey to end quickly. It will take about five years for healing and restoration of a healthy relationship. Feelings will not start to return much before three years. Anyone committed to walk this journey must plan to be there for the long haul.

8. **DON'T** give hurtful responses such as, "Are you still dealing with that?" or "Get over it."

9. **DON'T** abandon her. Keep in touch and offer encouragement and support.

Referrals for the traumatized wife may include:

1. A shepherd who listens well, is supportive, available, and will consistently pray for her.
2. Close trusted friends who can offer practical support.

3. A woman who has walked through this type of experience and has found healing.

4. A Spiritual Care Team.

5. A professional counselor who has training in these types of issues

Resources

Websites

http://www.tuffstuffministries.com: Tuff Stuff Ministries (TSM) Drs. Earl & Sandy Wilson are founders and codirectors of TSM, a national ministry for men and women.

http://www.bebroken.com: Be Broken Ministries

https://www.purelifealliance.org: Pure Life Alliance

https://www.hopeafterbetrayal.com: Hope After Betrayal

Books

Laaser, Debra. *Shattered Vows: Hope and Healing for Women Who Have Been Sexually Betrayed.* Grand Rapids: Zondervan, 2008.

Means, Marsha. *Your Sexually Addicted Spouse: How Partners Can Cope & Heal.* Liberty Corner, NJ: New Horizon Press, 2009.

Wilson, Earl, and Sandy Wilson, Paul and Virginia Friesen, Larry and Nancy Paulson. *Restoring the Fallen: A Team Approach to Caring, Confronting & Reconciling.* Downers Grove, IL: InterVarsity Press, 1997.

Wilson, Meg. *Hope after Betrayal: Healing When Sexual Addiction Invades Your Marriage.* Grand Rapids: Kregel Publications, 2007, revised and expanded 2018.

Video Series

http//wwwtuffstuffministries.com

Wilson, Sandy. "Lessons I Learned along the Way . . ." Albany, OR: Shepherd & Associates, christianvideos.net, 2014.

Resources for men addicted to pornography:

Carnes, Patrick. *Don't Call It Love: Recovery from Sexual Addiction.*
    Colorado Springs: Bantam Books, 1992.
Laser, Mark. *Healing the Wounds of Sexual Addiction.* Grand Rapids:
    Zondervan, 2004.
Leahy, Michael. *Porn Nation: Conquering Americas #1 Addiction.*
    Chicago: Northfield Publishing, 2008.
Roberts, Ted. *Pure Desire: How One Man's Triumph Can Help Others
    Break Free from Sexual Temptation.* Rev. and updated ed. Min-
    neapolis: Bethany House Publishers, 2008.
Schaumburg, Harry. *Undefiled: Redemption from Sexual Sin, Restora-
    tion for Broken Relationships.* Chicago: Moody, 2009.
Wilson, Earl. *Steering Clear: Avoiding the Slippery Slope to Moral
    Failure.* Downers Grove, IL: InterVarsity Press, 2002.

Video Series

    http//www.tuffstuffministries.com

Wilson, Earl. "Especially for Men." Albany, OR: Shepherd & Associ-
    ates, christianvideos.net, 2016.

Related Scriptures

Psalms 28:7; 34:18; 43:5; 46:1; 55:22; 91
Isaiah 41:10, 13
Matthew 18:15–17
John 3:16
James 1:13–15

AUTHOR BIO

DR. SANDY WILSON is a retired therapist and codirector, along with her husband, Earl Wilson, PhD, of Tuff Stuff Ministries. Tuff Stuff Ministries was created to help people with difficult things in their lives: sexual temptation, moral failure, betrayal, and broken relationships. Sandy's passion is providing help for women who have been betrayed by their spouse. Sandy is one of the six team members who authored *Restoring the Fallen: A Team Approach to Caring, Confronting & Reconciling*. Sandy is a retired counseling professor at Western Seminary in Portland, Oregon. She has five adult children, nine grandchildren, and three great-grandchildren.

Chapter 20

Spiritual Abuse

Gerry Breshears, PhD
Professor of Systematic Theology,
Western Seminary, Portland, Oregon
Elder at Grace Community Church, Gresham, Oregon

*S*andra felt so privileged to be executive assistant for Pastor James.[1] Many recognized her business skills, but he had helped her put them into the context of her spiritual life. Because he saw her as a very special person, she was able to believe in herself as a gifted and called person.

So when he asked her to leave her job in the law firm to serve Jesus at First Church, it was easy for her to give up her worldly compensation package. Balancing life as a widow with two preteen children and meeting Pastor James's needs pressed her energy levels. When she mentioned the pressures to Pastor James, he softly asked if she was really ready to walk in God's calling. Because Pastor James shared some of the secrets from his own home life with Sandra, she knew how important it was to apply Jesus' words captured well in *The Message*: "Anyone who comes to me but refuses to let go of father, mother, spouse, children, brothers, sisters . . . can't be my disciple" (Luke 14:26).

She refused to let her spirit be troubled by the financial pressures and the work that needed to be done after she got home. It helped when Pastor James gave her the beautiful calligraphy that said, "If anyone would come after me, he must deny himself and take up his cross and follow me" (Matthew 16:24 NIV 1984).

She hung it by her desk to remind herself that the extra hours spent on Pastor James's personal projects were really for Jesus. Lately there had been quite a few days when "I face death every day" (1 Corinthians 15:31), were the Lord's word to her. She just needed to be more considerate of Pastor James so he could triumph in the stresses ministry brought into his life. She understood how important it was to follow the command of God: "Have confidence in your leaders and submit to their authority, because they keep watch over you as those who must give an account. Do this so that their work will be a joy, not a burden, for that would be of no benefit to you" (Hebrews 13:17).

He was so sensitive to the Lord. Any time she allowed herself to lose the deep resonance between their spirits, it disrupted the work of the Holy Spirit in him. She respected his righteous wrath when that happened. In one of their personal discipleship times, they had worked through the story of Elijah (1 Kings 17–19). He helped her understand the Lord's Elijah-like anointing that was on him. He let her see that her support was essential so the Jezebels of the world could not hinder the Lord's work at First Church. God's Word was clear: "Do not touch my anointed ones; do my prophets no harm" (Psalm 105:15).

She was the only person in the world who truly understood and helped the pastoral side of his life.

Late Friday, Pastor James rushed to her desk with a quickly scribbled sketch of an announcement slide for the weekend services. She realized that his wording would infuriate some key leaders. Probably his mind was on his sermon and he missed how betrayed they would feel. When she gently pointed this out, his anger erupted. "Can't you just do what you are told for once?" She was glad he didn't see her tears as she inserted his words into the slide.

Tuesday's staff meeting was tense. The hostility the slide had unleashed weighed on everyone's spirit. Sandra's spirit sank when she saw Pastor James's troubled countenance. She wanted so much to help him feel better by communicating her caring support. Their eyes usually met as he came to the table, but today he uncharacteristically avoided hers.

After he opened with prayer, he immediately spoke directly to the controversy. Sandra felt so bad for him. She knew it was her fault that he had missed her warning about the wording. After he powerfully rebuked the opposition for their sinful attitudes, he turned to Sandra. "What's wrong with you? You should have known those words would infuriate people. Why didn't you just do the slide the way I told you to? Can't you ever do a simple job without undercutting me? Now I have to still the storm your incompetence caused. Of course I forgive you, but I really wonder about you these days."

Understand the Issue

Define Spiritual Abuse

Spiritual abuse exists when people with religious authority use their position of spiritual power to control or dominate another person in the name of God, faith, religion, or church, taking advantage of the victim's vulnerability to gratify personal needs such as needs for importance, power, intimacy, value, prosperity, sexual gratification, or spiritual fulfillment. The abuser exploits the power of the position to suck life from the victim. Power differential between abuser and victim is what distinguishes abuse from meanness. Friends are mean, but leaders abuse.

Sandra's story illustrates typical aspects of spiritual abuse. Loyalty to the leader is paramount. He is God's anointed and must be given the premier place in the organization. The victim is brought into a special place in the abuser's life, as small intimacies or personal revelations cement the specialness of the relationship. Disagreement or differences, especially in public, are simply not allowed. Scripture is twisted to support the sacrifices demanded. Serving the abuser is tantamount to serving Jesus. Subtle shame messages keep the victim in line.

Anything that competes with the abuser's priorities is framed as attacks from the evil one. It is always the responsibility of the victim to anticipate the needs of the leader, who is God's anointed. Suffering to meet the abuser's demands is a mark of God's favor. When something causes the victim to lose position, the abusive attack is personal, shaming, and savage, and the victim is often cast aside and left wondering what happened. Typically she continues to protect the abuser and keeps his secrets.

Incredible as it seems, Sandra worked all the harder for Pastor James, internally taking the blame for all the trouble even though she had warned him.

Spiritual abuse can come in many ways. Abuse in its more evil manifestations is destruction of life.[2] If the elements of life are such elements as feeling, personal expression, understanding, growth, or autonomy, then abusers destroy those facets in their victims.

Ritual abuse is the destructive use of a person to fulfill a prescribed ritual, in order to achieve a specific religious goal or satisfy the perceived needs of their deity. This can range from throwing Jonah overboard, to Mayan priests sacrificing a virgin before battle, to satanic ritual abuse. Jim Jones persuading more than nine hundred members of People's Temple to drink poison in 1978 was the final act in a premier example of cultic spiritual abuse. There were widespread spiritual and sexual abuses by Roman Catholic parish priests who were protected by diocesan hierarchy. In some cases bishops made payments to victims on condition that the allegations remained secret. Rather than being dismissed, the priests were reassigned to other parishes where, in some cases, the abuse continued.[3]

Many times spiritual abuse is perpetrated by well-meaning people in positions of spiritual power who minister in good churches. Here are some examples of abuse:

- The pastor uses a parishioner's personal story without permission to illustrate a sermon exposing the parishioner's vulnerability.
- Personal sins confessed in confidence are shared with others so they can pray.
- Leaders ask others to do things to avoid responsibility for unpopular actions.
- Teachers teach their personal views as the Word of God and shame those who question.
- A parishioner gets spiritual help from a pastor who then hints that the parishioner owes him support in the upcoming business meeting.
- A husband quotes Ephesians 5:22 as he demands sexual relations with his unwilling wife.
- A young man tells his girlfriend that she needs to learn to follow God's command to forgive when her pained response to his control moves her to decline his request for a date.

The Bible describes and condemns spiritual abuse. One example is the "shepherds of Israel" who eat the food that should go to the flock, who slaughter the sheep to clothe themselves, who rule harshly serving their needs.[4] Jesus raged against those who exploited worshipers by the money changers in the temple.[5] Jesus was angry at Pharisees whose concern was for human tradition rather than healing human suffering.[6] Jesus castigated abusive spiritual leaders for their abusive practices.[7] Stephen followed the example of his Lord as he exposed the abuses of the Jewish leaders.[8] In Galatians Paul pronounced eternal condemnation on those who demanded people follow human rules to gain entrance into the kingdom.

Recognize Spiritual Abuse[9]

1. Does her[10] personality generally become stronger, happier, and more confident as a result of being involved in the ministry?

Abusers typically use guilt, fear, and intimidation to control their victims as the abuse goes on. Her relatives and friends may see a noticeable change in personality. Victims often show patterns of loss of confidence as they feel beaten down by the abuse. Abusers teach their victims that asserting herself is not spiritual.

2. Do the leaders of the ministry seek to strengthen their family commitments?

Nearly all abusers attempt to minimize the commitments of their victims to their family, especially parents. The abuser will replace the husband/father as the source of wisdom and strength for the family. The group will be more important as family than the biological family. Because loyalty to family competes with loyalty to the abuser, family commitments are discouraged or viewed as impediments to spiritual advancement. Beyond this family members may see through the lies so they are dangerous to the abuser's agenda.

3. Does the leader encourage independent thinking and the development of discernment skills?

Spiritual abuse always comes out of a demand for authority and control. The abuser takes the role of priest and king, if not the place of God. Many times he will turn to passages such as 1 Corinthians 11 to emphasize that God operates among His people through a hierarchy, or "chain of command." Followers must come under the "covering" or "umbrella of protection" of the leader who will provide spiritual blessing so long as she submits fully. It is not her place to judge or correct his leadership—God will see to that.

Control-oriented leaders attempt to dictate what members think about important issues ranging from Bible interpretation to life issues such as whom to marry, where to live, how many children to have, or what jobs to accept. The process is so spiritualized that members usually do not realize what is going on. Many times the leader is widely recognized as a gifted teacher with insights into the depths of God's Word, and because he is uniquely anointed, the members of the group view him as one speaking with divine authority. Instead of checking to see if his

teaching is biblical, there is subtle but heavy pressure to submit and conform. Acceptable questions are limited to requests for further truth.

4. Is there allowance for individual differences of belief and behavior,
particularly on issues Christians generally consider to be of secondary
importance?

Abusive teachers often take strong stands on doctrines such as escha-
tology or demonology. These emphases distinguish them from "ordinary" Christians. Their adherence to unique doctrines and practices
validate their claim to be special to God. They judge the spirituality of
other groups because they fail to measure up to their special standards.

Their belief systems typically result in rigid lifestyle commitments.
For example, the leader manipulates victims by persuading them that
they must follow a rigid prayer regimen to protect themselves from
demonic attack. Because the rules are interpreted by the leader, victims who are out of favor can never keep the leader's impossibly high
standards. Their failure to live up to the standards reminds victims how
desperately they need the leader to guide them. The victim's guilt contributes to spiritual bondage.

5. Are high moral standards the norm both among members and
between members and nonmembers?

While abusers place special value on high moral standards in their
public image, they often transgress ethical norms in sexual and financial
areas. There is often a double standard between those in leadership and
those in the rank-and-file membership. While members are expected to
put in extra hours without pay, the abusive leader takes long expensive
vacations paid for by supporters. Abusers often carry on conversations
that are sexually charged, touch members in sexual ways, or enter into
sexual relations with them.

6. Do the leader and the organization invite advice, accountability,
and evaluation from outside its immediate circle?

Because abusers often violate community standards in ethics and organizational procedures, they refuse to submit to normal evaluations such as outside audits or professional organizations. They are virtually paranoid of outside evaluation. If there is a board, it only gets censored information from the abusive leader. Even so, the board is usually composed of people who are personally loyal to the leader. The members are given the explanation that they are judged by spiritual standards that would not be understood by the world. Abusers are quite secretive about some doctrines and the inner policies and procedures of the group.

7. Are group members encouraged to ask honest questions?

A cardinal rule of abusers is, "Don't ask questions. Don't make waves." Truth is settled and handed down from the top of the hierarchy. Questioning anything is considered a challenge to authority. Loyalty and submission cannot coexist with a questioning attitude, which would make her "rebellious" or "unteachable." Questioners are punished by being shamed, humiliated, or worse, being pushed out of the special relationship with the abuser, which amounts to being cut off from God's blessing and help.

Shepherding Insights

Spiritual abuse destroys soul and spirit. It damages life with people and, even more, life with God. Therefore, help needs to be both personal and spiritual.

Personal Help

HELPFUL THINGS TO SAY AND DO

1. **DO** be trustworthy. *You MUST be trustworthy.* What you say must match what you feel and do. If you are upset, say so but do it gently. Half-truths hurt rather than protect. Survivors have an

uncanny ability to detect anything you try to conceal. Clarify your intentions constantly.

2. **DO** hear her story. She needs to talk about the abuse and break the secrecy. Talking to her counselor is vitally important, but it is not enough because the relationship is still a confidential one that maintains the "secret." Listen caringly and actively. Ask the questions that come up, but keep the focus on her story, not your curiosity. The point is to meet her needs, not your own. Listen at the pace that she wants to share and to the extent that she wants to share. Encourage her to keep talking when she feels the shame and horror of what happened.

3. **DO** keep her confidentiality. Her experiences are hers to share, not yours. She—not you—needs to be the one to break the silence of secrecy, when she is ready and with whom she is safe and feels safe enough to do so.

4. **DO** help her express strong feelings. Be patient when she does so inappropriately. She needs someone to validate her feelings, especially the ones she finds so hard to accept. For example, you need to be able to deal with rage as an acceptable feeling, especially when it is directed at you. Help her understand that feelings are valid, but feelings are not facts.

5. **DO** help her to name her experience as abuse. Do not let her minimize what happened or take blame for what happened to her. Sometimes you may simply name it for her. But until she is ready to talk about it, do not press the issue.

6. **DO** help her sort through all the feelings. She needs to learn to differentiate disappointment from abandonment, "no" from "you're bad," anger from hate, "I can't" from "I don't like you." Help her learn to trust but only trustworthy people, to give and receive without strings, to choose for herself, to say no without anger, to say thank you.

HURTFUL RESPONSES TO AVOID

1. **DON'T** fall prey to the temptation to give her answers. You do not know why it happened, how God's glory will shine through the cracks in the abuse, nor how to heal the pain. It does not hurt to leave some things in tension.

2. **DON'T** judge her feelings and experiences. Some will be so far out of the realm of the ordinary that it is hard not to doubt them. Be careful how you answer when she asks, "You believe me, don't you?" You cannot verify the factuality of what happened. You can and should support and validate her feelings.

3. **DON'T** make it your job to make her feel better. When you take that as your responsibility, you will either deny her pain ("Don't cry. You are very loved"; "It's all going to be okay"; "God will use it for good") or abandon her when you cannot take away the pain. You are *not* Messiah! Get used to the idea of not being able to meet all needs.

4. **DON'T** let her take blame for abuse. Challenge her when she slips into thinking, "If only I'd been a little more . . ." Help her realize what he did to entrap and diminish her.

5. **DON'T** let her play the victim. She has the power of choice, the power of the Spirit, and the help of friends. She can make choices and take action.

6. **DON'T** do for her what she can do herself. When you do, you continue the dependency. When someone is hurting so much, it is a great temptation to make her life easier. But what you actually do is create dependency. Worse, you hinder her healing.

7. **DON'T** process your own feelings in her hearing. As you get involved with her story, it will trigger deep feelings in you. Do tell her about them. But do not reverse roles and reabuse her by letting her take the helper role.

8. **DON'T** promise more than you can give. The best support is consistent caring. Start your involvement slowly and increase it wisely and with careful consideration of what commitment you can make and keep. When you feel the urgency and intensity of her needs, you tend to fall into overwhelming levels of involvement. It is much better to commit a consistent thirty minutes a week for a year than be involved in a couple of all-nighters. Crisis mode leads to burn-out and abandonment that traumatizes her. Be concrete when discussing what you will do. What you intend as noncommittal responses will often sound like binding promises to her with resulting feelings of betrayal of trust.

9. **DON'T** become the therapist. She really needs healthy friends. Do ordinary things friends do together: go out to eat, share a hobby, take a hike, organize a garage sale, bake a cake, etc. Help her gain an identity as a "person" rather than as an "abuse survivor."

10. **DON'T** let her control you. For example, clarify time limits prior to or at the beginning of every meeting. Then hold to them when she wants to talk more. This helps her learn to set and live with boundaries as well as protects her from the feeling of abandonment due to misunderstood expectations.

Spiritual Help

Start the process of untwisting Scripture. We have already seen how all of the passages in Sandra's story were misused to establish the power of the abuser. Do Bible study with her, but do it wisely. Instead of preaching to her, tell her what the passage means to you, help her interact with and interpret Scripture herself. Most abuse survivors know the Bible as a source of guilt and condemnation, especially if her abuse was in a Christian environment. You do her a great service if you help her discover the Bible as a living, personal book about grace, telling of a God of justice and holiness as well as mercy and love. Discuss all of Scripture including the passages speaking of God's judgment and wrath. She needs to know that God forgives freely and completely those who come to Him seeking mercy but also that He judges severely those who serve Satan, hurt children, and continue to refuse His grace.

Spiritual abuse always distorts the Lord, portraying Him in the image of the abuser. Introduce her to the Lord of the Bible. Take her to Exodus 32. Show her how in the midst of Israel's terrible sin of the golden calf and the Lord's furious anger at their sin, the Lord processes His feelings with Moses. The result is that He has compassion on them even though they are still involved in their debauched party. But that is not the end of the story. Moses wants to see the Lord in His full glory (Exodus 33:18). But that would kill him, so the Lord invites him into the cleft of the rock. Then He reveals Himself to His partner in ministry. Exodus 34:6–7 is the most quoted verse within the Bible itself. That means it is supremely important. Have her read it out loud. In a context of grievous sin, the Lord's first statement about Himself is that *He is compassionate and gracious.* That is, He cares and He helps. He is slow to anger. Unlike the abusers, there is no hair-trigger anger, no irrational rage. His anger is at real sin and only after and in the context of compassion and grace.

The list goes on: He abounds in love and faithfulness. Remember this in the context of sinners, not perfectly obedient people. How different than the abuser. The Lord's delight is to forgive wickedness, rebellion, and sin. His justice requires that He will never leave the guilty unpunished. Unfortunately, the consequences of sin may extend to children of unrepentant abusers like her abuser. Anyone can be forgiven, but only if he confesses and repents of his sin. Help her see herself as one who will experience the Lord's compassion and grace as she comes to Him to talk about her sin. This will be hard for her to believe because it is so incredibly different than what happened with the abuser.

She has been told that because the Lord is holy, He is separated from all sin. He cannot tolerate sin in His presence. Since she is sinful, the holy Lord despises her. This is a very powerful lie, because it has a nub of truth. The Lord will not leave the guilty unpunished. She needs to see the truth of Isaiah 6. The Lord is not distant and removed. He appears in the earthly temple with all of its uncleanness. He invades Isaiah's presence who responds with horror because of his sin. But notice that the Lord does not withdraw from the sinful man. Rather He takes away Isaiah's guilt and atones for his sin. Help her remember the cost of this atonement by picturing this same Lord hanging on a cross to make atonement for her sin as well as Isaiah's (John 12:41).

Then the Lord asks for someone to help Him take the message to the people. Rather than groveling in the presence of the holy Lord, Isaiah jumps up and down like an excited child, eager to partner with the Lord. The message is Isaiah 1:18–20: The Lord calls for them to think with Him. Though their sin is like scarlet, it will be white as snow. He calls them to repent with the promise that they will eat the best of the land. But if they resist, they will be devoured by the sword. The Lord tells Isaiah the call to repentance will actually harden the people. Isaiah asks how long he should keep up this call. The compassionate, gracious Lord will continue His call to repentance until the day of judgment finally comes. Then the abuser will be chopped down, leaving only a stump. Help her compare this picture with the picture of the Lord she was taught in the abusive system.

Help her understand grace is the Lord's help to those who are open about their sin. It is not a free pass for the abuser to continue in his sin. Neither is it limited to a select few elite people. Rather the Lord's compassion and grace move Him to "Defend the weak and the fatherless; uphold the cause of the poor and the oppressed. Rescue the weak and the needy; deliver them from the hand of the wicked" (Psalm 82:3–4).[11]

She has been told that she must forgive everyone, especially the abuser. She must release him from all obligation, all expectations, all standards, and trust him with no hesitation because she must forgive as the Lord does, not remembering at all. *Help her to see the lies around the truth here.* Take her to Numbers 14. The Israelites once again rebel against the Lord's leadership and He responds with wrath. Once again Moses calls on the Lord to forgive His sinful people, citing Exodus 34:6–7. The Lord does forgive them (Numbers 14:20), but He does not trust them with the blessing of dwelling in the land. He forgives but does not trust them. Neither does He kill them. In fact, He takes care of them, providing food, water, and protection for them. Even their sandals do not wear out. But they live out their natural lives in the desert rather than in the Promised Land.

Take her to the forgiveness story in Luke 17. Jesus says, "If your brother or sister sins against you, rebuke them; and if they repent, forgive them" (Luke 17:3). Keep doing it, Jesus says. But don't miss the need to rebuke the brother for his sin. This is not silence toward sinners, not ignoring the reality of sin. The brother must repent if forgiveness is to occur. In the parallel story in Matthew 18, Peter asks how many times he must forgive. Not seven times, but seventy times seven, Jesus responds. There is no end to forgiveness. But this follows the command to rebuke one taken in sin leading to repentance.[12] The one who refused to repent is as a pagan or a tax collector, meaning one who is outside the community of the Lord. The sin must be identified, confessed, and repented before forgiveness is complete. Jesus, whose forgiveness has no limit, does not pass by unrepentant sin. In fact, He blasts the teachers and the Pharisees for their spiritual abuse.[13] But even this promise of judgment ends with a compassionate cry for the very sinners who will be judged.[14]

Help her see that Jesus' model of authority is not lording it over people, not exercising authority over them, but serving them even if it costs comfort and life.[15] Take her to 1 Peter 5 to see that leaders care for the people. They are not greedy for money but eager to serve. They do not lord it over people but live as examples of service. Take her to the garden of Gethsemane to learn what true submission looks like. Jesus gives the Father His feelings ("My soul is overwhelmed with sorrow to the point of death"), His desires ("Take this cup from me"), and only then His trust ("Yet not what I will, but what you will").[16] We can see the Father's response to such groaning in His response to Israel in Exodus 2:24–3:10. He hears, remembers, cares, sees, comes, and rescues. Ask her how this compares to her abuser and what he taught about authority and submission.

Help the spiritually abused woman to deal with her own sin in light of compassion and grace. In the abusive system, any sin resulted in shaming, humiliation, and despair. How different in the kingdom of light, the complete forgiveness and cleansing Jesus gives to all who come to Him.[17]

Resources

Websites

http://www.spiritualabuse.com: Spiritual Abuse Recovery Resources

https://www.biblicaltraining.org/spiritual-abuse/gerry-breshears: Free on line class on spiritual abuse

https://www.connieabaker.com: Connie Baker helps religious abuse survivors find courage, hope, and freedom on their journey to healing

Books

Baker, Connie. *Traumatized by Religious Abuse: Courage, Hope and Freedom of Survivors.* Eugene, OR: Luminare Press, 2019.

Ball, Glenn. *Let Us Prey: The Plague of Narcissist Pastors and What We Can Do About It.* Eugene, OR: Cascade Books, 2017.

Blue, Ken. *Healing Spiritual Abuse: How to Break Free from Bad Church Experiences.* Downers Grove, IL: InterVarsity Press, 1993.

Diederich, F. Remy. *Broken Trust: A Practical Guide to Identify and Recover from Toxic Faith, Toxic Church, and Spiritual Abuse.* Self-pub., 2017.

Dupont, Marc. *Toxic Churches: Restoration from Spiritual Abuse.* Grand Rapids: Chosen Books, 2004.

Enroth, Ronald. *Churches That Abuse.* Grand Rapids: Zondervan, 1993.

———. *Recovering from Churches That Abuse.* Grand Rapids: Zondervan, 1994.

Johnson, David, and Jeff VanVonderen. *The Subtle Power of Spiritual Abuse: Recognizing and Escaping Spiritual Manipulation and False Spiritual Authority Within the Church*. Grand Rapids: Bethany House, 2005.

VanVonderen, Jeff, Dale Ryan, and Juanita Ryan. *Soul Repair: Rebuilding Your Spiritual Life*. Downers Grove, IL: InterVarsity Press, 2008, 2012.

Related Scriptures

Psalms 68:4–6; 103:6–13
Isaiah 58:6–9
Matthew 11:28–30
James 1:27

AUTHOR BIO

GERRY BRESHEARS has been professor of theology at Western Seminary since 1980. In addition to teaching and lecturing at a number of colleges and seminaries around the world, he speaks in many churches and is a pastor to pastors. He works with a wide variety of people and issues in the pastoral side of his life. Gerry and his wife, Sherry, have two sons, Donn and David, and a daughter, Cyndee, and four wonderful grandchildren. He is an elder and a member of the preaching team at Grace Community Church of Gresham, Oregon.

Chapter 21

Sexuality

Dr. Juli Slattery
Clinical psychologist, author, speaker and the president/cofounder of Authentic Intimacy

I met Bree* (names in this chapter have been changed) in a crowded coffee shop. A mutual friend connected us for no other reason than for me to hear Bree's story. Although she is twenty years younger, Bree grew up so similar to me. She was raised in a small, Midwest town, attending church and youth group. She, like me, had committed her life to Christ as a young girl. But now, our lives looked very different. After some small talk of getting to know each other, Bree dove into the deep end: "I don't believe in God anymore—at least the God I grew up learning about. And honestly, Juli, it's all because of sex."

Bree told me stories, similar to ones I'd heard from so many in her generation. Well-meaning Christians had taught her about purity, which she translated as "don't make the boys around you stumble, and don't have sex until you get married." Although she wanted to be a good Christian, Bree was naturally curvy—so much so that the boys in her youth group called her sexual names and teased her.

She was sixteen when Bree's youth pastor began showing her special attention that eventually led to sexual violation. Bree stopped attending church, gained thirty pounds, and sank deep into depression. Her Christian parents tried to force her to go to church and youth group. She knew she could never tell them what had happened. They wouldn't believe her anyway. Because she was "damaged goods," she no longer saw any point in purity rings or modesty.

When Bree went to college, she experienced a world of sexual freedom. Her shame seemed to disappear as everyone could have sex with anyone they wanted to. She developed an attraction to a close female friend and the relationship became sexual. Bree continued to date guys and wondered what she was. Gay? Bisexual? Or just confused? Now in her late twenties, Bree is single but dating a woman and she thinks she may be in love.

Bree eventually told her parents about what happened to her as a sixteen-year-old. They said they believed her, and then they asked if she had been "leading him on." Her parents still try to convince Bree to come back to God, with little understanding of the threads of pain that led her away from Him.

As Bree recounted her adolescence, she can see that her parents and teachers meant well, but that they were misguided following an "antiquated, misogynistic religion that promotes rape culture through guilt and shame."

I've heard many versions of Bree's story. The details vary. Some involve a gay brother, a transgender friend, sexual abuse that was blamed on the girl, a young woman shamed for promiscuity, a "submissive" wife abused by her husband, a hypocritical preacher who condemns sexual immorality found sleeping with his personal assistant . . . but they all lead to the same conclusion. Christianity must be dismantled because its teaching on sexuality is hurting good people.

Sexuality is one of the primary reasons why young women are running away . . . not just from church, but from God. Sure, some hang on to vestiges of Christianity, but a postmodern form of it that edits the Bible and invites us to create God as we would like Him to be.

Here is what I've learned from ministering to women like Bree: when sex becomes confusing, God becomes confusing.

Reaching women who are struggling with sexual pain and confusion (even if they don't identify it as such) is perhaps the greatest mission field of our day. It is not primarily about convincing them of a biblical sexual ethic. Instead, our mission must be rooted in connecting, or reconnecting, them to the deeper truth of Jesus Christ. Christianity is not primarily a lifestyle or code of ethics. It is a love relationship with God, the Creator and Lord. We talk about sexual abuse, homosexuality, porn addiction, and the hookup culture not just because these represent sin and pain, but because they are often the barrier and sometimes the bridge to the only conversation with eternal significance.

Jesus modeled this for us so clearly in John 4 when He talked with the Samaritan woman at the well. She avoided personal conversation, but Jesus intentionally brought up the subject of her sexual immorality. Why would He do this? Not to shame her but to invite her to address the deepest area of need and pain in her life. This was the source of her "thirst" for which He offered living water.

Understand the Issue

Most of us have been indoctrinated with an unspoken rule that we just don't talk about sex in church. If we do address sexuality, our conversations tend to be awkward and carefully managed to avoid the issues that people really struggle with. What woman goes to church to ask about whether or not using sex toys is a sin, to talk about her porn struggle, or to ask how to deal with an attraction to another woman? We just don't speak bluntly about such things.

Because of our silence and hesitance to address sexual issues from an honest and godly perspective, many people have an invisible but effective barrier separating their sexuality from their spirituality. They never think to ask God about sexual healing or to acknowledge that He never leaves us, even when we are looking at porn or having sex. God isn't shy about sexuality. He created us as sexual people and understands our sexual pain, questions, and struggles.

Helping them recognize the link between sexuality and spirituality is central to ministering to anyone dealing with a sexual issue. To be a Christ follower means pursuing Him in every area of life, including our sexuality. Many women experience their sexuality as "split off" from their relationship with God. In fact, the two can never truly be separated. Every sexual issue is also a spiritual issue. Here is why.

Our beliefs about sex come from our beliefs about God.

Think about the changes we have witnessed in recent years related to our beliefs about what is sexually moral and normal. There has been a consistent, predictable slide toward accepting pornography, same-sex marriage, gender fluidity, no-fault divorce, premarital sex, cohabitation, and hooking up. Why? Technologies like the internet and smartphones have played a role in these societal changes, but there is a more foundational reason. These changes have nothing to do with what we have learned about humanity and everything to do with what we have forgotten about God.

In Romans 1:18–32, Paul portrays the ancient Roman culture as undergoing relational, sexual, and moral chaos. He describes homosexual practices along with a host of other indicators that the culture had become corrupt, including greed, rebellion against authority, self-indulgence, and inventing new ways of doing evil. What we must realize is that Paul isn't primarily discussing the moral decadence of the Roman culture. He describes this brokenness in response to what the Romans chose to do with God. His invisible traits were evident to them through creation. But rather than worship God, they created and worshiped their own gods.

This is the same explanation for the moral changes we have seen within our culture, including our Christian subculture. We have become a humanistic society, elevating human experience and reason above God's authority. As a result, we have given ourselves permission to define God as we see fit. His plan and moral intentions for our sexuality are negotiable. After all, He loves us and wants the best for us, right? So why would a loving God ask a person to deny their sexual needs and desires?

A. W. Tozer wrote, "The question before us, and the question that really matters, is simply, what do you think of Christ? And what are you going to do with Christ? Every question we might ever have can be boiled down to the subject of Jesus Christ."[1]

At their core, all questions about sex involve questions about God, His Word, human nature, and redemption. My new friend, Bree, walked away from God because she no longer views Him as loving and trustworthy. She does not acknowledge God as the Creator who is intimately involved in her life. And because Bree and I disagree about God, we will disagree about sex. My ministry to her is not directed toward arguing about biblical sexual morality but listening and sharing about the foundational issues of God, love, truth, and what makes us thrive as human beings.

The "sexual revolution" is the result of a fundamental shift in our understanding of truth. Rather than acknowledging a Creator whose wisdom is far greater than ours, most Western Christians find "truth" through their feelings and experiences. *We define God's love as His embrace of the "authentic me" rather than an invitation to know and worship Him.*

As you minister to women, remember that many of them are beginning with a completely different orientation of how we find truth and how we define the moral categories of right and wrong.

What we might assume is a conversation about morality between two Christians may actually be a discussion between people who worship a very different God, even if they call Him by the same name. Before we dive into whether or not a certain sexual lifestyle is moral, we must be sensitive to the more pressing issue of a woman's relationship with God. Our view on any sexual issue is rooted in what we believe about God's character, authority, and trustworthiness. A woman who believes that being a Christian shouldn't cost her anything will quickly explain away any biblical teaching encouraging her to deny her desires, sexual or otherwise.

Our sexual experiences inform what we believe about God.

Carol has three young adult children, two daughters and a son. From the time they were small, Carol and her husband, Glenn, took their kids to church and taught them about God. Along with the rest of Christian teaching, Carol's children learned about God's standards for sexuality. As they navigated the teen years, one of her daughters began experimenting sexually with other young women. By her freshman year of college, she identified as bisexual. Carol and Glenn had barely gotten through their shock when a year later their teenage son announced that he was gay. "I've always liked boys," he told his parents.

While Carol and Glenn certainly were not perfect parents (who is?), they had done their very best to raise their children right. How did they fail? As this couple worked to make sense of their situation, it caused them not only to examine their parenting, but also their belief in God. Was faith in God worth risking the alienation of two of their children? They met many other Christians walking through similar circumstances who reconciled their pain by rejecting a traditional understanding of God and sexuality. Should Carol find a church that embraces God while also celebrating LGBTQ lifestyles? If not, what would it look like for her to love her children well?

Whenever we have an experience that doesn't line up with our beliefs, we feel "cognitive dissonance." This is the term psychologists use to explain the stress and discomfort that exists when we try to hold to two mutually incompatible ideas. Carol believes that the Bible defines bisexuality and homosexuality as broken and sinful expressions of sexuality. Yet she also loves her kids and wants them to be happy. They seem to be happier being able to fully express their sexuality without risking the love of their mom.

Much work around sexual issues involves enduring with people through such cognitive dissonance. When a woman is wading through betrayal in her marriage or the loneliness of singleness, she needs to process whether or not what she has believed about God is really true. Another example of this is making sense of God through tragedy and trauma. How could a loving God allow a little child to be sexually abused? Why doesn't God put an end to human trafficking and sex slavery? Surely, He could!

These are clearly involved and complicated questions that have no simple answers. Don't feel pressure to resolve a woman's cognitive dissonance with a theological explanation. Job's friends made this mistake and ended up adding to Job's suffering. Remember that God Himself did not give Job a logical answer to these questions. Instead, He revealed His power and sovereignty personally to Job. The woman asking these questions is in pain and ultimately wants to know, "God, can I trust You?" Validating her doubt and suggesting that you ask the Lord together to meet her in her pain may be your most helpful response.

When you are ministering to women on any sexual issue, make sure the conversation doesn't stop at sexual sin, shame, or longings. During His earthly ministry, Jesus often rebuked His disciples, but not for sexual thoughts or petty arguments. He most often rebuked them for their unbelief. At the core of every sexual struggle is this: Will we believe that God is the Creator and Healer? Is He worthy of building our lives upon?

Shepherding Insights

Issues like homosexuality and gender dysphoria/fluidity may intimidate you. How do you minister to a woman who herself is going through this or loves someone who is? If the current trends are any indication, this will be a massively growing proportion of women seeking help. If we avoid women in this type of pain because it makes us uncomfortable, they will likely seek help from communities that readily embrace them but may not readily embrace God.

Take comfort in the fact that you are equipped to minister to the underlying spiritual questions even if you are not an expert on LGBTQ or other sexual issues. The woman in front of you is a person who struggles with many of the same doubts, questions, and wounds that you carry. While you may not understand a woman's sexual choices and temptations, you can understand the longing to be loved, safe, respected, and accepted. You can understand how difficult it is to make sense of God when you have been hurt and don't know where to find truth.

Walking with a woman through her questions and doubts about God can be scary for you too. There have been times when the stories a woman has told me have been so devastating that I go home with my own unanswered questions. *God, how could You allow such pain in the world?*

I've gained great confidence and comfort in knowing that there is no question, no pain, and no brokenness that is too great for God. Even when my mind doesn't understand His ways, my faith in God's character keeps me grounded. Walking with women through sexual pain and doubt requires that we are willing for any question to be asked without fear. Instead of shutting down a woman's questions and doubts with platitudes or even Bible verses, we must be willing to sit in the tension of her pursuit for God.

We may shy away from women with sexual pain because these situations are often messy. Sexual experiences and sin get "locked away" for a reason. They represent shame and vulnerability. The details of sexual trauma, sexual addiction, and even of sexual dysfunction in marriage are unsettling. As a woman walks toward healing, her life may temporarily get worse before it gets better.

Shannon is a good example of this. When she and her husband, Sam, were walking through years of conflict, Shannon had an affair with a coworker. Their relationship lasted about six months before Shannon was convicted by God to break it off. Now, Sam and Shannon's relationship is back on track, better than it has ever been. They are invested in a small group through church and are learning to work through conflicts that formerly plagued intimacy in their marriage. Shannon asked me, "Do I have to tell Sam about the affair? It would break his heart and mess up all of the progress we have made."

I told Shannon that true intimacy is impossible with secrets. Telling Sam the truth would, in the long run, be the right thing for their relationship, but I understood why she wanted to keep the secret from her husband. The truth is messy.

You can anticipate such "messy" scenarios as you endeavor to minister to sexually broken women. The road to healing can be fraught with setbacks and relapses. This work is not for the faint of heart!

A special note to men in ministry

There is a genuine tension and concern for men ministering to women on sexual issues. As the #metoo movement demonstrates, great care and forethought is necessary to protect vulnerable women from violation and their caregivers from nebulous accusations. Your kneejerk response may be to avoid these situations altogether. I encourage you not to circumvent ministering to women who are experiencing pain related to sexuality issues. For many, their sexual histories include being objectified and sexually used by men. Part of their healing often involves engaging with spiritual fathers and brothers who value them as individuals and treat them with dignity. How will they heal if the healthy men around them are distant?

Without question, be wise about both physical and emotional boundaries when ministering across genders. You should not be in a building or car alone with a woman to whom you are ministering. Don't engage in private conversations through social media, texting, or email even with the intent of wanting to help. Involve your female staff when you sense conversations or interactions are too detailed or blurring healthy boundaries. Respect the professional guidelines established by counseling and pastoral organizations. These are for your protection as well as for the woman's safety.

HELPFUL THINGS TO SAY AND DO

1. **DO** get used to difficult conversations. This is the new
   normal. While in the past, it has not appeared "Christian" to
   talk about sexual things, it's a new day. Frankly the silence
   among Christians related to sexuality has caused a lot of pain.
   Women who have needed help or have been wounded were

silenced rather than embraced. Ministering to women in this generation means getting comfortable with conversations about pornography, sexual abuse, sexual problems in marriage, masturbation, and LGBTQ issues. Normalizing these conversations is not the same as embracing the behaviors.

2. **DO** listen and ask questions. Value every woman's story. The old saying goes, "People don't care how much you know until they know how much you care." James says it even better, "Be quick to listen, slow to speak and slow to anger" (James 1:19). At the heart of a woman's struggle is the question of her value. She doesn't want to be viewed as a problem to be fixed but embraced as an individual. LGBTQ may define categories of sexuality, but people never fit into categories. Each woman is a person who has a story to tell behind her pain. Even our most spiritual agendas can interfere with our willingness to listen and care.

3. **DO** be prayerful even in the moment, asking the Holy Spirit to give you wisdom. Although my full-time job is to study and to teach on sexual issues, there is still much I don't know. Even if I knew all of the latest research and worked with hundreds of women, I still don't know exactly what each woman needs to hear in the moment. We need the Holy Spirit to give wisdom. He can direct us in when to speak, when to stay silent, and when to simply cry with a woman in pain.

4. **DO** validate the hurt this woman has experienced, even if it came from the church. Very often, sexual issues have been exacerbated by church people. Pastors may have dismissed a report of sexual violation. Legalistic teaching may have added to a woman's shame. Sometimes well-meaning Christian people say things that are deeply hurtful. This has certainly been true related to LGBTQ struggles, including criticism and judgment toward parents whose children identify as LGBTQ. They can feel shunned by their Christian friends and condemned for

how they handle every situation from Thanksgiving dinner to attending a gay wedding.

5. **DO** lean into the relationship. Sexual issues are complicated and very vulnerable. Walking with a woman through them is messy and takes time. You can't rush into such sensitive topics without building a bridge of love, acceptance, and trust. There are no shortcuts to that work.

6. **DO**, with discretion, admit your own brokenness and pursuit of sexual wholeness. One of the greatest barriers to sexual issues is that women feel categorized by them. Often there feels like an "us" vs. "them" dynamic. One of the best ways to break down this barrier is to be appropriately vulnerable about ways that you have struggled with sexuality or sin. Even if your story isn't the same as the woman in front of you, the humility of admitting that you have experienced pain in this area too builds a bridge. Just think of the power of saying "ME TOO." It invites connection rather than judgment. The woman you are ministering to doesn't need to know the details of your story. It's enough to personally identify with her pain and need for hope.

7. **DO** sit with cognitive dissonance without having to defend God. A woman in pain needs a safe place to ask questions like, "How could a loving God allow this to happen?" or "If God loves me, why did He make me like this and then tell me to fit into a mold that looks nothing like me?" or "If God loves me, why are His people so cruel to me?" You do not have the answers to these questions, so don't try to make them up. God can and will defend Himself. As mentioned earlier, Job's friends would have been far more effective had they simply wept with and struggled with their friend's pain rather than forming theological reasons for it.

HURTFUL RESPONSES TO AVOID

1. **DON'T** give prescriptions of what healing looks like. Christine came to know Jesus Christ as Savior while identifying as a lesbian. She had a girlfriend and many of her friends were LGBTQ. Shortly after coming to Christ, she was invited to a women's Bible study where she felt like a major misfit with her short-cropped purple hair, tats, and nose ring. The ladies in the study tried to make her comfortable. One befriended her and asked her over for lunch. When Christine showed up at the woman's home, this dear lady took Christine in her closet and offered to show her how to dress more like a Christian woman. She also gave her a Christian book on dating so she could start forming a romantic relationship with a man. Christine left as soon as she politely could exit and has never again attended church. We can't possibly know God's journey of healing for a woman and shouldn't assume that we do. It is enough to show love and patiently shepherd her toward God's Word.

2. **DON'T** confront any further than you have connected. Think of your relationships as bank accounts. Every caring exchange, hour spent listening, kind thing you do for someone is a deposit. Each time you speak a hard truth or ask a difficult question, you are making a withdrawal from the emotional bank of that relationship. Every shepherding relationship will require times of gentle confrontation. Yet you must have built enough equity in your relational bank before this happens. In some relationships, these deposits take a lot of time to accumulate. Be patient!

3. **DON'T** try to convince or win a debate. Let me say it clearly: it is not your job to convince anyone that their sexual choices are sinful. There is a big difference between speaking God's truth and taking it upon yourself to win an argument about it. Realizing this has been one of the most freeing burdens in

ministering to people on sexual issues. It means I get to love God and love people without taking on the additional burden of owning the results. Only God can change a heart!

4. **DON'T** shy away from sharing your convictions when asked. You may be so invested in the relationship with a woman that you are afraid of speaking truth, even in love, because you don't want to hurt her. You do a woman no favors by pretending that brokenness is wholeness. We are called to "speak the truth in love" (Ephesians 4:15). As I mentioned earlier, this right is earned through humility and relationship. However, we are the light of the world. If the light blends in with the darkness, we are ultimately ineffective in making an eternal difference in someone's life. The gospel message is offensive, and we must never change that in order to win friends.

5. **DON'T** pretend that you have it all figured out. I was speaking at a conference on sexuality when a woman in tears approached me. She explained that her eight-year-old son was transitioning to a girl. Her words tumbled out, "Do you know how painful it is to hear your son cry every time he takes a shower because he can't look at his naked body? I've tried everything I know to do to help him. Why do people who have no idea of this pain talk about the Bible and sex?" This was not a time to teach but a time to listen. I don't know the pain this woman has walked through. I can't imagine how tortured and torn she has felt. While I may teach on biblical sexuality, I must also constantly be in a posture of learning. What this woman shared did not change my views on God and gender, but it impacted the way I communicate those truths.

6. **DON'T** stop learning. We are confronting questions and scenarios that feel totally unfamiliar to the average shepherd. Yet God is raising up teachers, scholars, and counselors who have wisdom and compassion. The church will need this expertise as we encounter new questions and challenges. Even as I pen

these words, I'm aware that much may have changed within the sexual landscape of our culture by the time you read them. There are theological arguments among Christians supporting homosexuality, same-sex marriage, cohabitation, and gender fluidity. You will be confronted with these. Like the Bereans in the book of Acts, go back to study, comparing everything you hear to the unchanging truths of God's Word.

7. **DON'T** put the cart before the horse. Remember the Great Commission that Jesus left with His disciples to go into all the world and make disciples (Matthew 28:19). While sexual integrity is part of surrendering our lives to Jesus' lordship, discipleship begins with an authentic encounter with God. One of the biggest mistakes I see people making is they want to address a woman's sexuality while neglecting her greater need for Jesus. We were made for intimacy. We were created for God, for the deepest passion and intimacy imaginable. Sexuality is a powerful physical way that we experience those longings for intimacy but is not the ultimate answer of what we are searching for.

Finally, remember that we are called to represent both the truth and character of Jesus. Don't fall for the trap of compromising truth for the sake of compassion or vice versa. John described Jesus as a man full of grace and truth. May this describe us as well.

Resources

Websites

https://www.authenticintimacy.com/: Authentic Intimacy
https://centerforfaith.com/: Center for Faith, Sexuality & Gender
https://www.himhministries.com/: Hole in my Heart Ministries
https://www.restoredhopenetwork.org/: Restored Hope Network

Books

Butterfield, Rosaria. *The Gospel Comes with A House Key: Practicing Radically Ordinary Hospitality in Our Post-Christian World.* Wheaton, IL: Crossway, 2018.

Hill Perry, Jackie. *Gay Girl, Good God: The Story of Who I Was, and Who God Has Always Been.* Nashville: B&H Books, 2018.

Harper, Brad and Drew Harper. *Space at the Table, Conversations Between an Evangelical Theologian and His Gay Son.* Portland: Zeal Books, 2016.

Kaltenbach, Caleb. *Messy Grace: How a Pastor with Gay Parents Learned to Love Others without Sacrificing Conviction.* Colorado Springs: WaterBrook, 2015.

Slattery, Juli. *Rethinking Sexuality: God's Design and Why it Matters.* Colorado Springs: Multnomah, 2018.

———. *25 Questions You're Afraid to Ask about Love, Sex and Intimacy.* Chicago: Moody Publishers, 2015.

Sprinkle, Preston. *People to Love: Why Homosexuality Is Not Just an Issue.* Grand Rapids: Zondervan, 2015.

Stanton, Glenn. *How to Love your LGBT Neighbor, Being Friends in Grace and Truth.* Chicago: Moody Publishers, 2014.

Wildenberg, Lori. *Messy Parenting: Powerful and Practical Ways to Strengthen Family Connections.* Birmingham: New Hope Publishers, 2018.

Yarhouse, Mark. *Understanding Gender Dysphoria: Navigating Transgender Issues in a Changing Culture.* Christian Association for Psychological Studies Books. Downers Grove, IL: IVP Academic, 2015.

Yuan, Christopher. *Out of a Far Country: A Gay Son's Journey to God. A Broken Mother's Search for Hope.* Chicago: Moody Publishers, 2011.

Related Scriptures

Matthew 19:5
Luke 7:36–50
John 4:4–26; 8:1-11
Romans 1:18–32
1 Corinthians 6:9–7:9
Galatians 6:1–5
1 Peter 2:11–12

AUTHOR BIO

DR. JULI SLATTERY is a clinical psychologist, author, speaker, and the president/co-founder of Authentic Intimacy. Juli earned her college degree at Wheaton College, an MA in psychology from Biola University, and an MS and a Doctorate degree in Clinical Psychology from Florida Institute of Technology.

From 2008–2012, Dr. Slattery served at Focus on the Family writing, teaching, and co-hosting the Focus on the Family Broadcast. In 2012, she left Focus on the Family to start Authentic Intimacy, a ministry devoted to reclaiming God's design for sexuality.

Juli is the author of ten books and host of the weekly podcast "Java with Juli." Juli and her husband, Mike, are the parents of three sons; they live in Akron, Ohio.

Healing Women in Pain

What the Healing Community Needs to Know

Chapter 22

Environments of Grace Offer Acceptance

Women whose lives have been marked by pain and suffering live in our neighborhoods, work in our marketplace, attend our local schools. The number of women suffering is astounding and includes women who populate our local evangelical churches.[1] Often their pain is hidden; women are fearful of being misunderstood or judged.[2] Women are significantly affected emotionally by the quality of their interpersonal relationships.[3] The risk of diminishing the quality of a relationship may be too great for a woman to reveal an emotionally painful trauma. The silence of women should not be interpreted as an absence of emotional pain.

Context for Spiritual Intervention

The church is in a strategic position to offer informed interventions. The deep wounds of the soul can best be healed in the context of biblically based grace-filled church communities where deep personal relationships can be developed.[4] Pastor Peter Scazzero is an example of a church leader who admittedly was not aware of his own lack of emotional health and therefore could not discern the emotional pain of those in his church.[5] His eyes were opened to his need through the painful threat of losing his marriage and his ministry. The positive impact of seeking intervention to work through the pain of his past not only brought positive benefit to his relationship with his wife, but has since been multiplied in the lives of his leadership team and congregants.

Scazzero observes that too often the church relegates emotional issues to the therapist's office and takes responsibility only for "spiritual" problems. The two are inseparably linked and critical to a healthy church.[6] People come to counselors and ministers seeking help for many reasons, but mostly it is for help with emotional pain.[7] Exposure to the unique needs of women in pain will prepare leaders to minister effectively to the high number of women in churches who suffer with emotional needs. The church is in a strategic position to offer such intervention.

Faith in Jesus Christ provides the essential components that support a woman in crisis. A crisis is defined as a juncture of her life in which "the trend of all future events . . . is determined."[8] This turning point may lead a woman to embrace Jesus Christ or turn away from His advances. Faith in Jesus Christ provides understanding and empowerment for repentance, forgiveness, and trust, and rebuilding trust once it has been damaged does not happen automatically or easily. Environments of grace offer unconditional acceptance, which fosters increased trust.

A woman needs to be valued for who she is and respected for her own skills and talents. She needs to feel strong and that it's safe to voice her opinions. The grace-filled church environment serves a critical role in the life of a wounded woman at a crossroad.

Christ sent a strong message to His followers that framed serving people in need as a picture of serving Christ Himself.[9] Jesus Christ modeled His intentions for the church by encouraging the downhearted, comforting the afflicted, and releasing the oppressed.[10] Although the biblical directive is reason enough to offer pastoral care, the additional voice of social agencies further compels us to respond.

For example, among the recommendations published in 2002 by the American Psychological Association to improve recognition and understanding of depression in women is to "develop collaborative outreach efforts with other professional organizations . . . including nontraditional partners *such as religious organizations* (italics added by author) . . ."[11] They recognize that the need cannot be met solely by social agencies.

The staff at most local community shelters, police precincts, law and medical offices is trained to respond to emergency needs of women, but seldom will know how to guide a woman in her spiritual journey in a time of crisis. Every crisis has a spiritual dimension. These concerns can either help or hinder progress in the healing journey. A woman working with secular agencies may be inclined to deny or hide her identity as a follower of Jesus Christ rather than include integration of her beliefs in processing her trauma. She will likely struggle with how to interpret the circumstance in light of the Bible or her church's worldview as she understands it.

The need for church and seminary leaders to develop awareness, understanding, and attending skills is evidenced by the assessment of community and professional organizations that work with women experiencing emotional pain. Churches and seminaries who respond to this need will more adequately prepare future leaders for ministry in the local church.[12] There is an urgent need for the church to become a safe place, to create an environment of grace for wounded women.

Environments of Grace

So what is an environment of grace?

The word "gracious" is used often in the Old Testament especially in two main ways. First, people repeatedly describe God as *gracious and compassionate* reflecting God's own description of Himself.

> And he [God] passed in front of Moses, proclaiming, "The LORD, the LORD, the *compassionate and gracious God*, slow to anger, abounding in love and faithfulness." (Ex. 34:6, emphasis added)

Second, people in the Old Testament testified that because "the gracious hand of God was on me" they were able to accomplish the purpose for which God sent them out.[13] God's graciousness and compassion are extended to us; we in turn reflect Him well when we are compassionate and gracious. His gracious hand will guide and empower me in the process of following Him. Those solid beliefs will enable me to receive grace and give it to others.

In the New Testament, the word "grace" is used often.

> The Word became flesh and made his dwelling among us. We have seen his glory, the glory of the one and only Son, who came from the Father, full of *grace* and truth. (John 1:14)

> This righteousness is given through faith in Jesus Christ to all who believe. There is no difference between Jew and Gentile, for all have sinned and fall short of the glory of God, and all are justified freely by his *grace* through the redemption that came by Christ Jesus. (Romans 3:22–24).

God, who is Himself gracious, sent His Son, who is full of grace and truth, to our planet. This Son lived among humans for over thirty years, enabling us to see what grace looks like—grace and truth in perfect harmony. This grace has been extended to us in ways that are not fully comprehensible. Certainly, we are justified when we believe. Jesus Christ is "full of grace" and it is His freely given grace that provides our redemption and the forgiveness of our sins. Ephesians 2:8–9 removes any assumptions that our salvation might be something we earn or accomplish ourselves: "For it is by grace you have been saved, through faith—and this is not from yourselves, it is the gift of God—not by works, so that no one can boast."

In addition to salvation, redemption, sanctification, and eternal life, God's grace provides more than we can comprehend. A partial listing includes:[14]

- One blessing after another
- An abundance of all we need in every good work, at all times
- Christ's power in our weakness
- Using our gifting is "faithfully administering God's grace"
- The promise of restoration in suffering, resulting in making you strong, firm, and steadfast
- Confidence in prayer, that we will receive grace in the time of need

Paul asks two summarizing questions—"If God is for us, who can be against us?" and "He who did not spare his own Son, but gave him up for us all—how will he not also, along with him, *graciously give us all things*?" (Romans 8:31–32, emphasis added).

Did you miss it? Reread this list in view of shepherding. This demands repeating. In this life we are given all we need for life and godliness.[15] This includes when we step out to shepherd another; we are given *all we need* to graciously and compassionately walk alongside a woman in pain. God's grace provides an abundance of whatever we need, "at all times." No matter the situation, Christ will be power in our weakness. He will give one blessing after another. We will receive grace in time of need when we approach Him in prayer. We have the promise that there will be maturing benefits in suffering. We are administering God's grace when we minister in our gifting. Wow! In case we missed it, Paul summarizes in Romans 8:31–32 that *God is for us.* He has already given the most precious thing for us, His Son; He will also "graciously give us all things." So, what more are we lacking? Are you willing to trust God's Word as you move forward into what might be new territory for you?

These Scriptures bring great encouragement and empowerment to the shepherd, and thus to the woman in pain. If God's grace is so lavishly given to us, how can we do less than extend it to others, particularly to people in pain? The greater our personal understanding of what God has lavished upon us, the more easily we will extend it to others and be a catalyst for a community of grace.

What does grace look like in relationship? Jeff VanVonderen, in *Families Where Grace Is in Place*,[16] says grace and shame are opposites. In a shame-based family system, members are given constant messages about themselves that something is wrong with them. Love is conditional and based on performance. Acceptance is earned by performing certain behaviors and avoiding others. *People* are not loved and accepted for who they *are* but for what they *do*. *Behavior* is all-important.

In contrast, grace-filled family relationships are characterized by:[17]

1. *Words of affirmation that are consistently communicated verbally.*
2. *A people-oriented, rather than performance-oriented, environment.* What is *real* is more important than how things look. A grace-filled home or church is a safe, unconditionally accepting place where a person's outside can match her inside. Life is seen as a process rather than an event. Members do not have to fix one another; rather, they encourage one another in making good choices.
3. *Boundaries and expectations are clearly communicated.* Unspoken rules and coded hinting are not life-giving. It is not appropriate to hold someone accountable for rules they did not verbally know were in operation. Speaking the truth in love is a biblical injunction.
4. *People are acceptable and valuable because of God's love and grace toward them.* God is the source of everything we believe and do.
5. *Family members are responsible and accountable.* This increases maturity. Faultfinding, making excuses, blaming, and shaming do not. Unacceptable behaviors are about poor choices, not about our value and acceptance as people.

6. *Feelings are valid and useful.* They are a God-given means of expression and connection to others.

Is it possible to change a shame-filled family or church into a grace-filled community? That is the same as asking, "Is it possible to become more like Christ?" How can we better reflect Christ in the community of people in which we currently belong or wish to belong? The obvious answer is to spend time in the Bible identifying what such a community really could look like. Certainly the first few chapters of Acts provide an example of a Spirit-filled community. The Epistles give the details of what godliness looks like, personally and in community. Certainly the Gospels expose the compassionate, gracious Jesus who embodies both grace and truth.

A second place to look may be books such as the one you are currently reading. Follow the journeys of the women's stories in section 2. Work through chapters of my previous book, *Shepherding a Woman's Heart*, with others who have a similar desire. Try gathering two or more people to study with you, pray together, and seek God's direction on how you can become grace-filled people. It is likely God will begin with your own heart. It could be risky, but so hope-filled.

What difference might it make in your life if grace were fully embraced? Five truths about grace are cited in *TrueFaced*.[18]

1. *Humility attracts grace.* Certainly the Bible is clear on this: "God opposes the proud, but shows favor to the humble."[19] Humility and trust escort us to grace. I am likely to be more humbly transparent when I trust God with me, and then trust others with me. This is different than trusting my own assessment of myself and taking credit for my relative goodness.
2. *Grace changes our life focus.* Instead of focusing on my sin issues, my life focus needs to be on trusting God and who God says I am. This shift will bring incredible freedom.

3. *Let God handle my sin.* Sin will not be managed. Behavior change
   and sin management are deceptively tricky boxing opponents. We
   may win some early rounds, but soon we realize this is a losing
   battle. Grace trusts that God and only God can handle our sin.
4. *Grace melts masks.* Striving drives us to hide, which breeds compulsive sinning. Grace creates authenticity.
5. *Grace changes how we treat one another.* Our character is actually
   formed in relationships.

An environment of grace provides me with truth, acceptance, healing, safety, perspective, freedom, and power that other environments do not provide. This is fundamental to resolving my own sin issues. The community of grace begins to break the cycle of sin issues that kept us bound. We see one another as saints who sin, rather than as sinners who are saved. We believe what God says about us is true. We can now be exactly who we are, in the midst of all our issues and unresolved stuff, and still fully experience grace, love, and acceptance. The final objective is maturing us into who God says we are[20] and fulfilling His purpose for us in our generation.[21]

The biblical story of Christ's love and grace gives meaning to life and pain. A woman gains strength when others in the faith community offer a listening ear, practical support, and spiritual tools to assist in times of crises. This is most effective when the caregiver enters the woman's painful experience with a grace-filled heart and an understanding of the context of her pain.

This book is birthed out of a desire to bring understanding to that context. Section 3 provides models of shepherding ministries in both the local church and parachurch settings. This section outlines the development, implementation, and evaluation of ministries that provide short- and long-term caregiving in environments of grace.

Each chapter in section 3 will provide the process an effective healing community walked through to construct an environment of grace. Our hope is that you will begin to see the possibilities of what you could do in your community of faith, as each writer addresses the following:

- What was your perception of the needs of women that moved you to action?
- Describe the healing community of which you are currently a part.
- What were the five key steps you took toward designing and developing community care?
- How did you influence other people to embrace your vision?
- How did you provide training for caregivers?
- How did you overcome key obstacles?
- What are your greatest challenges and your greatest joys?
- What specific advice would you offer others who would like to develop a healing community?

As you read section 3, ask the Spirit of God to open your mind and heart to what He may lead you to do in your church or community.

Chapter 23

Wounded Healers Reflect God's Power

Jan Marshall, Founding Director of Shepherd's Door,
a ministry of Portland Rescue Mission

*A*s a young woman, I knew nothing of rescue missions and homelessness. My future husband, however, was born and raised in rescue mission culture. His father had directed a mission for over forty-nine years. My first introduction into this work was when I visited his family. Rescue mission work did not appeal to me, nor could I imagine doing this type of work. Yet, I married into it and felt for some years that rescue mission work was settling for second best.

When I attended Bible school, my intention was foreign missions, which was persistently upheld in my church, so my belief system drove me to follow that direction. My motive, however, was to be good and therefore loved. I felt that to do anything else would be of great disappointment to my church and family. It never occurred to me that God might have a different plan. Slowly He began to unveil how He had indeed prepared me for frontline work with homeless women.

The culture in my home as I grew up was one of anger and reaction. I grew up angry, resentful, unforgiving, and dishonoring to my imperfect parents.

My husband and I worked in various rescue missions, gleaning community respect; no one knew the deep dark struggles I carried inside. Outwardly I was the ideal pastor's wife, conference speaker, teacher, and leader. My closest friends knew of my struggles and unforgiveness because I talked incessantly of my parents' mistakes. I can only imagine how my friends felt. They probably felt like running the other way when they saw me coming.

My personality was basically joy-based and optimistic, though I had carried a level of depression throughout my childhood. But one day when I was in my early thirties, I woke up deeply depressed, something I had never experienced before. In fact, I had disrespected people who could not "get over" their depression and move forward.

I thought being a better wife, mother, housekeeper, and Christian would take care of my depression. I blamed Satan and tried to defeat him by being more "spiritual," to no avail. I asked my husband to pray for me. No relief. I memorized Bible verses. No reprieve. I read books on self-help. No release. Nine months later I was *still* depressed. Whether awake or asleep, I felt a dark cloud hovering over my head.

God had me right where He wanted me. It was while reading Catherine Marshall's book *Beyond Ourselves* that my heart opened to God. In the chapter "The Prayer of Relinquishment," Marshall tells the story of Nathaniel Hawthorne's gravely ill twelve-year-old daughter dying of a virulent form of malaria.

Una could not, must not die. This daughter strongly resembled her father, had the finest mind, the most complex character of all the Hawthorne children. Why should a capricious Providence demand that they give her up? Moreover, Una had been delirious for several days and had recognized no one. Were she to die this night, there would not even be the solace of farewells.

As the night deepened the young girl ceased her incoherent mutterings and lay so still that she seemed to be in the anteroom of death. The mother went to the window and looked out on the piazza. There was no moonlight; heavy clouds scudded across a dark and silent sky.

"I cannot bear this loss—cannot." Then suddenly, unaccountably another thought took over. "Why should I doubt the goodness of God? Let Him take Una, if He sees best. I can give her to Him. No, I won't fight against Him any more."[1]

Una lived.

Marshall continues.

Jesus said, "Resist not evil." In God's eyes, fear is evil because it is acting out the lack of trust in Him. So Jesus is advising "Resist not fear."

In other words, Jesus is saying: "Admit the possibility of what you fear most. And lo, as you stop fleeing, as you force yourself to walk up to the fear, as you look it full in the face, never forgetting that God and His power are still the supreme reality, the fear evaporates." Drastic? Yes. But effective.[2]

It was the Prayer of Relinquishment that brought me to a place of full surrender. Under all my anger and bitterness was deep fear—of failing; of what others think of me; that others would find out what a failure I was. These were all lies from Satan and the only way they could die was for me to look my fear in the face and say, "Enough!"

Unable to sleep in the quiet darkness of the night, I lifted my hand and said, "Though You slay me I will exalt You. If this depression is from

You, I accept it. I don't understand why but I surrender to You." What He did for me in the seconds that followed my prayer of surrender will be forever chiseled in my heart.

I was a wounded listener subdued with no fight left. At various points in our lives, God requires the place of self-death. Even for active, high-achieving, articulate leaders. That spot is both sweet and bitter. But it is a place of heart change nevertheless. Did it happen instantly? No. Remember, God allowed nine long months of depression to subdue my performance-based spirit. Yet He patiently loved me every inch of the way. He was preparing my heart during those nine grueling months.

As I uttered the words "Though You slay me I will exalt You," a little word entered my heart . . . anger. I argued with Him. "Not me, I'm not angry; I'm sweet. Ask anyone!" Again the quietness of His presence brought back the word . . . anger. He spoke to my heart. *"You are not responsible for what was done to you as a child. You were not a bad girl. But you are responsible for your reaction to it. Your anger is no less a sin than your parents' lack of parenting. Lay the anger at My cross . . . give it up."* I knew it was true. I gave it to Him. He forgave me.

Then He spoke to my heart again and said, *"Forgive them for what you think they did to you."* Good wording. As a bitter woman I had blown everything out of proportion and could not remember any good things from my childhood. Forgiving my parents was actually easy at this point because we stood on equal ground. We both needed God's forgiveness. I was repentant for my bitterness and God forgave me . . . I could forgive them.

God continued to speak. *"Give up your rights to ever be loved by them. They will never be able to love you the way you want. I want to be your father and mother. I am enough for you."* I felt relief. I did not need to earn their love anymore. I no longer expected their love and approval of me. God approved and that was enough. The last thing God said was, *"Agape them."*[3] I was free to love without condition because I had given up my rights. In the quietness of that night, God and I had a profound interaction that changed me forever and gave what I call the "formula of recovery."

Much of the vision for Shepherd's Door is based on that profound experience.

- Acknowledge and repent of my anger. Lay my reaction at the cross.
- Forgive what you think they did to you.
- Give up your rights to ever get their love and approval. God's love is enough.
- Agape them.

When God whispered words of truth to my heart, my surrender immediately became deliverance. The next morning I awoke happy, optimistic, and free from depression, never to be depressed to that extent again. I began to remember the good things from my childhood and I felt God's agape love for my parents grow in me in the months to follow.

When my own selfishness, arrogance, and unforgiveness lifted, I began to feel free and in tune to those around me. I saw women and children entering our mission with the same heaviness and sorrow I had carried. Suddenly I understood the value of pain and the brokenness of childhood. Surrendering to God and forgiving others allowed me to fully experience the joy of God's love and presence. My past prepared me to more effectively put in place the biblical concepts I had learned and to assist other hurting women who carried deep grief from their pasts. I gained understanding as I identified more fully with women in pain. I felt grateful and ready to serve homeless women and children.

What was your perception of the needs of women that moved you to action?

To perceive the needs of another comes from passion ordained by God. God equips us with personality gifts, spiritual gifts, and experience that strengthen this perception. My understanding of the broken and hurting woman began early in my childhood and continues to this day.

Describe the healing community of which you are currently part.

Shepherd's Door strives to be a repentant and authentically relational community. Jan David Hettinga's work *Follow Me* articulates well this concept.

> In the book of Acts there is a description of the tremendous experience of true community in the young Christian church. The relational warmth and camaraderie were palpable. It hung in the air like the smell of jasmine on a warm summer night. It radiated from hearts on fire with love for Jesus and each other. It's no surprise that the watching world was eager to get in on it. Their nose prints on the windows of the early church revealed how attracted they were to the breathtaking marvel of the kingdom of God among men.[4]

Authentic relationship means seeing another through Jesus' eyes. This is the challenge. Not only are we not comfortable with a broken homeless woman, she is not comfortable with relationship. In fact, because rejection has been a lifelong experience for her, she will try to get you to reject her because she is most comfortable with rejection. She has not yet learned the freedom of authentic relationship. Imagine how trust could be built if we could look at her and see the finished product. She needs to receive the message "I love you. I will never stop loving you. You can do nothing to make me stop loving you. It is your behavior I don't love. Let's talk about your behavior." This is the kind of healing community that reflects God's love and opens the door to experience His healing power.

What were the five key steps you took toward designing and developing community care?

For nearly forty years, I have served alongside my husband at five different rescue missions in the United States. Those years of experience converged when we arrived at the Portland Rescue Mission (PRM) in Portland, Oregon. I was given freedom at PRM to develop staff, program structure for ministry to women, and building design. I started my tenure at PRM amidst the capital campaign to build the facility in which we would house and minister to homeless women and children. The following steps were crucial in designing and developing the community of care at Shepherd's Door.

1. Understand the target group.

I spent years reading every book on bereavement and loss I could get my hands on. It was during that time that He showed me that I had been a grieving child and had to walk through the same stages of grief as a bereaved person to finish my grief work. The hurting woman who comes to us has taken great loss in her childhood and is stuck in grief work. I also came to understand that her belief system bought into lies in early childhood and that she demonstrated survival behaviors that kept her safe in her family. Also, she used drugs, alcohol, and men to sedate the pain caused by the lies she believed. Understanding this profile became crucial.

Most people believe the source of homelessness is poverty, domestic violence, and/or drugs, but the root cause actually goes deeper. *The root cause of homelessness is unresolved issues of early childhood abandonment.* This view of the homeless woman was not initially accepted in rescue mission culture. I knew God had shown me this, so I persevered in teaching this concept, literally for years. Eventually doors of understanding and acceptance opened. Today missions come from all over the country to train at Shepherd's Door.

2. Program design should reflect the profile of the target group.

Curriculum that addressed the root cause of homelessness needed to be the essence of our program design. The following are current examples.

> *Genesis Process*[5]—a biblical relapse prevention curriculum that focuses on the false belief system from childhood.
> *Basic Bible*—a daily class taught by local pastors or volunteers; or a time of community worship.

Education—Because a woman may not have a high school diploma,
and may believe the lie that she is stupid, we offer classes to assist
her in getting her GED.

Life Skills—Parenting, budgeting, how to rent a home, cooking
within a budget, and so on are taught to equip the woman as she
transforms to learn how to live in society.

Vocational Training—Our facility is designed to help a woman learn
a vocation such as culinary kitchen management, administrative
work, day-care work, facilities and grounds.

3. Staff is more crucial than the program.

Because authentic relationship is crucial to recovery, it is most
important to find not only a diverse staff but staff that will embrace transparency. One of the joys of this work has been to see a staff person confess
to a resident that she has sinned, asking forgiveness. Imagine the trust
that can build with the resident.

Staff is trained in how to create a safe and healing environment. This
fosters trust. Staff is also trained in the Genesis Process,[6] which is our
biblical and professional recovery curriculum. This curriculum deals
with the false belief system developed in early childhood that supports
destructive behaviors. Through the study of this process, the ground is
leveled as we discover that we all have lies and addictions. This encourages both staff and residents to humbly walk in gratefulness and recovery.

4. Building design

Because we were building a campus from scratch, we were able to
view the profile of our residents and build accordingly. The following
four examples give greater insight into some of the values of the ministry
at Shepherd's Door.

• *Large day care certified by the state*—Missions are notorious in our
country for not keeping children safe—the next generation. As
Mom heals, the children need a safe place where they can learn to

be children again. Most children who come to us have lost their childhood by the age of six. Our choice to be certified and pay our teachers higher wages assures safety, excellent teaching, and recovery for the children of the residents. While their brains are growing, children's false belief systems can be changed more quickly than if they were adults. This is a crucial window of opportunity for ministries to help children make positive memories. Even if Mommy leaves the program of Shepherd's Door prematurely, we believe the time spent in this incredible day care will enable the Lord to intervene and turn the generation toward a positive direction.

- *Large windows that almost go to the floor*—Lots of sunlight brought into a building encourages an optimistic environment. Also, ledges are added to some of the windows so children can sit and look out anywhere in the building.
- *Sound system built in*—Positive worship music can be piped throughout the building, encouraging women and children to worship God. (I have walked into the building early in the morning and seen children dancing in the hallways . . . what a blessing!)
- *Long, wide hallway between buildings*—On a cold and rainy day children can ride their indoor bikes down the hallways. This also gives lots of space for visitors and volunteers during a busy day.
- *Private residential rooms*—Women never enter each other's rooms nor care for one another's children. This is a safety policy. As women are dealing with difficult issues in their lives, they need a quiet and uninterrupted space to nest with their children and feel safe.

5. Create a homelike atmosphere.

No residential facility should look institutional. In creating Shepherd's Door, we intentionally designed the building to initiate value and dignity in those who come to us. At intake sometimes a woman looks like a deer in headlights. I can almost hear what she's thinking: *I'm not worthy of this place. It's too beautiful. If they only knew about me, they wouldn't want me here.* It is important that she know she is worth it. While the resident is transforming within the program of Shepherd's Door and becoming comfortable with the environment, her eye for beauty is surfacing as well. When she graduates from our program, she will desire to create a comfortable and beautiful home for her children. It is important she live in one first.

How did you influence other people to embrace your vision?

It clearly was God's plan all along. In the summer of 2000, the executive director of Portland Rescue Mission called me to help with the project of an eighty-bed facility for homeless women and children. At that time the board of directors consisted only of men, not uncommon in those days. Wisely realizing the need for a woman's perspective, they called me to come.

At that time I had been in rescue mission work for thirty-two years during which I watched the attitude toward homeless women and children move from apathy to mild interest to panic. Boards were pressuring directors to move forward. Missions were not ready for this fast-growing population, and few knew how to proceed. As far as I knew, I was the only consultant in this arena. Many were in the process of a capital campaign to build a building and assumed the program could be implemented exactly like the men's program. Typically men work in a different paradigm than women. A women's and children's ministry could not be run the same as the men's. Needless to say, I received many calls from around the country only to discover that although they were desperate for help, they were not ready for counsel. Frustrating!

During the flight to Portland, I prepared myself for more of the same attitude. Instead I was pleasantly surprised at the board's willingness to design a building that was program-focused, which meant redesigning the existing rendering. The redesign would include a 3,000-square-foot center for children, which increased the cost considerably. God moved the hearts of the board and the director to embrace the vision.

Because Portland was in the middle of a capital campaign and because over four million dollars had already been raised, we had to go back to the neighborhood association as well as the local businesses and major donors to explain the changes in the building plans. The president of the board and I went door-to-door asking to explain the new vision. Amazingly it went well and the campaign finished and the building was completed in 2003.

There were voices in the local media who told me that they loved my vision but believed it was too big and unrealistic. The path to completion was not without disbelievers and naysayers. But God gave strength to continue the pursuit. A passage that kept me going during this time was

Therefore, since we are surrounded by such a great cloud of witnesses, let us throw off everything that hinders and the sin that so easily entangles. And let us run with perseverance the race marked out for us, fixing our eyes on Jesus, the pioneer and perfecter of faith. For the joy set before him he endured the cross, scorning its shame, and sat down at the right hand of the throne of God. (Hebrews 12:1–2)

How did you provide training for caregivers?

We focus on authenticity. How does authenticity and selflessness happen within a staff? At Shepherd's Door they are strongly encouraged to focus on the disciplines of the faith. It is not possible to love with deep authenticity unless we are willing to die to self. How can we help a bitter woman if we are bitter? How can we help the addicted if we continue to sedate pain with food, television, sleep, laziness? To be on staff with the Portland Rescue Mission the staff must sign a statement of culture. This culture statement has wording such as

- We joyfully pursue the privilege of intimate abiding in Christ by which we daily receive God's love and grace through the Holy Spirit's transforming power, enabling us to fulfill our transformational purpose as participants in God's work.

- We maintain a relational environment, rich in both mercy and truth, by emphasizing repentant living that produces honesty, humility, transparency, and gratitude.
- We encourage all staff, partners, and people we serve to diligently practice the disciplines of the faith so that we may better understand our identity in Christ and more fully live in His promised peace.

Our executive director insists that staff of all levels take these thoughts seriously and be willing to be made accountable for our walk with Jesus. Interestingly, as we begin to die to the besetting sins in our lives, we become repentant and grateful. This qualifies us to humbly speak to the same issues in others' lives.

How Did You Overcome Key Obstacles?

Recruiting Supportive and Gifted Staff

A good leader surrounds herself with people who know more about what they do than she does. Shepherd's Door's new building opened in February 2003. It was with much trial and error that I finally found the staff who was able to complete my leadership. Because I am not a great people manager, I made many mistakes.

God graciously and eventually brought me skillful staff to assist me in my leadership. They are made up of all generations, diverse in personality and skills. I have been most impressed with the young zealous generation who is highly skilled in recovery and called to ministry. The older generation watches as new methods are put in place while making sure that in zeal the message is never compromised.

Selling Vision to Board and Community

I learned that boards do not always buy into a vision. I could have picked up my marbles and gone home but I believed that God gave me the courage and energy to stay the course. At one of my most difficult times, the Lord led me to Psalm 91 (NLT): "Those who live in the shelter of the Most High will find rest in the shadow of the Almighty." Psalm 59:16–17b (NLT) says, "For you have been my refuge, a place of safety when I am in distress . . . you, O God, are my refuge, the God who shows me unfailing love." Remember that it is healthy for boards to question vision. Because of board intervention, I was able to avoid mistakes. For that I will always be grateful. Full buy-in may take time and lots of prayer.

God is our Source. He is the lifter of our heads and our sure anchor. He allows difficulties so we can watch Him part the waters for us to walk through safely. Whatever difficulties I've gone through have only left me grateful and ready to worship Him.

What are your greatest challenges and your greatest joys?

My own belief system is both a challenge and a joy. I have much improved in the area of dying to lies and embracing truth but sometimes a lie will raise its ugly head. *I can't do this job. If they only knew about me, they would neither love me nor like me.* The temptation is to run the other way, eat a whole chocolate cake, or hide and hope no one finds me. Throughout my years in ministry, I have never felt capable. Yet, God has repeatedly put me in new circumstances . . . it never stops . . . I am rarely ever comfortable. I have studied for years but still know very little. Technology continues to change and challenge me. I am hearing myself say, "What happened to the good old days when . . ." Scary. Yet, God is God. He never changes. His call is sure. "Love as I love," He says.

On the other hand, I have to pinch myself because I have the privilege of serving in a frontline ministry to hurting homeless women and their children. God called me as a four-year-old to follow Him. He allowed difficulties of childhood and adulthood but He never left me. He knew that I needed to die to self and depend on Him. Yes, we will still believe lies this side of heaven. On this side of heaven, we only know in part (see 1 Corinthians 13:12). Someday we will know fully but until then we are to grow in the knowledge of His great love. Then we can give to others effectively.

What specific advice would you offer others who would like to develop a healing community?

Many years have passed since my personal experience of recovery. God entered different times of my life to equip me. All were profoundly personal and life changing. First Corinthians 2:10–12 (NLT) says, "But it was to us that God revealed these things by his Spirit. For his Spirit searches out everything and shows us God's deep secrets. No one can know a person's thoughts except that person's own spirit, and no one can know God's thoughts except God's own Spirit. And we have received God's Spirit (not the world's spirit), so we can know the wonderful things God has freely given us." His Holy Spirit will do an incredible work in the heart of the submitted and humble person. Walking in His presence expecting to hear Him speak through His Word and the Holy Spirit is of great value in ministry and in the personal walk with Him. If your heart is hungry for more, expect miracles. He wants to give us more so we can serve others on their journey.

AUTHOR BIO

JAN MARSHALL became the director of women's ministries for the Portland Rescue Mission in 2000. She designed the overall building project for Shepherd's Door's new women and children's shelter in Portland, Oregon. She established and trained staff and developed the long-term program for women and their children at Shepherd's Door. Previously, Jan served as founder of the Evergreen Training Center for women and their children in Erie, Pennsylvania. She sat on the national board of the Association of Gospel Rescue Missions, as the chairperson of the Women and Family track of the AGRM. Jan reconstructed the Moriah House Shelter program for women and their children in Memphis, Tennessee. She established aftercare programs for bereaved women and children in New Castle, Pennsylvania. She established her consulting business to assist missions across the country in management of leadership programs for women and family shelters.

Chapter 24

Authentic Soul Care Givers Generate Health

Mary Kalesse, Cofounder and
Director of Soul Care Resources, Inc.

*I*magine a congregation of 1,200-plus people, over half of them women. Imagine a staff of eight pastors, only one of them female. Now imagine a sincere desire to meet the spiritual and emotional needs of hurting women with no compelling vision, rigorous training, or consistent accountability in place. It is in this setting that Soul Care came to be.

I joined our church staff as Director of Women's Ministries. As the only female pastor, it was my assignment to coordinate and direct the discipleship, mentoring, and equipping of women. As a pastor, I was also assigned the care of women with emotional and spiritual needs. The truth is that when I entered that role, my perception of women's needs was very limited in terms of scope—the kinds of struggles they faced, the severity, or how very deeply those needs were experienced.

I had made many friends and casual acquaintances at church over the decade that I had attended. Some of them had serious problems and personal pain with which to contend. Yet most seemed pretty stable, fairly happy, and surviving the circumstances of life. When I moved into the role of pastor, women slowly began to share with me on a different level. I became acquainted with the deeper pain and anxieties that they carried within.

As my awareness increased of the spiritual and emotional needs of women, the limitations of my time and my own preparedness also became more apparent. What I encountered in terms of need defied the realities of my limits—marriage and family issues, serious health issues, grief and loss issues, depression, addiction, loneliness, sexuality confusion, and lack of spiritual freedom were all waiting for my attention. It became clear early on that addressing all these needs was an impossible and unwise undertaking for one person.

Describe the healing community of which you are currently a part.

The formal Soul Care Team, a group of about ten women who are actively participating in the ministry of giving care. The group meets regularly to pray, process the work of meeting with hurting people, and supporting each other in times of distress.

The healing community of Soul Care at our church goes well beyond our small team. Each class of 20 to 25 women who take the "Equipped to Care" course forms a special community where in the atmosphere of safety and encouragement bonds of friendship grow. Many participants show an eagerness to continue the intentional journey toward Christ-likeness together. Following the conclusion of the nine-month course, several class groups have continued to meet for book studies, fellowship, and support.

The healing community generated by Soul Care in our church family has expanded dramatically over the past decade. Because of the shared vision, experience, language, and skill among this large group of women, a sense of camaraderie develops not only within class groups but also among the classes that have been taught over the years. And this has impacted our whole church. Men began developing a Soul Care ministry dedicated to meeting the needs of men three years ago. Now 250 to 300 men and women have taken the course. They are for the most part actively involved in ministries throughout the church using what they have learned as they live out their personal callings. Each one who has been affected is more able to give away the hope and understanding of transformational healing to others.

One of the great blessings that we have received in teaching the course is to hear how the ministry of Soul Care has impacted class participants' families. Relationships have deepened, rifts mended, grace extended, and compassion and patience have grown in the soil of humility.

Another Soul Care healing community has developed in the country of Kazakhstan, which had been under the harsh domination of communism for decades. This church of young, first-generation Christians said they simply did not know how to give care to one another. We were overwhelmed with the eagerness with which they received and absorbed the content of the course. We have now mentored a group of women in that church who have developed a deep community of care within their church. This has truly amazed us and Kazakhstanis who felt that their cultural background would limit the effective transfer of such a ministry.

We are now convinced that "healing community" is not a Western church phenomenon but is the spiritual fruit of a God who cares and who commands and empowers His children to love and care for each other, partnering with Him in deep transformational work.

What were the five key steps you took toward designing and developing community care?

Creating a ministry to provide community care was a process involving many steps. Prayer and pondering, listening and talking wound their way through each of the steps as we moved forward in the process. We frankly did not approach the task with a very businesslike or linear mind-set. I would describe our work during those days as more organic and serendipitous. However, in the midst of this process, I could see that the Lord definitely led us through some very specific steps. Five of those key steps in our design and development stages were definition, recruitment, education, curriculum, and launching.

1. Definition

Vision and mission were significant parts of the defining process. Out of the growing awareness of the need and the certainty of my limits, a conversation developed with other like-minded women that began to shape a vision *for* and the mission *of* Soul Care. We had to decide what the ministry would BE and DO and what it would NOT BE and DO.

The fundamental beliefs that shaped our vision and mission are that

- true and lasting change and healing happen best in community
- the church, the body of Christ, has a unique calling to come along-side those who are in pain
- the church's calling to care is a privilege with profound import
- the community of faith described in Christ's words and the apostles' teachings is a community of hope and healing where every member is charged to love and care well for others
- we all need help learning to love effectively.

With these beliefs as our starting point, we determined that Soul Care would

- be spiritually focused
- be offered as a free and confidential ministry
- serve women who were churchgoers
- serve unchurched women
- move women toward community and connection
- be short-term, and

- be offered only at the church building (rather than in homes or restaurants).

Just as critical to our definition of the ministry as determining what we would BE was the determination of what Soul Care would NOT BE. Soul Care would not

- offer professional counseling, mentoring, or friendship building
- meet with children or adolescents
- attempt to compete with professional counseling but would refer women to professionals as appropriate.

To effectively embrace these fundamental beliefs about the church and God's call to walk with others in love, we envisioned a ministry that had both an equipping arm and an action arm. The equipping is done through "Equipped to Care," a nine-month course. The action arm is the formal caregiving ministry called Soul Care. Trained and supervised laypeople meet individually with those seeking care for emotional and spiritual needs.

2. Recruitment

It was essential in the early days to find and cultivate leadership support for the team's vision. This was no small thing and has required ongoing attention. But the truth is that if we had not had leadership buy-in for our vision, the ministry would have faltered along the way. We took our need and our plan for developing the ministry to our elders for approval and with one adjustment we were given freedom to move forward.

Another piece to the recruitment step was recruiting partners to help in the development of a training program. Out of the groups of women who took part in various stages of the visioning step, several women stood out as keenly interested in being part of the development of the ministry. Lu Hawley, in particular, was uniquely qualified to lead in this kind of work because of her extensive experience in the field and joined me as coleader.

3. Education

A third critical step in the development of Soul Care was our own preparation. We needed to become as knowledgeable as we could about the nature of women's needs, the biblical foundations for care, and human behavior. We also had to become knowledgeable about available resources and other ministries that had similar missions. We accomplished these goals through participation in a wide variety of conferences, seminars, and training courses. Although this educational step was essential especially in the beginning days of the ministry, we have continued investing many hours over the years attempting to keep on the growing edge of our knowledge as the ministry has grown.

4. Curriculum

As we grew in knowledge and experience in the field of soul care, we began planning a training curriculum relying at first on the thoughts and ideas of others. Each year the curriculum was enhanced and rewritten, becoming more truly aligned to our vision and mission. Through continual revision, the curriculum we now use, "Equipped to Care," is entirely our own.

5. Launch

Once the curriculum was determined, we began the initial training, described later in this chapter. It was after the first training course was completed, a full year and a half later, that we formed a small team and began the formal giving of care to women at our church. Launching the actual ministry of caregiving had many steps within the broader plan, such as team administration, team supervision, publicity, creation of a system of accountability, informing pastoral staff, and elders. And finally attracting our first care seekers!

How did you influence other people to embrace your vision?

I think that our own enthusiastic belief in the vision for Soul Care had the greatest influence on others. We tried as best we could to talk it up and live it out in our own lives. We wanted excellence in both the training and the ministry of care, so we set the expectations high for the class. We let women know that the course would require work, commitment, and the willingness to take risks. We have not lacked for people willing to take this challenge and to do the hard work required. People want to be part of something meaningful that challenges them to think and grow. Setting the standards high, I think, has helped others embrace our vision.

It was easiest to "sell" this new ministry to women. They caught it best perhaps because they were aware of their own needs and were looking for a place where their spiritual and emotional needs would be addressed. As women took the class or came for and received care, they became our advocates.

We also had an important advocate who was on staff and on the board of elders. He was a champion for the ministry in its early days, helping us thread our way through the administrative and legal issues of such a ministry. Now several staff and elders, along with many leaders of the church, have taken the course and continue to recommend it to others, becoming our "influencers."

How did you provide training for caregivers?

Training was one of the most important pieces of the ministry right from the start. It was one of the greatest needs I saw when I began as pastor to women. There was no consistent preparation for women who wanted to work as caregivers. Since as pastor to women I would be the "buck stops here" person, I was committed to a plan that would truly equip those who worked with the most broken and hurting in our congregation. I wanted us all to be on the same page in our language, in our vision, in our skills, in the outcomes we sought, and in the processes of giving care. It was imperative for me that the training piece be in place before we ever began the ministry of caregiving.

So we developed a nine-month, weekly three-hour, intensive course that is divided into trimesters—"Revealing, Relating, and Renewing." The first trimester focuses on coming to know ourselves and God through our understanding of who we are in Christ. The second trimester focuses on moving in relationship with one another with a skills emphasis on building safety, respect, and compassion in relationship. The third trimester focuses on growth, change, and transformation with a skills emphasis on the caregiving process as it relates to God's purposes.

This course is offered to anyone willing to make the commitment. We determined from the beginning that we would not select people for the class that we thought would make good caregivers, but have trusted the Lord to bring whomever He would, for whatever reason they wanted, to take the training. It is always a surprise to see who enrolls each year and how God works in their lives during the nine months we are together. People come to the class for all kinds of reasons. Most people taking the training do so for personal reasons without aspirations to become formal caregivers but for those wishing to participate in the formal caregiving ministry, training is nonnegotiable.

How did you overcome key obstacles?

We are still overcoming obstacles! They keep us on our toes; they keep us on our knees; they keep us vision-centered and mission-minded. They have sharpened our personal belief in and commitment to the work of Soul Care. Obstacles have been the impetus for continuing our own education in the areas of spiritual and emotional health and transformational living. Sometimes the obstacles have made us change our plans; at other times they have just slowed us down.

An early game changer obstacle was the reluctance of the elders to allow us to include men as class participants or in the caregiving ministry. They felt the lines of authority would be compromised. Although we didn't agree, nevertheless we shaped our course and the ministry specifically for women. There were great benefits in doing so. The level of risk-taking, relating, and sharing in the classes has been much deeper than a mixed class could have experienced. The ministry to women flourished with this change in the plan and we were thankful for it.

The downside that came later with this obstacle was when men desired to start a Soul Care ministry to men. It required additional changes to the manuals used and engendered numerous challenges to the format and administration of the ministry that could have been avoided had we begun both men's and women's Soul Care during the same period of time.

What are your greatest challenges and your greatest joys?

The greatest challenges we have faced have to do with maintaining the integrity and vitality of the vision and mission. The vision and mission of Soul Care require a paradigm shift from our human and cultural bent toward fixing, doing, and a problem focus. When we get off track, our default is always to this old and unhealthy, unhelpful focus. Keeping the vision and mission central is constant and hard work as the ministry matures and leaders change and new programs within the church abound.

One challenge has been repeated requests to alter or shorten the training course to accommodate the fast-paced culture we live in. This challenge has come up several times from those who have not taken the course. Our commitment is to the nine-month, weekly three-hour course because we understand that it takes time for participants to not only learn new ways of relating and caring, but most importantly, it takes time to absorb the paradigm shift from fixing to partnering with God.

In conjunction with this challenge is the desire by some to ease the level of accountability required of Soul Care teams and the formal format for caregiving. To these direct challenges, we have learned to speak up and hold the line on things we believe are essential to training caregivers and maintaining a quality level of care for those who seek help. We continue to explain and teach about Soul Care whenever we get a chance in informal conversations and more formal settings.

The greatest joys come from the transformational focus of Soul Care. Soul Care is about life change and we are able to observe it firsthand. We watch this personal transformation first in the participants of the Equipped to Care course who experience nine months of study and practical skills that for many are life changing. Then we watch as care seekers find hope and peace, even when their circumstances do not change. It is our privilege to watch as many of them experience inner change that releases them to move in their struggles toward God and others.

What specific "advice" would you offer others who would like to develop a healing community?

The things that have been crucial for us and we confidently recommend to others are the following:

• Live out your vision.

Maintain your personal integrity in relationship to your vision for ministry. If you believe community is where God intends to mature, grow, and heal, then you must be in serious community yourself. If you believe that relationships are the proving ground for love, then intentionally develop, maintain, and challenge yourself in a few soul friendships—relationships established in honesty, with the invitation for feedback and correction, in which the giving and receiving of affirmation and support are the hallmarks. *Authentic soul care givers generate health.*

• Be sold out and committed to your vision for life.

A pit bull hanging on, unwilling to let go, best depicts this mind-set. Determine to be involved long term.

• Create a team of like-minded, vision-committed people.

This should include at least one pastor/leader who will work with you through the maze of your church's leadership structure. Most churches have a labyrinth that can be daunting and deadening for someone on fire with a vision. It is essential that you not work alone in the formation or training.

• Plan to start small.

The need may be huge but the shoulders of your new ministry need time and experience in order to lift the heavy load. This is particularly true if you are pioneering a new ministry, rather than implementing a long-term proven curriculum.

• Be patient!

This kind of work requires it. Don't bypass the foundational work of training people to do your ministry in an attempt to get it off the ground quickly. Remember biblical characters such as Paul, in the desert for three years preparing to do the work God called him to. David was placed in the school of suffering for years while he waited for God's timing to take the throne. And Jesus is our best example of one who responded according to the Father's timing, in authentic preparation and service to others.

The authentic soul care giver is one who generates healing. If you believe community is where God intends to mature, grow, and heal, then you must be in community yourself.

Prepare well and serve with passion.

AUTHOR BIOS

MARY KALESSE was cofounder and director of Soul Care Resources, Inc., a nonprofit ministry committed to the church becoming a place of spiritual and relational restoration and healing. Mary's desire is to see those served by the church become people who experience belonging, emotional health and spiritual growth. Mary also served on her church's Soul Care Team and taught "Equipped to Care" courses. Mary previously served on a church staff as pastor to women. She is the mother of two grown children, grandmother of five. Her husband, Armond, was also involved in the ministry of Soul Care for men at their church and served on the Soul Care Resources Board.

LU HAWLEY, MASF, is cofounder of Soul Care Resources, Inc., and currently serves with Co-Serve International.

Chapter 25

Communities of Support Bring Hope

Kathy Rodriguez, PsyD, Psychologist

My own journey with Jesus Christ began in a little nondenominational church in Germany. At the time my husband and I were both in the military. Once we met the Lord, both of our lives were turned around 180 degrees. Our desire for alcohol was gone and within three years we knew we wanted to go into some sort of ministry. We agreed the next step was to return to the United States for more education.

Nine years into the Christian life, I began feeling a dichotomy grow within me. After I accepted Christ into my life, I earned both a master's degree and a doctorate in clinical psychology and was daily counseling people toward wholeness. But I found it hard to live an authentic life in the church. I had grown up in a dysfunctional, emotionally neglectful, and verbally abusive family, and I knew I had scars on the inside and probably on the outside that needed God's healing touch.

The tragedy was that the only place I found that could tolerate my honesty was a Christian counselor. As much as it pains me to say it, I could not find a church community that could tolerate real people like me. The church that we attended at the time seemed more like an exclusive country club of people who wore the "happy face" and never talked about anything except crafts, their last vacation, or their kids. But they said nothing about how God was working in their lives.

Church began to pose an integrity problem for me. I had to live with myself and I knew I had problems, though I was a psychologist. It did not matter how good I looked or how good I smelled or even how many letters appeared after my last name, I knew I needed a place to heal and grow. Yet the church was not a safe place to heal because I had to wear a mask that looked like I was put together like everyone else. If I was not careful, church—the bride of Christ and my supposed household of faith—was in danger of becoming only another performance arena, not a safe place to yield myself to God's healing power.

There was a huge gap between the outward image and inward reality. The reality is people have problems. People sin. We make wrong choices. People are victims and perpetrators. People in all of these categories are found in the Bible—they are not edited out of the text. The Bible and reality agreed. But I found that people in the church worked especially hard to hide their reality.

In the early nineties my husband, Rocky, and I stumbled into East Hill Church trying to find a Saturday night English speaking service because we ministered in a Hispanic church on Sundays. Looking to be fed, but truthfully not expecting much based on our previous experience with church, we were in shock and awed to hear the senior pastor matter-of-factly confess that he had been a drunk and addicted to pornography. Rocky and I could relate to him, because we had been drunks too before we came to Christ! So we hung around for a while to see if this was truly real. Over the weeks, months, and subsequent years, we have realized we finally came home to church, a place that has remained home for sixteen years. We do not wear masks anymore and neither do most folks who are involved at East Hill.

In 2001 God called me to come on staff at East Hill Church. They had several specialized classes and small groups on specific healing topics and even some generalized classes to heal family-of-origin issues. It was not very long before I knew that I was finally in "my sweet spot." This was the job that God had been preparing me for all my life. The experience with my own dysfunctional family—the neglect, the abuse, my own therapy, and education—all of it has been used by God to accomplish His healing purposes in making church a safe place for imperfect people to grow.

All of our classes are open to the public. People come from all over, including other churches. Therapists go through these classes. Therapists refer clients to these classes. The classes are not a substitute for counseling but they greatly aid the counseling process.

Today I am even more passionate about the church being a hospital that heals. The Protestant church split in the early 1920s between conservative and liberal denominations. The conservative side focused on its doctrinal underpinnings of sin and humans needing a Savior. The liberal church saw the pain of humankind; this emphasis gradually degenerated into humanism, and thus the divide.

In the last twenty years, there has been a moving closer together to form a more integrative perspective. There is one Author of truth. He reveals Himself in His Word and He reveals Himself in His world. He cannot be divided against Himself. Once we lay hold of that truth, our concept of God gets bigger. We can see that God is the Master Psychologist. He is the One who created the psyche. So when things are going wrong with our personality, minds, or emotions, the first place we need *not* go to get fixed is a program. Instead, we go to see how God would heal us through His Word, shepherds, trusted Christian counselors, pastors, church classes, or small groups. The greatest impact we can have is through the church. Today, more than ever, I firmly believe the church is the hope of the world.

What was your perception of the needs of women that moved you to action?

People have problems. Women are wounded and in emotional pain, as are men. Men and women need to be brought into spiritual, physical, and emotional wholeness. Where do people in pain go for help? I believe there is a calling on the church at large to bring men and women to wholeness. There is a biblical basis for what we have been called to do. Matthew 25:34–46 is a startling passage that equates providing food for the hungry, drink for the thirsty, hospitality for the stranger, clothes for the needy, visits to the imprisoned, and care for the sick with doing all this for Jesus Himself. "Whatever you did for one of the least of these . . . you did for me." James 1:2–4[1] gives reasons for trials in life. It is a testing of your faith with the intended outcome of becoming *mature and complete.* This is wholeness. My life verse is 2 Corinthians 1:3–4: "Praise be to the God and Father of our Lord Jesus Christ, the Father of compassion and the God of all comfort, who comforts us in all our troubles, so that we can comfort those in any trouble with the comfort we ourselves receive from God." God clearly "comforts us so that we can comfort" others. His purpose is clear.

If the church refuses to provide answers, opportunities, and resources, we force people out into the world to find secular answers that may or may not have sound biblical and godly foundations. Sometimes people bring back into the church the secular information they have gained and want us to fully embrace it. (For example, Alcoholics Anonymous is a good program that has helped many stay sober. Christians need to be careful of the dependence on a "higher power," moving the emphasis from the Savior who empowers us to change, to the program itself.)

Too often we view the ongoing war between psychology and Christianity as a competition, when in reality both desire healing. Psychology is the study of human behavior.[2] Understanding human behavior is very helpful, but the power to change comes from Jesus Christ. He is the Author of truth who reveals Himself in the Word and in the world. It is an integration of the Word of God and some clinical understandings that result in healing the broken, bringing back the scattered, strengthening the sick, and seeking the lost (Ezekiel 34:16). We need to figure out ways in which we can empower the church to do its calling. The church needs to be a hospital that heals. This is my life work.

Describe the healing community of which you are currently a part.

Restoration Ministries clarified its mission in 2001, to reach out to the unchurched, heal the brokenhearted, and equip and release healed healers into leadership. We desire to do that in a threefold way.

1. We provide resources to bring men and women to spiritual, physical, and emotional wholeness.
2. We encourage personal and corporate opportunities for discipleship through relational small group growth.
3. And we mentor the God-given natural and supernatural giftedness of men and women and train them to be released as healed healers in the body and in the community.

I envisioned this happening in a three-step approach but it was not until I got to East Hill Church that I saw it in action. My response was, "That's it! That is what I have learned in school but I never have seen it in any church." The three-step plan is about prevention. This needed to be synthesized in ways that are workable in a two-year, five-year, or ten-year plan. The broad, general categories of the three necessary components are as follows.

1. *Primary prevention—sound biblically relevant teaching.* Expository preaching is great but if the communicator cannot connect it to application that is relevant in today's world, it is not helpful. People come to church for help. A lot of people will be helped just by good, solid teaching that they can apply to their lives and their families. In order for that to occur, the pastor/speaker/teacher has to be transparent. He/she has to be willing to pull down the mask and essentially say, "This is where I

struggled. This is where I messed up. This is from what I had to repent. This is the kind of help I am getting." And he/she has to also be willing to mentor people who have some of those very same issues and bring them to a point where they are raised up as healed healers. The healers then can give testimony to God's healing path in their lives.

This is what makes teaching come alive for people through testimony. Hearing someone in leadership say in essence, "I was lost. God came to me when I was feeding in the pigpen. This is what He did to pick me up and clean me off. This is how He is healing me and this is how He is using me." The response is nearly always, "Wow. If God can do that for him/her, maybe He can do that for me." And suddenly that person's understanding of God expands. "Perhaps God is big enough to help me, to bring me to a place of healing. Maybe there is hope after all." This level of intervention will serve the greatest number of people but it comes from good, solid relevant teaching from the Bible.

2. *Secondary prevention—specialized help.* This is for people who need more specialized help than just coming to church once a week and getting biblically relevant teaching. Secondary prevention is providing resources and opportunities within the church, such as Bible studies, growth groups, or healing groups on different topics, as a place for people to get more specialized help. Another aspect of secondary prevention is compiling a resource list of competent Christian counselors in the surrounding area with which the church can partner. For example, if I learn that Lora has a depression that is putting her in bed more days a week than she is up, then I have a Christian counseling resource to which I can refer her. The counselor will provide the needed evaluation and recommendations. As shepherds, we have a responsibility to attend to the needs of the flock. To prevent shepherd burn-out, shepherds would be wise to access additional resources and team members when needed.

Secondary prevention provides specialized help that may be as varied as learning how to be a wife, establishing better boundaries in relationships, or working on a specific problem such as sexual abuse or an addiction.

3. Tertiary prevention—a healing community. Identify your church as a place that welcomes both people who are considered "misfits" and people with run-of-the-mill problems. Promote the fact that your church is a healing community. Make this known in your church, your local community, and in your region. East Hill Church is sometimes spoken about as, "You know what is at East Hill? A lot of addicts." When a former acquaintance found out we were at East Hill, she said, "What are you doing there? That's a dumping ground." It is a picture of the church in case you have not looked in your pews lately. We are all sinners saved by God's incredible grace! But it is true that many people come to East Hill because they have been able to find loving understanding and help that was not available in their previous church.

Each church has specific strengths. Do you know what those are in yours? What is the history of your church? Who is the primary audience your church intends to reach? Once you discover these answers, then you need to ask, where does my gifting fit here? If you believe it does not fit, you should first pray, "Lord, is this a signal that I should go elsewhere, or is this a signal that I am supposed to be a catalyst here? How would You use me, Lord?"

Second, meet with the lead pastor. What is his dream? What does he see this church doing? How is this church encouraging shepherds to care for the flock? Share your heart and discover if there is a common vision. If you really have a heart for building a healing program, you must have the lead shepherd in agreement for it to become a reality. Too often such a ministry fails simply because leadership's focus is in a different area. Even if you initially feel like a salmon swimming upstream, if God is the source of your vision of bringing a healing ministry to your church, then He will prevail. He will find a way. He will soften that pastor's heart. He will direct you and the leadership. I have often seen it happen.

What were the five key steps you took toward designing and developing community care?

1. *Research.* Do your homework. Discover your church's perspective on healing, deliverance, spiritual warfare, professional counseling, and community care. Read everything you can on the subject matter. Try to get a lot of different resources so you can become aware of what is available. Talk to others who are involved in community care. Observe other ministries, if possible. Talk to others in your church who might be interested. Above all, pray, pray, pray!

2. *Think in terms of providing the broad followed by the specific.* Use small group format and begin layering in one class at a time. Obviously East Hill did not create this method overnight. When I came to East Hill in the midnineties, they did not have all they do now. They used books such as *Wounded by Shame, Healed by Grace* by Jeff VanVonderen; *Love Is a Choice* by Hemfelt, Minirth, and Meier; and *Boundaries* by Cloud and Townsend. Later, Pat Springle's *Untangling Relationships: a Christian Perspective on Codependency,* and *Families Where Grace Is in Place* by Jeff VanVonderen were used. These general classes were open to anyone. These were focused on emotional healing. There were multiple entry points into Restoration Ministries during the two years of teaching these general topics.

Each book was divided into a twelve-week study. Each session began with the small group discussing, for thirty to sixty minutes, the homework completed the week before. This was followed by a teaching segment, then a return to the small group to process the questions on this new material before going home and working on the new homework. It is important to have both small group sessions and a teaching segment each week. The teaching segment can accommodate more people, but to process it, the people should be in small groups.

3. *Specific studies were added to the general.* Small group studies gradually layered into the general studies, as people completed their two years.

Topics such as sexual addictions, sexual abuse, chemical addiction, men's anger, and women's anger groups were added. It was essential that people first had the general understanding of the pain of their childhood and processed some of that before moving into deeper, more specific issues. It also provided a resource for them to refer back to, if needed.

4. *Learn how to screen leaders.* Make sure leaders are healed enough and trained in small group dynamics. Often I find people wanting to start a ministry for their own healing, which can be harmful to groups. Leaders need to get healed first so that they can hand off the comfort they have received.

5. *Raise up coaches.* As you begin to find more leaders, raise up coaches who can have several leaders underneath them. Coaches can mentor/coach leaders for growth, maturity, and accountability. This also frees you not to be in multiple roles. It also gives others an opportunity to learn and grow.

How did you influence other people to embrace your vision?

When you are the one who has the heart and passion, finding people who can hand off the comfort that they have received[3] is a key piece. That is why our pastor's wife is so effective to minister to women whose husbands are sexual addicts. She lived it with her husband as he was coming out of his pornography addiction.[4] She understands what wives with sexually addictive husbands are thinking and feeling. She can hand them comfort in a way that only comes from someone who has been through it.

However, being wounded in itself does not qualify someone to lead; neither does having a PhD qualify someone. Everyone who comes to our program must go through the stuff herself. Even if a person has a PsyD, she does not start in the middle just because she has completed her studies. I was no exception. I went to that first class at East Hill and the teacher/facilitator was right in my stuff. I thought I was further along in my healing but he had a lot to offer me. Integrity in your healed healers demands that they go through the process individually. People will observe and listen because of their walk. Without this, leaders will never have the kind of integrity that matches walk with talk. And then there is on-the-job-training.

How did you provide training for caregivers?

Healing and accountability prepare people to give stable support and hope to others. East Hill uses the Genesis Process[5] in many of our small groups for accountability, as well as in our sexual addictions program and in our Restorations program. The Genesis Process is good for building relapse prevention and showing people how to do accountability. There are currently twelve groups of sexual addicts at our church: five of those were formed at East Hill but have since become part of other churches. National and international opportunities have emerged to give seminars called Pure Desire[6] and teach people how to set up these kind of sexual addiction ministries in their church. This introduction includes information on legal liabilities in setting up sexual addiction and other programs.

What is the process of training leaders?

- Adequately prepare the leader-to-be by asking her to read several resources on the topic and be prepared to share her responses with you. Set up time to discuss and process this with her.
- Check out her background. Discover her issues and what she has done to heal. Talk to her spouse, if she has one. Ask her to go through church membership classes (if required in your church), giftedness class, and small group training.
- Observe her as a follower. While you are working on the elements listed above, discover her ability to follow. I have found that a good follower means that she will be a good leader. Every great leader was once a good follower.
- Set up pieces of accountability as you are building up these leaders. It usually takes about a year to prepare somebody to colead a class.

(If someone is not suited, she will drift away.) Then your challenge becomes how to use this individual and not burn her out.

- Establish from the beginning that she will have to go through healing classes. In your circumstances if there are no healing classes, is she willing to go to a Christian counselor? If someone wants to lead a class for the sexually abused, ask where she is in her own healing process. Has she gone to private counseling and received help with this? What is her marriage like? Talk to her spouse about their relationship. Is it stable and able to take on something like this? This is important, because we do not want people to get into leadership and then wallow in their pain and not get any better. We need to set boundaries so people do not get worse or hinder their own healing.

All of our leaders in Restoration Ministries must go through the healing classes.[7]

- Have them colead a class with another more experienced leader. They may teach a session or two but their primary job is to assist that leader. Then eventually they will lead as a small group facilitator for that particular group. After more small group experience, they may eventually teach that class.

How did you overcome key obstacles?

One of the things we learned the hard way is not laying hands on potential leaders too quickly. Rather, see if she is the person God intends to lead this ministry. Coach leaders to *I lead you, you watch; I lead, you help; you lead, I watch; you lead, and I check in with you.* That is the primary model we follow. We do not just turn people loose; instead, we monitor them. They are always surrounded by other leaders.

What are your greatest challenges and your greatest joys?

One of my greatest challenges is how to answer the question, how do you educate the "perfect" people in the church to understand and accept the fact that there are imperfect people in their church? This is a question I am often asked. I am still working on the answer! The greatest contribution to changing this mind-set often starts with a pastor/preacher/ teacher who does not hesitate to talk publicly about difficult topics. And no matter what your role is in your church, risk speaking about your own life struggles, which gives others freedom to speak of theirs. It is life-giving to know I am not alone in my struggles, and to know there really is healing power in Jesus Christ. And I pray a whole lot.

The greatest joy is repeated many times in stories like this one. A woman came to see me; she had come to East Hill years ago for our Domestic Violence program. She said that her significant other just got out of jail and she went back to him. I realized she had significant bruises. "I've got to get out," she said. I contacted our attorney and he told her how to get a restraining order. After talking with her, he said, "This has got to be reported. You have to do something about it." Usually it takes about seven times before a woman will leave for good. This was only her third time. I thought it might help her case if she had pictures, so we took pictures of the big bruises all over her body.

The next morning I had a call from her about 10:15. Her significant other left for a doctor's appointment. She said she was gathering a few things, then she and her baby would leave and walk to the church. She lived about five miles outside of town. We picked her up, got the restraining order, then found a place for her to stay in a shelter. This was Thursday. We figured she would probably leave the shelter soon and go to her brother's house in Alaska. On Sunday we received a call from her. Her abuser had committed suicide. The story does not have a Cinderella ending; it has an East Hill ending. This is real life. Real issues. This is where people are and what our society is like.

I was so glad that our church had resources so we knew where to go and how to help her. Otherwise, he might have killed both her and her baby before he killed himself. This is a picture of why we have to have a healing church and why the church is the hope of the world.

What specific "advice" would you offer others who would like to develop a healing community?

Network with those who have already developed a healing community. Make connections with licensed Christian professional counselors and social service providers in your community. It takes a village or church to help people become whole. The church is bigger than the people who occupy one building on a weekend. Know what the other churches in your community are doing; cross denominational lines. Learn from parachurch organizations. The church includes Christian professionals who are out there in the community with whom we can network. The church and the local community can become an emotional incubator where people are trying to heal from what has gone wrong in their lives. The church provides a vital component for people to grow up emotionally and spiritually. Spiritual maturity affects your emotional maturity and vice versa.

I would also recommend you read, read, read. Keep up on the current literature on issues that cause emotional pain.

Always keep as a priority prayer and the reading of Scripture. The good news of forgiveness and grace because of Jesus Christ's death and resurrection is "the power of God that brings salvation to everyone who believes" (Romans 1:16).

AUTHOR BIO

DR. KATHRYN RODRIGUEZ is a retired psychologist who specializes in healing the emotional wounds of dysfunctional families, childhood sexual abuse, father wounding and eating disorders. She taught seminary and grad classes in counseling, integration, and ethics. Along with caring for one of their two granddaughters, Kathy and her husband, Rocky, continue to disciple young parents in their church. They have two adult children and two grandchildren.

Acknowledgments

My brief experience in playing college basketball came to mind several times while working on this challenging project. Like basketball, the kaleidoscope of abilities, temperament, expertise, and energy exhibited by each player must all come together in a way that fosters unity of focus. My own ability as a 5'4" lone basketball player would have been considerably less had we not functioned as a team. The opportunity to score baskets for my team was greatly enhanced because we shared a common goal and we worked as a team to achieve it. We understood that working as a team only increased our chances of winning.

This project certainly embodied a kaleidoscope of people who were willing to give of their time, expertise, and experience for the greater purpose of influencing others toward health and wholeness. This resource has clearly been strengthened by each person on the team.

Prayer Team

Only God knows the number of people who prayed for this project. This project would not have become a reality without your prayers. Eight women agreed to pray specifically on the days each contributing author and I wrote, edited, and rewrote. These women were faithful to their commitment. The impact of each prayer was felt with humanly impossible results. Thank you SO much, Kathy Crannell, Sandi Phillips, Daisy Santos, Carolyn Smith, Kenine Stein, Julie Tadema, Sue Walt, and Sandy Wellman.

Contributing Authors

All of the contributing authors are active in their fields of ministry. I understand that time is of the essence for you and so value even more highly the treasured gift of your contribution to this book.

A few chapters began as interviews, were transcribed, and formatted by Kenine Stein. Thanks, Kenine, for your good work and willingness to fill your days "off work" with this project. Your work was essential in getting this project off the starting block.

Western Seminary

I am grateful for the many students who have participated in a "Women in Pain I or II" class or other pastoral care to women courses at Western Seminary, either on campus in Sacramento, San Jose, California, Portland, Oregon, or online. Thank you for sharing your stories and affirming the need for greater understanding and shepherding skills. Thank you for increasing my desire for this information to be made available to men and women in leadership in our churches, nonprofit ministries, communities, friends, and families.

The encouragement and support shown by President Randy Roberts and by the faculty and staff at Western Seminary was essential in my ability to see this project through to the end. Thank you for the flexibility in scheduling and opportunity to provide needed resourcing for people in the trenches of ministry.

Moody Publishers Team

I felt this project was "home" from my first conversation with Steve Lyon. Steve's initial comment, "as a pastor what I would have given for a resource like this," told me he "got it!" Further conversation with Holly, Pam, and others on the Moody team reinforced this perception that they understood the value this project could be in the hands of those who care about bringing healing to the pain in others' lives. The expertise of each player on this team has been strategic in strengthening the value of this resource. It has been great working with you! Thanks for understanding that working as a team increases our chance of winning. You just scored.

Family

This project has been in my heart for many years. I appreciate the many men and women who knowingly or unknowingly have contributed to the passion of this project. I am especially grateful to church families in Germany, Orlando, Portland, North Palm Beach, Gresham, and Clackamas. Only eternity will fully reveal the full impact of your love for Jesus Christ and His bride in my life.

I am especially thankful to my own family. I appreciate your encouragement especially during times of limited family involvement when my focus remained on this project. Lorraine and Gene, Dan and Maureen: Thanks for exhibiting your own desire for more effective care given to people experiencing emotional pain and for your involvement in the lives of hurting people. May we pass a heart like Jesus' on to the next generation: Hannah, Zach, Matthew, Madeline, Katie, and Emma. I especially appreciate my husband Jim's ability to shepherd people with grace and understanding. How blessed I am to feel your full support and encouragement with this project.

NOTES

Chapter 1: How Can I Stop the Pain?

1. John W. James and Russell Friedman, *The Grief Recovery Handbook* (New York: Harper Collins, 1998), 3.
2. Gerald L. Sittser, *Grace Disguised: How the Soul Grows through Loss* (Grand Rapids: Zondervan, 1995), 25.
3. Ibid.
4. James and Friedman, 3.
5. H. Norman Wright, "Crisis Intervention and Emergency Practice," in *Competent Christian Counseling*, vol. 1, Timothy Clinton and George Ohlschlager, eds. (Colorado Springs: WaterBrook Press, 2002), 613.
6. James and Friedman, 5.
7. Melody Gilbert, director/producer, *A Life without Pain, a Documentary* (Frozen Feet Films) 2005. http://alifewithoutpain.com. *A Life without Pain, a Documentary*, is an exploration into the day-to-day lives of three children who literally feel no pain. Three-year-old Gabby from Minnesota, seven-year-old Miriam from Norway, and ten-year-old Jamilah from Germany have a genetic defect so rare that it is shared by just one hundred people in the world. Their parents must watch their every move, but even their vigilance hasn't shielded the girls from many serious, life-altering injuries. Congenital insensitivity to pain and congenital insensitivity to pain with anhidrosis (CIPA) are part of a family of disorders called HSAN, which stands for hereditary sensory and autonomic neuropathy. People with an HSAN disorder have trouble perceiving pain and temperature. For more information on this disorder, see http://health.howstuffworks.com/cipa.htm/printable.
8. Sandra Wilson, *Hurt People Hurt People* (Nashville: Thomas Nelson, 1993), 5.
9. Pain is defined as "a mental or emotional suffering or torment," *Webster's Encyclopedic Unabridged Dictionary of the English Language* (San Diego: Thunder Bay Press, 2001), 1394.

10. Ibid.

11. H. Norman Wright, American Association of Christian Counselors World Conference 2003, pre-conference extended training on "Crises Counseling," Nashville, September 2003.

12. James and Friedman, 61.

13. Henri Nouwen, *The Wounded Healer* (New York: Doubleday, 1990), 96.

Chapter 2: When Will Life Be Normal Again?

1. NASB.

2. Joanna North, "The 'Ideal' of Forgiveness: A Philosopher's Exploration," in *Exploring Forgiveness*, Robert D. Enright and Joanna North, eds. (Madison: University of Wisconsin Press, 1998), 18.

3. Paul W. Coleman, "The Process of Forgiveness in Marriage and the Family," in *Exploring Forgiveness*, 92.

4. Adapted from Sandra D. Wilson, *Into Abba's Arms* (Carol Stream, IL:Tyndale House, 1998), 164–69.

5. Adapted from "Forgiveness," notes written by Julie Tadema, Brush Prairie, Washington, accessed November 6, 2009.

6. Richard Fitzgibbons, "Anger and the Healing Power of Forgiveness: A Psychiatrist's View," in *Exploring Forgiveness,* 65–66.

7. Beverly Flanigan, *Forgiving the Unforgivable* (New York,: Macmillan, 1992), 167.

8. Louis A. Barbieri Jr., "Matthew," in *The Bible Knowledge Commentary* John F. Walvoord and Roy B. Zuck, eds. (Wheaton, IL: Victor Books, 1983), 62.

9. Luke 7:47. The entire story is in Luke 7:36–50.

10. Luke 23:34a: "Jesus said, 'Father, forgive them, for they do not know what they are doing.'"

11. Coleman, 88.

12. Flanigan, 99.

13. Adapted from Beverly Flanigan's listing, 1. Naming the Injury, 2. Claiming the Injury, 3. Blaming the Injurer, 4. Balancing the Scales, 5. Choosing to Forgive, 6. The Emergence of a New Self, in *Forgiving the Unforgivable* (New York: Macmillan, 1992), 73–170.

14. Coleman, 93.

Chapter 3: What Does Healing Look Like?

1. Hurricane Andrew was the costliest natural disaster in US history until surpassed by Hurricane Katrina of the 2005 season.

2. More than 250,000 people were left homeless; 82,000 businesses were destroyed or damaged; about 100,000 residents of south Dade County permanently left the area in Andrew's wake. Source: "Hurricane Andrew after the Storm Ten Years Later," *St. Petersburg Times*, http://www.sptimes.com/2002/webspecials02/andrew/.

3. Matthew 10:42 NLT.

4. H. Norman Wright, "Crisis Intervention and Emergency Practice," in *Competent Christian Counseling*, vol. 1, Timothy Clinton and George Ohlschlager (Colorado Springs: WaterBrook Press, 2002), 607.

5. Ibid., 608–14.

6. This information is drawn from several resources, such as Normajean Hinders, *Seasons of a Woman's Life* (Nashville: Broadman & Holman, 1994); AACC Workshop by H. Norman Wright on *Crises Counseling 2003, Recovering from the Losses of Life* (Nashville: Lifeway), 1995; H. Norman Wright, "Crisis Intervention and Emergency Practice," in *Competent Christian Counseling*, vol. 1, Timothy Clinton and George Ohlschlager (Colorado Springs: WaterBrook Press, 2002).

7. Carol Kent, *A New Kind of Normal* (Nashville: Thomas Nelson, 2007), 219.

8. BibleWorks, Strong's Concordance for 3648 "complete."

9. Walter Brueggemann, *The Message of the Psalms: A Theological Commentary* (Minneapolis: Augsburg, 1984). *Praying the Psalms*, 2nd ed. (Eugene, OR: Cascade Books, 2007).

10. It is the relationship and the consequent working alliance that determines primarily the quality and the quantity of change that occurs in the human. Michael J. Mahoney, *Human Change Processes: The Scientific Foundations of Psychotherapy* (New York: Basic Books, 1991), 264.

11. Gerald L. Sittser, *A Grace Disguised, How the Soul Grows through Loss* (Grand Rapids: Zondervan, 1995), 43.

12. Marion Duckworth, *Healing for the Empty Heart* (Grand Rapids: Bethany House, 1993), 165–69. Used by permission.

13. See ibid., 169.

Chapter 4: Where Is God in the Pain?

1. Leslie Montgomery, *Were It Not for Grace: Stories from Women after God's Own Heart* (Nashville: Broadman & Holman, 2005), 89.

2. Ibid., 89.

3. Isaiah 26:3 KJV.

4. Montgomery, 93. Joni, with the help of others, continued to process these hard questions of suffering. Joni and Steve Estes coauthored their findings in their book *When God Weeps: Why Our Sufferings Matter to the Almighty* (Grand Rapids: Zondervan, 1997). Joni's story today is known worldwide through her ministry, Joni and Friends, reaching people with disabilities and their families.

5. Jon Tal Murphree, *A Loving God and a Suffering World* (Downers Grove, IL: InterVarsity Press, 1981), 9.

6. William H. Willimon, *Sighing for Eden: Sin, Evil and the Christian Faith* (Nashville: Abingdon, 1985), 30–31.

7. The atheist believes in no deity; the agnostic believes we probably cannot know if deity exists; the polytheist believes there are many deities; the dualist believes there are two irreducible elements, such as mind and matter or good and evil; the naturalist believes natural processes only; the fatalist believes everything is predetermined and unchangeable; the materialist believes physical matter is the only reality. *Merriam-Webster Unabridged Dictionary*, computer program by Merriam-Webster, 2003.

8. David Atkinson, *The Message of Job: Suffering and Grace* (Downers Grove, IL: InterVarsity Press, 1991), 26.

9. Mike Mason, *The Gospel According to Job* (Wheaton, IL: Crossway Books, 1994), 29–30. See Job 1:8–12.

10. "God permits all sorts of things he doesn't approve of. He allows others to do what he would never do" (Joni Eareckson Tada and Steven Estes, *When God Weeps: Why Our Sufferings Matter to the Almighty* [Grand Rapids: Zondervan, 1997], 80).

11. Frank E. Gaebelein, gen. ed., *The Expositor's Bible Commentary*, vol. 4 (Grand Rapids: Zondervan, 1988), 880.

12. Unlike Job's friends who only spoke *about* God, not *to* Him.

13. John Ortberg, World Conference of the American Association of Christian Counselors, main session, Nashville, September 2005.

14. *Theodicy* comes from the Greek *theos*, "God," and *ieke*, "justice." Theodicy is the attempt to justify the ways of God to humanity, to think about what a good God does with evil and suffering. Theodicy deals with the meaning of pain in terms of sin, evil, human choice, the will of God, and God's response. Since Eden, evil influences mankind to use his free will to hurt other

humans. This perhaps accounts for four-fifths of the sufferings of humankind. This may be the greatest cause of pain—pain induced by other human beings, not God. But humankind does not generally see themselves as perpetrators of evil, as sinners deserving God's wrath. Human beings need to recognize this propensity to evil in order to receive redemption. Often it is the pain in life that shatters the illusion that all is well and leads to surrendering the self-will to God. Pain gets one's attention and challenges basic life assumptions. Willimon, 34.

15. Job 40:8, "Would you discredit my justice? Would you condemn me to justify yourself?"

16. Philip Yancey, *Disappointment with God* (Grand Rapids: Zondervan, 1988), 193.

17. God suggested that Job try answering questions like these: Did you participate in laying the foundation of the earth as God did? Who marked off its measurements? Who designed the ostrich, horse, or behemoth? "What is the way to the place where the lightning is dispersed . . . ? From whose womb comes the ice? Who cuts a channel for the torrents of rain, and a path for the thunderstorm, to water a land where no one lives?" (Job 38:4–5; 39:13, 19; 40:15; 38:24, 29; 38:25–26).

18. Atkinson, 157. See Job 42:3.

19. Tada and Estes, 78–79. See Job 42:2, 6.

20. Gaebelein, 431–32. See Job 42:7–8.

21. Ibid., 1057. See Job 42:7–9.

22. Ibid., 441–42. See Job 42:12.

23. "Nowhere in all the land were there found women as beautiful as Job's daughters, and their father granted them an inheritance along with their brothers" (Job 42:15). A father's money normally went to his sons, who would then take care of their father in his old age. Monies that went to a daughter would be used exclusively for her husband and his family—not returned to help her father in his old age.

24. C. S. Lewis, *The Four Loves* (New York: Harcourt, Brace and World, 1960), 169.

25. D. A. Carson, *How Long O Lord?* (Grand Rapids: Baker Book House, 1990), 245.

26. The biblical book of Ruth, chapters 1–4.

27. Carolyn Custis James, *The Gospel of Ruth* (Grand Rapids: Zondervan, 2008), 37.

28. Ibid., 45.

29. Ruth 1:13, 20–21.

30. Carson, 240–41.

31. Old Testament prophets such as Hosea use metaphors of married love, adultery, prostitution, unfaithfulness, and restoration. Note Hosea 1:2; 2:19–20; 3:1; 4:14; 6:1.

32. Luke 15:11–32.

33. Romans 3:23; 6:23; Deuteronomy 30:15–20.

34. Luke 13:4–5. "Or those eighteen who died when the tower in Siloam fell on them—do you think they were more guilty than all the others living in Jerusalem? I tell you, no! But unless you repent, you too will all perish."

35. Luke 13:1–3. "Now there were some present at that time who told Jesus about the Galileans whose blood Pilate had mixed with their sacrifices. Jesus answered, 'Do you think that these Galileans were worse sinners than all the other Galileans because they suffered this way? I tell you, no! But unless you repent, you too will all perish.'"

36. John 9:1–4.

37. Carson, 67.

38. Dr. Joy Elasky Fleming in *God's Words to the Woman in the Garden of Eden Retold According to the Hebrew* (Think Again Publishers, 2004) argues that the New King James Version more clearly reflects the Hebrew text. Dr. Fleming suggests 'itsebon in Genesis 3:16a is better translated "sorrowful-toil-because-of-the-curse-on-the-soil" and 'etsev is better translated "effort" or "work."

39. Genesis 3:17, "Painful toil" is the same Hebrew word, 'itsebon, used in Genesis 3:16a.

40. Genesis 6:6, *Atsab* is translated in English "to hurt, pain, or grieve." James Strong, *Strong's Exhaustive Concordance of the Bible* (McLean, VA: MacDonald Publishing), 90.

41. Genesis 6:5–6.

42. Matthew 26:39–44.

43. Matthew 27:46.

44. Willimon, 167. Also note Isaiah 53:4–5.

45. Murphree, 110.

46. Luke 13:1–4; John 9:3; Romans 8:17; Ezekiel 33.

47. Romans 5:3–4.

48. Revelation 21:4, "He will wipe every tear from their eyes. There will be no more death or mourning or crying or pain, for the old order of things has passed away."

49. Murphree, 89.

50. Ibid.

51. Stanley Hauerwas, *Naming the Silences: God, Medicine and the Problem of Suffering* (Grand Rapids: Eerdmans, 1990), 85.

52. Psalms 13; 35; 55.

53. Luke 23:42–43.

Chapter 5: Shepherding Insights

1. Not her real name.

2. Barney Self, EdD, a licensed marriage and family therapist who works in LifeWay's pastoral ministries as LeaderCare Counselor. Adapted from, "When to Refer Someone to a Professional Counselor, Part Two," www.lifeway.com/lwc/article_main_page. Accessed August 10, 2004.

3. Bruce Larson, Paul Anderson, and Doug Self, *Mastering Pastoral Care* (Portland: Multnomah, 1990), 28.

4. W. Clebsch and C. Jaekle, *Pastoral Care in Historical Perspective* (New York: Jason Aronson, 1964), 1, quoted by Catherine Clark Kroeger and James R. Beck, ed., *Women, Abuse and the Bible* (Grand Rapids: Baker, 1996), 158.

5. Frank Gaebelein, gen. ed., *The Expositor's Bible Commentary*, vol. 11 (Grand Rapids: Zondervan, 1978), 58.

6. Ephesians 4:12–13.

7. William McRae, *The Dynamics of Spiritual Gifts* (Grand Rapids: Zondervan, 1980), 86.

8. David Stancil, "The Ministry of Shepherding," *Preparing for Christian Ministry: An Evangelical Approach*, ed. David P. Gushee and Walter C. Jackson (Grand Rapids: Baker, 1996), 205–6.

9. Philip Keller, *A Shepherd Looks at the Good Shepherd and His Sheep* (Grand Rapids: Zondervan, 1978), 29.

10. Ibid., 40.

11. Ibid., 23.

12. Sue Edwards and Kelley Mathews, *New Doors in Ministry to Women* (Grand Rapids: Kregel, 2002), 64.

13. Beverly White Hislop, *Shepherding a Woman's Heart* (Chicago: Moody, 2003), 31.

14. John 10:10b. One of the best-known passages in the Bible, Psalm 23, gives David's description of the Lord as his shepherd. John 10 further elaborates on some of the characteristics of Jesus as the Good Shepherd. Ezekiel 34 gives further description of poor shepherds and good shepherds.

15. John 10:3–4, 10–15.

16. Tim Clinton and George Ohlschlager, "Introduction to Christian Counseling: The 21st Century State of the Art," in *Caring for People God's Way*, ed. Clinton, Hart, and Ohlschlager (Nashville: Thomas Nelson, Inc., 2005), 19.

17. Ron Hawkins, Edward Hindson, and Tim Clinton, "Pastoral Care and Counseling, Soul Care Centered in the Church," in *Competent Christian Counseling*, vol. 1, Timothy Clinton and George Ohlschlager, eds. (Colorado Springs: WaterBrook, 2002), 403. Referenced D. Hart, *The Anxiety Cure* (Nashville: Word, 1999).

18. Ian F. Jones, Tim Clinton, and George Ohlschlager, "Christian Counseling and Essential Biblical Principles," in *Caring for People God's Way*, 54.

19. Jim Kallam Jr., *Risking Church: Creating a Place Where Your Heart Feels at Home* (Colorado Springs: WaterBrook, 2003).

20. Siang-Yang Tan, "Lay Helping, The Whole Church in Soul-Care Ministry," in *Competent Christian Counseling*, Timothy Clinton and George Ohlschlager, eds. (Colorado Springs: WaterBrook, 2002), 425. Dr. Tan is senior pastor at First Evangelical Church in Glendale and Arcadia, California, and professor of psychology at the Fuller Seminary Graduate School of Psychology in California.

21. Larry Crabb, *Connecting: Healing Ourselves and Our Relationships* (Nashville: Word, 1997), xv.

22. Ibid., xvi.

Chapter 6: Depression

1. William C. Shiel Jr., "Medical Definition of Depression," MedicineNet, https://www.medicinenet.com/script/main/art.asp?articlekey=2947.

2. Ibid.

3. "Depression in Women," eMedTV.com, http://depression.emedtv.com/depression/depression- in-women.html, accessed 2009.

4. Although many of these facts are true for men, the feminine pronoun will be used for the purpose of this book.

5. Mark A. Sutton and Bruce Hennigan, *Conquering Depression: A 30-Day Plan to Finding Happiness* (Nashville: Broadman & Holman, 2001), 47.

6. Ibid., 103.

7. Ibid., 150.

8. Frank B. Minirth and Paul D. Meier, *Happiness Is a Choice* (Grand Rapids: Baker, 1994), 191.

9. Luke 5:12–13.

10. The law commanded strict segregation of a person who had leprosy, for it was a graphic picture of uncleanness. A leprous person could not worship at the central sanctuary; he was ceremonially unclean and therefore cut off completely from the community. According to the Mosaic law, one who was leprous was not to be touched by anyone who was ceremonially clean, because the clean would then become unclean. John Martin, "Luke," in *The Bible Knowledge Commentary*, N.T. edition, eds., John F. Walvoord, Roy B. Zuck (Wheaton, IL: Victor Books, 1983), 216.

11. Proverbs 15:22.

12. See John 8:1–11, John 4:1–42, and Mark 5:25–34 for examples.

Chapter 7: Infertility

1. *Merriam Webster Dictionary.*

2. Resolve: the National Infertility Association website "Infertility Diagnosis" www.resolve.org/site/PageServer?pagename=lrn_wii_id.

3. John and Sylvia Van Regenmorter, "Infertility: Facts & Fiction," *Stepping Stones* 20, no. 2 (Apr/May 2002): 1.

4. Pat Schwiebert and Chuck DeKlyen, *Tear Soup: A Recipe for Healing after Loss* (Portland, OR: Grief Watch, 1999).

5. Resolve, "The Hidden Emotions of Infertility" Hidden No More, Resolve http://www.resolve
.org/site/PageServer?pagename=lrn_wii_he.

6. Elisabeth Kubler-Ross, *On Death and Dying: What the Dying Have to Tell Doctors, Nurses,
Clergy and Their Own Families* (New York: Macmillan, 1969).

7. John and Sylvia Van Regenmorten, "When a Friend or Family Member Faces Infertility:
Here's How to Help," *Stepping Stones* 21, no. 8 (Sept/Oct 2003): 2.

8. Elizabeth Price, "I Go Not to the 'Yes' but to the 'No,'" *Stepping Stones* 20, no. 4 (Aug/Sept
2002): 3.

9. 9. See Diane Clapp and Merle Bombardieri, "Talking About Infertility: Just for Family and
Friends: How Can I Help? The Dos and the Don'ts of Support," Resolve, n.d., http://
familybuilding.resolve.org/site/PageServer?pagename=cop_tainf_jffaf.

Chapter 8: Terminal Illness

1. Examples of God's divine intervention: 2 Kings 4:8–37; 20:1–11; Acts 9:36–42.

2. Although the process is similar for men and women, for the purpose of this chapter, feminine pronouns will be used.

3. *Understanding the Process of Dying*, Hospice and Palliative Care in Washington County, OR.

4. *The Dying Process*, "Common Myths about Pain," excerpt from Hospice Foundation of
America's Clergy Education Project Curriculum, 15–16.

5. "To My Family with Love, Personal Directives," Beaverton Foursquare Church, Beaverton,
OR, 2009.

Chapter 9: Physical Disabilities, Chronic Pain, and the Aging Process

1. Vulvodynia is chronic, diffuse, unremitting sensation of burning of the vulva—(the female
external genital organs including the labia, clitoris, and entrance to the vagina)—a painful
sensation that may extend to the perineum, thigh, or buttock and is often associated with
discomfort in the urethra and rectum. This is a seemingly minor disease of major consequence for a woman's quality of life. It is a condition of unknown cause without a proven
mode of treatment. Source: Medicine Net.com http://www.medterms.com/script/main/art
.asp?articlekey =14090.

2. Chart compiled from information written by Ev Waldon for class handouts, PCW512Y,
Women in Pain II, taught at Western Seminary, fall 2009.

3. For the purposes of this chapter, we will use feminine pronouns, although men also have
many of these experiences.

4. American Academy of Family Physicians. http://www.aafplearninglink.org/Webcasts/
Practical-Aspects-of-Chronic-Pain-Management-A-Case-based-Approach.aspx.

5. Chart compiled from information written by Ev Waldon for class handouts, PCW512Y,
Women in Pain II, taught at Western Seminary, fall 2009.

6. The economic impact of chronic nonmalignant pain (CNP) is staggering. Back pain,
migraines, and arthritis alone account for medical costs of $40 billion annually, and pain is
the cause of 25% of all sick days taken yearly. The annual total cost of pain from all causes is
estimated to be more than $100 billion. CNP also causes many psychological problems, such
as feelings of low self-esteem, powerlessness, hopelessness, and depression. Sources: Brown-
lee, Shannon, and Joannie M. Schrof, "The Quality of Mercy," *U.S. News and World Report*,
March 17, 1997: 55–57, 60–62, 65, 67. American Academy of Pain Medicine and American
Pain Society. "The Use of Opioids for the Treatment of Chronic Pain." *Clinical Journal of Pain*,
vol. 13, March 1997: 6–8. Canine, Craig. "Pain, Profit, and Sweet Relief." *Worth*, March, 1997:
79–82, 151–57. Liebeskind, J.C., "Pain Can Kill," *Pain* 44, no. 1 (January 1991): 3–4.

7. Proverbs 17:22: "A cheerful heart is good medicine, but a crushed spirit dries up the bones."

8. Chart compiled from information written by Ev Waldon for class handouts, PCW512Y Women in Pain II, taught at Western Seminary, fall 2009.

9. Tips on how to communicate with people with a variety of disabilities can be found on this website: http://www.dol.gov/odep/pubs/fact/comucate.htm, accessed November 9, 2009.

Chapter 10: Addictions

1. American Psychiatric Association. *Diagnostic and Statistical Manual of Mental Disorders*, 4th ed. (1994).

2. Patrick Carnes and Joseph Moriarity, *Sexual Anorexia: Overcoming Sexual Self-Hatred* (Center City, MN: Hazelden, 1997).

3. Second Corinthians 12:7–10 (See Related Scriptures).

Chapter 11: Abortion Recovery

1. HEART is a ministry of Pregnancy Resource Centers in Greater Portland, OR. HEART and Healing a Father's Heart exist to provide a safe confidential environment for individuals to experience the hope and healing through a Bible study support group for women and men. Our vision is "Reconciliation and restoration for those who are struggling with a past abortion(s) and seek healing and forgiveness through God's Word and relationships with others."

2. U.S. Dept. of Health and Human Services 2002, quoted on http://www.portlandheart.org/resources.htm

3. 17% teens, 33% aged 20–24. "Facts on Induced Abortion in the United States," Guttmacher Institute, July 2008. http://www.guttmacher.org/pubs/fb induced abortion.html.

4. "Facts on Induced Abortion in the United States," Guttmacher Institute, July 2008. http://www.guttmacher.org/pubs/fb induced abortion.html.

5. "Between Two Worlds": Number of Abortions since 1973. http://theologica.blogspot.com/2009/01/number-of-abortions-since-1973.html.

6. Men are not exempt from some of these feelings, although men typically process them differently. More physicians and mental health professionals along with the Pregnancy Resource Centers of Greater Portland recognize the real need to help mothers and fathers grieve the loss of their children to abortion. The aftermath of abortion paralyzes many in their emotional, mental, and spiritual growth. It is strongly recommended that men also process through a group study, such as Healing a Father's Heart (see resources for men at the end of this chapter). www.portlandheart.org/stress.htm. For the purposes of this chapter, we will focus on PAS in women.

7. Research psychologist Dr. Vincent Rue gathered data from 765 post-abortive women in the US and Russia and concluded that 87% of the US women reported high to overwhelming stress after abortion. 78% of the Russian women reported the same. Source, "Trauma Symptoms Following Induced Abortion," Dr. Vincent Rue, PhD, Institute for Pregnancy Loss, Portsmouth, NH. (1996).

8. "Post-Abortion Stress (PAS) Awareness," handout from HEART, Healing Encouragement for Abortion Related Trauma, a ministry of Pregnancy Resource Centers in Oregon, January 24, 2000, distributed by Mindy Johnson in PCW512x, Women in Pain I course at Western Seminary, Portland, OR, January 23, 2009.

9. www.portlandheart.org/stress.htm, the website for HEART.

10. Adapted from *Helping People Get Through Grief*, by Delores Kuenning (Grand Rapids, MI: Bethany House, 1987). Used by permission, "Post-Abortion Stress (PAS) Awareness," handout from HEART, Healing Encouragement for Abortion Related Trauma, a ministry of

Pregnancy Resource Centers in Oregon, January 24, 2000, distributed by Mindy Johnson in PCW512x, Women in Pain I course at Western Seminary, Portland, OR, January 23, 2009.

11. "Facts on Induced Abortion in the United States," Guttmacher Institute, July 2008. http://www.guttmacher.org/pubs/fb induced abortion.html.

12. "Post-Abortion Stress (PAS) Awareness," handout from HEART, Healing Encouragement for Abortion Related Trauma, a ministry of Pregnancy Resource Centers in Oregon, January 24, 2000, distributed by Mindy Johnson in PCW512x, Women in Pain I course at Western Seminary, Portland, OR, January 23, 2009. Source, 1989 CAC Conference, Copyright PRC's of the Greater Portland area.

13. Written by Lisa Heacock, 2004, former HEART Director, Greater Portland Pregnancy Resource Center (PRC), taken from Post-Abortion Stress (PAS) Awareness PRC publication.

14. Heacock.

Chapter 12: Eating Disorders

1. Eating is controlled by many factors, including family, peers, and cultural practices. American Psychiatric Association Work Group on Eating Disorders. Practice guideline for the treatment of patients with eating disorders (revision). *American Journal of Psychiatry*, 2000; 157 (1 Suppl): 1–39.

2. *Science*, October 10 issue, http://mentalhealth.about.com/b/2003/10/16/rejection-feels-like-pain-to-the-brain.htm.

3. Dieting to a body weight leaner than needed for health is highly promoted by current fashion trends, sales campaigns, media, and in some activities and professions. Women are especially vulnerable to these demands because a woman's body holds a primary focus of American cultural mores. Joan Jacobs Brumberg, *The Body Project: An Intimate History of American Girls* (New York: Vintage Books, 1997).

4. "For God so loved the world that he gave his one and only Son, that whoever believes in him shall not perish but have eternal life. For God did not send his Son into the world to condemn the world, but to save the world through him. Whoever believes in him is not condemned. . . ." John 3:16–18.

5. As told (2009) by Laura Roberts, Psy. D, a clinician at Cornerstone Clinical Services, who specializes in treatment of anorexia, bulimia, and compulsive overeating. CCC has facilities in both Milwaukie and Tigard, OR.

6. Compared to one million men. Crowther et al., 1992; Fairburn et al., 1993; Gordon, 1990; Hoek, 1995; Shisslak et al., 1995 as cited on http://www.nationaleatingdisorders.org/p.asp?WebPage_ID=294.

7. Approximately 90–95 percent of anorexia nervosa sufferers are girls and women. About 50 percent of people who have been anorexic develop bulimia or bulimic patterns. American Psychiatric Association. Diagnostic and Statistical Manual for Mental Disorders, 4th ed. APA: Washington, DC (1994).

8. Disorders have been reported in children as young as six and women as old as seventy-six. "Statistics: How Many People Have Eating Disorders?" Anorexia Nervosa and Related Eating Disorders, Inc., 2002. http://www.anred.com/stats.html.

9. http://www.nationaleatingdisorders.org/information-resources/general-information.php#terms-definitions, accessed October 2009.

10. Ibid.

11. Ibid.

12. Anorexia nervosa has one of the highest death rates of any mental health condition. A young woman with anorexia is twelve times more likely to die than other women her age without

anorexia. P. F. Sullivan. Mortality in Anorexia Nervosa. *American Journal of Psychiatry* 152 (1995): 1073–74.

13. http://www.disordered-eating.co.uk/disordered-eating/disordered-eating.html; http://www.medicalnewstoday.com/articles/159485.php.

14. Constance Rhodes, *Finding Balance*, "What Is EDNOS?" http://www.findingbalance.com/articles/disorders/ednos.asp.

15. http://www.findingbalance.com/videoplayer/video.asp?clip=FBA1184.

16. Sources: Science Daily, National Eating Disorder Association; http://www.emaxhealth.com/1275/85/32431/cause-anorexia-linked-brain-circuitry.html.

17. Daniel G. Amen, MD, "Healing the Hardware of the Soul," http://www.amenclinic.com/bp/articles.php?articleID=20.

18. William R. Miller and Stephen Rollnick, *Motivational Interviewing* (New York: The Guilford Press, 2002), 6, 41.

19. http://en.wikipedia.org/wiki/Pro-ana. Pro-ana refers to the promotion of anorexia nervosa as a lifestyle choice rather than an eating disorder. It is often referred to simply as "ana" and is sometimes affectionately personified by anorexics as a girl named Ana. The lesser-used term pro-mia refers likewise to bulimia nervosa and is sometimes used interchangeably with pro-ana.

20. See Remuda Ranch, "The Remuda Model of Treatment," http://www.remudaranch.com/general/outcomes/index.php.

21. *Science and Spirit*, "Mayo Clinic Releases Studies on Spirituality and Health," http://www.science-spirit.org/archive_cm_detail.php?new_id=396.

22. The invalid had been in this condition for thirty-eight years. Jesus asked a question with a seemingly obvious answer. Yet Jesus used this approach on several occasions in the Gospels. See also Matthew 20:32; Mark 10:51; Luke 18:41.

23. "The thief comes only to steal and kill and destroy; I [Jesus] have come that they may have life, and have it to the full" (John 10:10). "For the Spirit God gave us does not make us timid, but gives us power, love and self-discipline" (2 Timothy 1:7). "For God gave us a spirit not of fear but of power and love and self-control" (2 Timothy 1:7 ESV).

24. *E. D Referral.com*; Mary Anne Cohen, "Sexual Abuse and Eating Disorders," The New York Center for Eating Disorders; http://www.edreferral.com/sexual_abuse_&_ed.htm.

Chapter 13: Incarceration

1. FITS is a worldwide organization reaching incarcerated women and women in transition from prison to their communities with the life and love of Jesus Christ.

2. Fran Howard and Marlee Alex, *Beyond the Bars: What Happens When Jesus Goes to Prison*, Freedom in the Son, Inc., 23.

3. Psalm 9:9 (NLT), "The LORD is a shelter for the oppressed, a refuge in times of trouble."

4. Howard and Alex, 25.

5. More in-depth studies using expanded measures of abuse have found that nearly all girls and women in prison samples have experienced physical and sexual abuse throughout their lives (Bloom, Chesney-Lind, & Owen, 1994; Browne et al., 1999; Fletcher, Rolison, & Moon, 1993; Gilfus, 1987, 1992; Owen, 1998; Richie, 1996). Not only was the prevalence of abuse extremely high, but the abuse was also severe and cumulative over the life course of the women. Gilfus, M. (2002, December). Women's Experiences of Abuse as a Risk Factor for Incarceration. Harrisburg, PA: VAWnet, a project of the National Resource Center on Domestic Violence/Pennsylvania Coalition against Domestic Violence. Retrieved October 26, 2009 from: http:// www.vawnet.org. This statistic is also cited by Kathryn Grant, founding

vice president of Prison Fellowship International, in the foreword of *Ministry Manual for Volunteers to Women in Prison and in Transition*, Howard, Vaubel, and LeDai, 1997, p. 4.

6. Nationwide 61.7% of incarcerated women (black, Hispanic, and white) have minor children. Lauren E. Glaze and Laura M. Maruschak, BJS Statisticians, U.S. Department of Justice, Bureau of Statistics Special Report, *Parents in Prison and Their Minor Children*, revised January 8, 2009, page 14. http://www.ojp.usdoj.gov/bjs/pub/pdf/pptmc.pdf.

7. An estimated 809,800 prisoners of the 1,518,535 held in the nation's prisons at midyear 2007 were parents of minor children, or children under age 18. Parents held in the nation's prisons—52% of state inmates and 63% of federal inmates—reported having an estimated 1,706,600 minor children, accounting for 2.3% of the US resident population under age 18. Unless otherwise specified in this report, the word *parent* refers to state and federal prisoners who reported having minor children. The word *children* refers to youth under age 18. Between 1991 and midyear 2007, parents held in state and federal prisons increased by 79% (357,300 parents). Children of incarcerated parents increased by 80% (761,000 children) during this period. Lauren E. Glaze and Laura M. Maruschak, BJS Statisticians, US Department of Justice, Bureau of Statistics Special Report, Parents in Prison and their Minor Children, revised January 8, 2009, page 1. http://www.ojp.usdoj.gov/bjs/pub/pdf/pptmc.pdf.

8. Grant, 4.

9. Ephesians 6:12 NLT.

10. 1 John 4:4 NLT.

11. Fran Howard, Dedrea Vaubel, and Marlee LeDai, *Ministry Manual for Volunteers to Women in Prison and in Transition*, Freedom in the Son, 25.

12. See also 2 Timothy 2:2.

13. Howard, Vaubel, and LeDai, 16.

14. FITS serves the women and the Department of Corrections throughout the state of Oregon. Coffee Creek Correctional Facility is a 1684 bed facility located on 108 acres and costing $171 million. It is the only women's prison in the state of Oregon with a current population of 950 women ages 17–67. There are 450 employees. FITS provides teaching, mentoring, lay-counseling, and support for the women's prayer warrior weekly meeting. Special programs are held for the residents on Thanksgiving and Christmas day each year. When their sentence is complete inside, FITS volunteers walk with them in transition from prison back to their homes and communities. This may include picking them up at the gate to safely escort them to their parole officer, buying them breakfast, and just spending that first day of release with them.

Chapter 14: Homelessness

1. Merriam-Webster's Unabridged Dictionary online.

2. Loris Hanson Sheets, *Sisters of the Road: Stories of Homeless Women in America* (Lincoln, UT: Pine Canyon Press, 1999), 25.

3. Ibid., 26.

4. Michael Dye and Patricia Fancher, *The Genesis Process—A Relapse Prevention Workbook for Addictive Compulsive Behaviors* (Genesis Addiction Process & Programs, 4th ed., 2004), 40. Genesis Process is founded and directed by Michael Dye CADC, NCAC II; www.genesis process.org.

5. "For he chose us in him before the creation of the world to be holy and blameless in his sight. In love he predestined us for adoption to sonship through Jesus Christ, in accordance with his pleasure and will—to the praise of his glorious grace, which he has freely given us in the One he loves" (Ephesians 1:4–6 NIV).

6. "Even before he made the world, God loved us and chose us in Christ to be holy and without fault in his eyes. God decided in advance to adopt us into his own family by bringing us to

himself through Jesus Christ. This is what he wanted to do, and it gave him great pleasure" (Ephesians 1:4–5 NLT).

7. "Christ will make his home in your hearts as you trust in him. Your roots will grow down into God's love and keep you strong. And may you have the power to understand, as all God's people should, how wide, how long, how high, and how deep his love is" (Ephesians 3:17–18 NLT).

8. Such as in silence and solitude, pray, read the Bible, worship, and fast. See Donald S. Whitney's *Spiritual Disciplines for the Christian Life* (Colorado Springs: NavPress, 1997) for more specifics.

Chapter 15: Suicide

1. American Association of Suicidology: AAS Suicide Data Page (based on 2006 statistics), website (http://www.suicidology.org), August 2009. The American Association of Suicidology is a nonprofit organization dedicated to understanding and preventing suicide. The website provides current information and links to other helpful resources.

2. Centers for Disease Control and Prevention website (http://www.cdc.gov/ViolencePrevention/pdf/Suicide-DataSheet-a.pdf), August 18, 2009.

3. Centers for Disease Control and Prevention. Web-based Injury Statistics Query and Reporting System (WISQARS) [Online]. (2009). National Center for Injury Prevention and Control, Centers for Disease Control and Prevention (producer). [cited 2009 Jun 17]. Available from: URL: www.cdc.gov/injury/wisqars/index.html.

4. Term coined by Edwin Schneidman cited in R. W. Maris, A. L. Berman, M. M. Silverman, *Comprehensive Textbook of Suicidology* (New York: Guilford, 2000), 261.

5. Cited in "Niagara Falls Survivor Says Depression, Not Derring-do, Fueled Plunge," Nation/World Section, *News-Review*, Roseburg, OR, October 22, 2003.

6. Website (http://cfasggb.tripod.com/Suicide/patrols_help_reduce_golden_gate_Suicide.htm) January 11, 2004.

7. Although much of this information is not gender specific, for the purpose of this book, feminine pronouns will be used predominantly.

8. B. W. Walsh and P. M. Rosen, *Self-Mutilation: Theory, Research, and Treatment* (New York: Guilford, 1988).

9. "Strictly speaking, suicidal ideation means wanting to take one's own life or thinking about suicide without actually making plans to commit suicide. However, the term suicidal ideation is often used more generally to refer to having the intent to commit suicide, including planning how it will be done." Marcia Purse, "Suicidal Ideation," About.com Guide, July 6, 2009, http://bipolar.about.com/od/suicide/g/suicidalideatio.htm.

10. P. G. Quinnett, *Counseling Suicidal People: A Therapy of Hope* (Spokane, WA: The QPR Institute, 2009), 70. Dr. Quinnett has developed extensive training and quality resources in suicide prevention that can be found at www.qprinstitute.com.

11. Website: www.1000deaths.com 1/2004.

12. I am indebted to N. Gregory Hamilton, MD, for the wisdom and insights shared in his supervision of my work with suicidal patients.

13. J. M. McGlothlin, *Developing Clinical Skills in Suicide Assessment, Prevention, and Treatment* (Alexandria, VA: American Counseling Association, 2008), 199.

14. John 10:10.

Chapter 16: Domestic Abuse

1. Name changed to protect her identity.

2. "Her Journey" is a 15-week study and support group for women suffering from domestic abuse/violence offered by A.R.M.S. in several states of the US.

3. "Fear No Evil: A Faith-Based Approach to Ending Domestic Abuse," Abuse Recovery Ministry & Services, 2006, p. 2.

4. "Domestic Violence Facts," National Coalition against Domestic Violence, 1633 Q St NW #210, Washington, DC 20009. http://www.ncadv.org/files/DomesticViolenceFactSheet (National).pdf.

5. "Fear No Evil," adapted from page 4.

6. "Domestic Violence Facts," National Coalition against Domestic Violence, 1633 Q St NW #210, Washington, DC 20009. http://www.ncadv.org/files/DomesticViolenceFactSheet (National).pdf [source cited: I.H. Frieze, A. Browne (1989) Violence in Marriage. In L. E. Tonry, eds. *Family Violence*. Chicago: University of Chicago Press.]

7. In 92% of all domestic violence incidents, crimes are committed by men against women. http://www.marriage-relationships.com/domestic_violence_statistics.html.

8. Female pronouns will be used for the abused in this chapter.

9. American Bar Association—Commission on Domestic Violence: Key Statistics. Stalking. http://www.abanet.org/domviol/statistics.html [source cited: Stalking Resource Ctr., *The Nat'l Ctr. For Victims of Crime, Stalking Fact Sheet*, http://www.ncvc.org/src/Main.aspx, citing Patricia Tjaden and Nancy Thoennes, US Dept of Justice, NCJ 169592, Stalking in America: Findings from the National Violence against Women Survey (1998)].

10. Domestic Violence Resource Center / Domestic Violence Statistics. (Bureau of Justice Statistics, Intimate Partner Violence in the US 1993–2004, 2006.) http://www.dvrc-or.org/domestic/violence/resources/C61/. And "Domestic Violence Facts," National Coalition against Domestic Violence, 1633 Q St NW #210, Washington DC 20009. http://www.ncadv.org/files/Domestic ViolenceFactSheet(National).pdf.

11. "Fear No Evil: A Faith-Based Approach to Ending Domestic Abuse."

12. Domestic Violence Resource Center/Domestic Violence Statistics. http://www.dvrc-or.org/ domestic/violence/C61 [source cited: The Centers for Disease Control and Prevention and the National Institute of Justice, Extent, Nature, and Consequences of Intimate Partner Violence, July 2000. The Commonwealth Fund, Health Concerns Across a Woman's Lifespan: 1998 Survey of Women's Health, 1999].

13. Domestic Violence Resource Center / Domestic Violence Statistics. http://www.dvrc-or .org/ domestic/violence/C61 [source cited: (Bureau of Justice Statistics, Crime Data Brief, Intimate Partner Violence, 1993-2001, February 2003. Bureau of Justice Statistics, Intimate Partner Violence in the US 1993–2004, 2006.)]

14. Battered women seek medical attention for injuries sustained as a consequence of domestic violence significantly more often after separation than during cohabitation; about 75% of the visits to emergency rooms by battered women occur after separation (Stark and Flitcraft, 1988). About 75% of the calls to law enforcement for intervention and assistance in domestic violence occur after separation from batterers. One study revealed that half of the homicides of female spouses and partners were committed by men after separation from batterers (Barbara Hart, Remarks to the Task Force on Child Abuse and Neglect, April 1992). http:// www. hawthornedvrt.org/Women-and-Domestic-Violence.htm.

15. When stress hormones (cortisol) remain active in the brain for too long they injure and even kill cells in the hippocampus, the area of your brain needed for memory and learning. http://www.fi.edu/learn/brain/stress.html#top.

There is now evidence that points to abnormal stress responses as causing various diseases or conditions. These include anxiety disorders, depression, high blood pressure, cardiovascular disease, certain gastrointestinal diseases, some cancers, and even the process of aging itself. Stress also seems to increase the frequency and severity of migraine headaches, episodes of asthma, and fluctuations of blood sugar in diabetics. There also is scientific evidence showing that people experiencing psychological stress are more prone to develop colds and other infections than their less-stressed peers. Overwhelming psychological stress (such as the events of 9–11) can cause both temporary (transient) and long-lasting (chronic) symptoms of a serious psychiatric illness called posttraumatic stress disorder (PTSD). Medicine Net.com http://www.medicinenet.com/stress/page8.htm

16. Survey of men involved in "Mankind," a program of A.R.M.S. for male abusers.

17. "Fear No Evil: A Faith-Based Approach to Ending Domestic Abuse," Abuse Recovery Ministry & Services, 2006, 2.

18. Ibid., adapted from page 3.

19. Ibid., 6.

20. Ephesians 5:25–28.

21. This is a quote from one of the women who went through our Her Journey class.

22. Adapted from "Responding to Domestic Violence: Guidelines for Pastors and Rabbis," Faith Trust Institute, Center for the Prevention of Sexual and Domestic Violence. Seattle, WA. 1998.

Chapter 17: Sexual Abuse

1. Adapted from Kathy Rodriguez and Pam Vredevelt, *Surviving the Secret: Healing the Hurts of Sexual Abuse* (Gresham, OR: East Hill Church, rev. 2003), 15–16.

2. Kathy Rodriguez and Pam Vredevelt, *Surviving the Secret: Healing the Hurts of Sexual Abuse* (Grand Rapids: Revell, 1987), 26.

3. Ibid.

4. Ibid.

5. Ibid.

6. Ibid.

7. Sexual assault includes rape, forced vaginal, anal or oral penetration, forced sexual intercourse, inappropriate touching, forced kissing, child molestation, and the torture of the victim in a sexual manner. Frequently Asked Questions about Women's Health: Sexual Assault, National Women's Health Information Center, US Department of Health and Human Services.

8. Prevalence, Incidence, and Consequences of Violence against Women Survey 1998. National Institute of Justice & Centers for Disease Control & Prevention. http://www.rainn.org/get-information/statistics/sexual-assault-victims, accessed November 13, 2009.

9. 2003 National Crime Victimization Survey, US Department of Justice. http://www.rainn.org/get-information/statistics/sexual-assault-victims, accessed November 13, 2009.

10. World Health Organization, 2002. http://www.rainn.org/get-information/statistics/sexual-assault-victims, accessed November 13, 2009.

11. Rodriguez and Vredevelt, 23.

12. Ibid., 51–53.

13. Patrick J. Carnes, PhD, DAS, lists nine predominant ways that trauma continues to affect people over time. Three of those are (1) Trauma blocking—efforts to numb, block out, or overwhelm residual feelings due to trauma; (2) Trauma repetition—repeating behaviors and/or seeking situations or persons who re-create the trauma experience. Reenactment, efforts to resolve the unresolveable. 3) Trauma bonds—dysfunctional attachments that occur in the presence of danger, shame or exploitation. To read more, see article by Patrick J. Carnes, PhD, DAS, "Trauma Bonds," pages 8, 17, 19. Means Family Counseling Center, http://www. markmeans.com/clientimages/36010/sexaddictionfiles/csattraumabonds course.pdf (cited November 16, 2009).

14. Rodriguez and Vredevelt, 85–92.

15. Ibid., 157.

16. Ibid.

17. Perry Draper, *Haunted Memories: Healing the Pain of Childhood Abuse* (Grand Rapids: Baker, 1996), 34–35.
18. Rodriguez and Vredevelt, 142.
19. Please see section III for more information on healing communities.

Chapter 18: Divorce

1. Exodus 33:19; Psalm 27:13; 31:19; 69:16; 2 Peter 1:3; God's love for us 1 John 3:1, 16; 4:7–21.
2. Although there are similarities between the process men and women experience in divorce, for the purpose of this chapter, feminine pronouns will be used.
3. For more explanation of each, see Welby O'Brien, *Formerly a Wife* (Camp Hill, PA: Wing-Spread, 2007), 9–16.
4. See www.DivorceCare.org for groups in your area.
5. See http://www.aacc.net/resources/find-a-counselor/American Association of Christian Counselors for a Christian counselor in your area.
6. See section 5, "Related Scripture References," for a complete list of verses that specifically ministered to me in my pain.
7. To see a full list of Scriptures that ministered to Welby in her journey of survival, growth, and healing, see *Formerly a Wife* by Welby O'Brien, © 1996, 2007 by Welby O'Brien. Used by permission of WingSpread Publishers, a division of Zur Ltd.

Chapter 19: Pornography

1. Spiritual Care Team is a group of mature Christians who voluntarily commit themselves to support and assist a person with acute spiritual needs through a process of returning that person to fellowship with God, family, and fellow believers.
2. Earl and Sandy Wilson, Paul and Virginia Friesen, and Larry and Nancy Paulsen, *Restoring the Fallen: A Team Approach to Caring, Confronting & Reconciliation* (Downers Grove, IL: InterVarsity Press, 1997), 31–40.
3. See resources for men at end of chapter.
4. Wilson et al., 60.
5. Matthew 16:23, "Jesus turned and said to Peter, 'Get behind me, Satan! You are a stumbling block to me; you do not have in mind the concerns of God, but merely human concerns.'"
6. See more on the forgiveness process in chapter 2.

Chapter 20: Spiritual Abuse

1. Sandra and Pastor James and their story are composites of many true stories I've worked with over the years.
2. The best account of evil is M. Scott Peck, *People of the Lie* (New York: Touchstone, 1998). He notes that "evil" is "live" spelled backward.
3. There are many accounts of these kinds of abuse. See "Peoples Temple," "Catholic sex abuse cases," and "Cult and Ritual Abuse" in *Wikipedia*.
4. Jeremiah 23:1–40; Ezekiel 34:1–10; Micah 3:5–12.
5. Matthew 21:12–13; Mark 11:15–18; Luke 19:45–48; John 2:13–17.
6. Mark 3:1–6.
7. Matthew 23.
8. Acts 7.
9. The following questions are adapted from Ronald Enroth, *Recovering from Churches That Abuse* (Grand Rapids: Zondervan, 1994). His book is oriented to abusive churches and systems. While that is a huge danger, abuse also happens within seemingly healthy churches.

10. This chapter uses masculine pronouns for the abuser and feminine pronouns for abused. However, abuse is not unique to men, nor being abused to women.

11. See also Isaiah 1:16–17; 58:6–7; Micah 6:8; Matthew 25:31–46; James 1:27.

12. Matthew 18:15–17.

13. Matthew 23.

14. Matthew 23:37.

15. Matthew 20:25–28.

16. Mark 14:32–36.

17. "If we confess our sins, he is faithful and just and will forgive us our sins and purify us from all unrighteousness" (1 John 1:9).

Chapter 21: Sexuality

1. A. W. Tozer, *The Crucified Life: How to Live Out a Deeper Christian Experience* (Venture, CA: Regal, 2011), 25.

Chapter 22: Environments of Grace Offer Acceptance

1. Women comprise nearly 60 percent of congregants. There is a total of between eleven million and thirteen million more born again women than men in American evangelical churches. George Barna, *Women Are the Backbone of the Christian Congregations in America*, Barna Research Online, March 6, 2000, 1. Barna notes: "The term 'born again Christian' does NOT refer to people calling themselves by this label. Barna Research surveys include two questions regarding beliefs that are used to classify people as born again or not born again. To be classified as a born again Christian an individual must say they have made a personal commitment to Jesus Christ that is still important in their life today, and that after they die they will go to heaven because they have confessed their sins and accepted Jesus Christ as their Savior. People who meet these criteria are classified as born again regardless of whether or not they would say they are born again Christians."

2. Catherine Clark Kroeger and James R. Beck, eds., *Women, Abuse and the Bible* (Grand Rapids: Baker, 1996), 143.

3. Ibid., 140.

4. Siang-Yang Tan, "Lay Helping, the Whole Church in Soul-Care Ministry," *Competent Christian Counseling*, vol. 1, ed. Timothy Clinton and George Ohlschlager (Colorado Springs: WaterBrook, 2002).

5. Peter Scazzero, *The Emotionally Healthy Church* (Grand Rapids: Zondervan, 2003), 19.

6. Ibid., 20, 32.

7. Edward M. Smith, *Healing Life's Deepest Hurts* (Ann Arbor, MI: Vine Books Servant and Campbellsville, KY: New Creation, 2002), 85.

8. A crisis is "a stage in a sequence of events at which the trend of all future events, for better or for worse, is determined; a turning point." *Webster's Encyclopedic Unabridged Dictionary of the English Language*, 477.

9. Matthew 25:35–45.

10. Mark 5:25–34; 2 Corinthians 1:3–7; 1 Thessalonians 3:1–3; 2 Thessalonians 1:4–6.

11. Carolyn Mazure et al., "Summit on Women and Depression: Proceedings and Recommendations," American Psychological Association, March 2002, 37.

12. D. G. Hart and R. Albert Mohler Jr., eds. *Theological Education in the Evangelical Tradition* (Grand Rapids: Baker, 1996), 281.

13. Examples include Sarah when she became pregnant with Isaac (Genesis 21:1); Jacob's gifts to Esau possible because of God's graciousness (Genesis 33:11); God's own description of

Himself to Moses (Exodus 34:6); Hannah became pregnant with Samuel (1 Samuel 1:20); Ezra's five month journey to Jerusalem (Ezra 7:9); the king granted Nehemiah's requests for supplies and safety for his trip to Jerusalem (Nehemiah 2:8).

14. "Out of his fullness we have all received grace in place of grace already given" (John 1:16). "And God is able to bless you abundantly, so that in all things at all times, having all that you need, you will abound in every good work" (2 Corinthians 9:8).

"My grace is sufficient for you, for my power is made perfect in weakness" (2 Corinthians 12:9).

"Each of you should use whatever gift you have received to serve others, as faithful stewards of God's grace in its various forms" (1 Peter 4:10).

"Let us then approach God's throne of grace with confidence, so that we may receive mercy and find grace to help us in our time of need" (Hebrews 4:16).

"And the God of all grace, who called you to his eternal glory in Christ, after you have suffered a little while, will himself restore you and make you strong, firm and steadfast" (1 Peter 5:10).

15. "His divine power has given us everything we need for a godly life through our knowledge of him who called us by his own glory and goodness" (2 Peter 1:3).

16. Jeff VanVonderen, *Families Where Grace Is in Place: Getting Free from the Burden of Pressuring, Controlling and Manipulating Your Spouse and Children* (Minneapolis: Bethany House, 1992), 138.

17. Ibid., 140–47.

18. Bill Thrall, Bruce McNicol, and John Lynch, *TrueFaced: Trust God and Others with Who You Really Are* (Colorado Springs: NavPress, 2003), 110–30.

19. James 4:6 and 1 Peter 5:5.

20. The desired outcome of life's trials is in part perseverance. "Consider it pure joy, my brothers and sisters, whenever you face trials of many kinds, because you know that the testing of your faith produces perseverance. Let perseverance finish its work so that you may be mature and complete, not lacking anything (James 1:2–4). Gifts were given so the body of Christ may be built up, "until we all reach unity in the faith and in the knowledge of the Son of God and become mature, attaining to the whole measure of the fullness of Christ" (Ephesians 4:13).

21. "We will not hide them from their descendants; we will tell the next generation the praiseworthy deeds of the LORD, his power, and the wonders he has done . . . so the next generation would know them, even the children yet to be born, and they in turn would tell their children (Psalm 78:4, 6). Even when I am old and gray, do not forsake me, my God, till I declare your power to the next generation, your mighty acts to all who are to come (Psalm 71:18). Then we your people, the sheep of your pasture, will praise you forever; from generation to generation we will proclaim your praise" (Psalm 79:13).

Chapter 23: Wounded Healers Reflect God's Power

1. Catherine Marshall, *Beyond Our Selves* (Grand Rapids: Revell, 1994), 84–85.

2. Ibid., 87.

3. *Agape* is a Greek word for love, which is described as the kind of love God expressed to people through the gift of Jesus Christ. It was a deliberate choice, made without assignable human cause, except the nature of God Himself. "This is not the love of complacency, or affection, that is, it was not drawn out by any excellency in its objects." See Romans 5:8. Taken from W. E. Vine, *The Expanded Vine's Expository Dictionary of New Testament Words* (Minneapolis: Bethany House, 1984), 693.

4. Jan David Hettinga, *Follow Me: Experience the Loving Leadership of Jesus* (Colorado Springs: NavPress, 1996), 244.

5. Genesis Process is founded and directed by Michael Dye CADC , NCAC II www.genesis process.org.

6. Genesis Process Mission Statement: We believe the best evangelism is a changed life. Therefore it is the goal of the Genesis Process and Programs to be intimately involved as part of the body of Christ in the Great Commission through the successful restoration of broken lives.

Chapter 25: Communities of Support Bring Hope

1. "Consider it pure joy, my brothers and sisters, whenever you face trials of many kinds, because you know that the testing of your faith produces perseverance. Let perseverance finish its work so that you may be mature and complete, not lacking anything" (James 1:2–4).

2. http://en.wiktionary.org/wiki/psychology.

3. 2 Corinthians 1:3–4.

4. Her husband, Ted Roberts, writes of his journey and healing in his book *Pure Desire* (Ventura, CA: Regal, 15th print, 2008).

5. The Genesis Process was conceived by Michael Dye in the Santa Barbara rescue mission some years ago, www.genesisprocess.org.

6. Pure Desire Ministries International, led by Dr. Ted Roberts, has practical answers that deal not only with the personal shame of the struggle but the family systems that fuel the issues. To find group locations near you, check our website. If you would like your Pure Desire Men's or Women's group to appear on the group locations site, please send your information to DianaG@puredesire.org. http://puredesire.org/default.aspx.

7. This is healing from family wounds and healing from dysfunctional families. There are four layers to it even though there are five classes.

   Entry level—*Wounded by Shame, Healed by Grace* (written by Jeff VanVonderen. This resource is no longer available, but there are many quality resources that cover this introductory topic) is a good entry-level class. Most of our classes are DVD-driven. We show a DVD to the class and then break them up into gender-specific small groups to process the material and do homework.

   Level 2—once they have finished the first level (with no more than two absences), they can do either *Love Is a Choice* (Dr. Robert Hemfelt, Dr. Frank Minirth, Paul Meier, MD [Nashville: Thomas Nelson, 2003]) or *Healing the Father Wound* (Kathy Rodriguez [Gresham, OR: East Hill Church, 2008]). If their hurts primarily are from a dad who left the family, was abusive, distant, or emotionally uninvolved, they have a father-wound. Women who are codependent and have a love-addiction also have a father-wound. These women did not have a solid relationship with the first man in their lives. If the potential leader has more of a generalized family dysfunction, *Love Is a Choice* is the recommended class. Both books and workbooks are used.

   Level 3—*Boundaries* (Henry Cloud and John Townsend [Grand Rapids: Zondervan, 1992]) is an eight-week course. DVDs are used.

   Level 4—*Safe People* (Henry Cloud and John Townsend [Grand Rapids: Zondervan, 1996]) is available to those who are eligible by having taken previous classes. The prerequisite classes prepare people to hear the truth of *Safe People*. Participants want to attend *Safe People* to learn how to find safe friends. What they find is that, "I am not a safe person." That is the biggest problem—not finding safe people—but realizing I am the most unsafe person in my life. Participants find that God will heal them through character development in relationships. He always heals within the context of relationship so they find out what they are really made of in this context. This is essential in healing.

ABOUT THE AUTHOR

BEV HISLOP (D. Min., Gordon-Conwell Theological Seminary) has recently served as Professor of Pastoral Care for Women and the Executive Director of the Women's Center for Ministry at Western Seminary in Portland, Oregon. She also served on the board of Network of Women in Leadership and was the former host of the weekly radio program *Western Connection for Women.* Bev has authored *Shepherding a Woman's Heart: A New Model for Effective Ministry to Women.* She is also a contributing author to *Tending the Soul* and *Women's Ministry Handbook.* Bev and her husband, Jim, have two married children and six grandchildren. hislopbev@gmail.com

A New Model for Effective Ministry to Women

Shepherding a Woman's Heart issues a challenge for pastors to empower the women in their churches with the same spirit that moves them to care for their flock. This resource provides guidance on how to properly equip healthy women to nurture hurting women.

978-0-8024-3354-1 | also available as an eBook

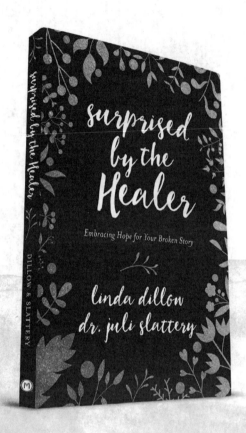

Advice from One Grieving Mom to Others

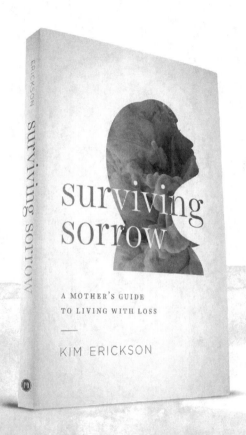

Any mother who is grieving the death of a child needs guidance for not only grieving, but also living. Drawing from her own experiences, Kim Erickson offers this profound and powerful resource that's invaluable for any mom in this situation—and for the friends and family who want to support her.

978-0-8024-1917-0 | also available as an eBook